What professionals say about the RISE program...

"The RISE program is an excellent model for illness prevention and health promotion. Its unique contribution is that it clearly integrates all the medically documented aspects of staying well. It integrates a sound theoretical base of information with a concise and practical daily application, i.e., information and skill development."

> Anthony Elite, M.D.
> Director, Office of Prevention
> California State Department of Mental Health

"RISE is very impressive to me. It offers a real, tangible approach to becoming an active participant in coping with illness, in meeting the challenges of the workplace, and in life."

> Edward S. Gallagher, M.D.
> Corporate Medical Director
> A T & T

"Of all the behavioral approaches to health and illness that I've seen, the RISE program stands out as the most effective by far and also the most compatible with our modern model of medical science."

> Chris Matthews, M.D.
> Medical Director, Owen AIDS Clinic
> University of California at San Diego School of Medicine

"RISE is a critical part of a whole-person approach to dealing with HIV infection and other serious conditions. In fact, I recommend it highly to all people who want to learn a way to control stress and improve their health."

> Charles Steinberg, M.D.
> Director, AIDS, Medicine, and Miracles, Inc.
> Boulder, Colorado

"The RISE program has been extremely well received from both the staff and patients of Kaiser Hospital. The basic principles of RISE are applicable to any person with a chronic condition, and we plan on encouraging many more patients to participate in the program."

Suzanne Furuya, M.P.H.
Director of Health Education
Kaiser Permanente
Santa Rosa, California

"The RISE program bridges the gap between accumulated academic knowledge of the mind and body with meaningful spiritual practices. I have watched RISE participants develop inner strength, discover meaning in their lives, and find a way out of suffering."

Jeanne Wismer, R.N., M.P.H.
Associate Professor
Community Health Care Systems
School of Nursing, Oregon Health Sciences University

"The RISE program has been extremely beneficial for our Health Plan Members living with HIV. In giving people with chronic illness the skill to reduce stress, slow down, and promote a healthier lifestyle, RISE offers tools for self-management. Perhaps the greatest strength of RISE is that it focuses on treating the mind, body, and spirit. Following the principles of RISE can and does enrich the quality of one's life."

Patricia Jones
HIV Health Educator
Kaiser Permanente
San Francisco Medical Center

"Many of our Foundation clients have attended RISE and reported beneficial results. The program is wonderfully compatible with the other early intervention services offered at AFSD."

Gordon Stewart
Director of Education & Outreach
AIDS Foundation of San Diego

"As the chief executive of a rapidly growing international development organization, I have found that the RISE program provides a set of life tools that have enabled me to cope with the constant and accelerating pace of change that dominates the global marketplace. Without this ability, I would be hard-pressed at times to do much more than just survive. I am grateful for the contribution the program has made to my life, and by extension, to the life of my organization."

Andrew J. Murokawa
President, World Share
San Diego

"Being involved with the HIV/AIDS ministry, I am privileged to have been a student of the RISE program. By emphasizing the wellness of the whole individual, the program has helped many HIV+/AIDS patients to strengthen their immune systems."

Fr. Nicholas Christiana
Director, San Diego AIDS Ministry

"We've tried so many other things in this country, and still continue to look for all the answers in status symbols or whatever, and yet here's a program that doesn't use anything but your own mind."

H. Albert Best, Ph.D.
Vice-President, Civil Service Commission
City of San Diego

"The RISE tools have helped me in my professional life as a nurse manager to remain calm and centered when attempting to initiate change in a resistant environment. I am more aware that I have a choice in the way I react to change, which allows me to foster a better work environment."

Ann Zalewski
Nurse Manager, Mercy Wound Care Center
Mercy Medical Center, San Diego

THE
RISE

RESPONSE

THE
RISE
RESPONSE

Illness, Wellness, and Spirituality

A proven program of relief for people coping
with cancer, HIV, chronic pain, and tension

Tim Flinders
Madeline Gershwin, R.N., M.A.
Rick Flinders, M.D.

CROSSROAD · NEW YORK

Grateful acknowledgment is made to The Blue Mountain Center of Meditation for permission to reprint selections "From the Vedas" and "From the Upanishads" from *God Makes the Rivers to Flow*, Nilgiri Press, 1991.

RISE logo design: Doug Stewart

1994

The Crossroad Publishing Company
370 Lexington Avenue, New York, NY 10017

Printed in the United States of America

Library of Congress Cataloging-in-Publication Data
Flinders, Tim.
    The rise response : illness, wellness, and spirituality : a proven program of relief for people coping with cancer, HIV, chronic pain, and tension / Tim Flinders, Madeline Gershwin, Rick Flinders.
      p. cm.
    Includes bibliographical references.
    ISBN 0-8245-1394-0
    1. Stress management. 2. Chronically ill—Mental health. 3. Self-care, Health. I. Gershwin, Madeline. II. Flinders, Rick. III. Title.
RA785.F584 1994
158.1—dc20
                                    94-3093
                                      CIP

To Sri Eknath Easwaran,
our teacher, guide, and
inspiration

Contents

Part ONE
THE RISE PROGRAM

I. Tools

II. Support

Part TWO
CHOICES

I. Coping with Illness, Disability, and Stress

II. Wellness: Building a Hardy Lifestyle

III. Meeting the Challenges of the Workplace

IV. Spirituality and Self-Empowerment

Acknowledgments

Six years is a long time in the life of an organization like RISE. So many people have crossed our path, and so many have made a contribution (*all* RISE trainers are volunteers) that it would be impossible to name them all. We'd probably do best simply to say thanks to everyone and leave it at that. But there are a number of people and institutions whose self-effacing contributions made this work what it is, and we can't help singling them out.

IN MEMORIAM

Kenny B., Robert E., David V., Del T., Daniel S., Dan F. — and those many unnamed RISE alumni who succumbed to illness, whose valor and grace continue to instruct and inspire us.

Northern California

Pat J., Suzane F., Robbin R., Darrel W., Wade W., Larry W., Duff, Ed F., JoAnne B., Jan S., John R., Jim and Claudia, Bert K., Michael N., Janet N., Ed G., Elizabeth G., John L., Snejzana A., Tom H., Winston F., Chuck R., Christian G., the Blue Mountain Center of Meditation and its office staff, Kaiser Permanente, the Family Practice Residency, Santa Rosa Community Hospital, Pacific Bell, the Sonoma County Academic Foundation for Excellence in Medicine, the Sonoma County Community Foundation, Sonoma County Public Health Department, Sonoma County Medical Association, Exchange Bank, Face to Face, Institute of the Treatment and Research of HIV, Davies Medical Center, Merritt Peralta Hospital, Mt. Zion Medical Center of the University of California Medical School, San Francisco, Student Health Services, University of California, Berkeley, Institute of Noetic Sciences.

Southern California

Joanne S., Don M., Kaye P., Gary P., Corinne G., Jill B., Jim K., Christine B., Sal V., Edward G., Frank M., Ann Z., Kathy M.,

Greg C., Carol S., Tyrone A., Barbara C., Suzie H., Jack C., Lloyd P., Jack M., Stan B., Greg R., Gary K., Al B., Bill R., Ruth R., Bob L., Father Nick, Dick S., the University of California at San Diego Medical Center, Owen AIDS Clinic, UCSD AIDS Clinical Trials Group, San Diego Community Health Care Alliance, AIDS Foundation of San Diego, San Diego Gas and Electric Company, Mercy Medical Center, San Diego Lesbian and Gay Men's Community Center, San Diego County Medical Services Complex, San Diego Community Research Group.

Pacific Northwest

Marcy M., Paul W., Don M., Jay R., Jeanne W., Scott B., Paul J., Seattle University, Cascade AIDS Project, Oregon Health Sciences University, School of Nursing.

Denver

Marty F., Ken G., Tom N., John H., Toby T., the Denver Public Health Department, Colorado AIDS Project.

Canada

Peter K., Bob B., Peter T., Sandra J., Glen P., Vivian C., Shirley B., Penelope P., Tom B., Spring G., Jeremy B., AIDS Committee of Toronto, St. John's Hospital, Toronto.

Elsewhere

Peter F., Mitch S., Greater Rochester AIDS Interfaith Network.

Personal Acknowledgments

Madeline

To Elizabeth Allen and Ben Young, whose talents have kept the San Diego RISE program going for the past five years. To Jackie Reid who never failed to be helpful. To my beloved teacher Sri Easwaran, who in addition to everything else gave me work with meaning; to Melissa Larson, for giving me a home away from home; to my husband, Warren, whose never-ending support and encouragement have sustained me through the last six years; and to SSB, life of my life.

Tim

I want to thank Candice Fuhrman, our literary agent, whose friendship, quiet persistence, and encouragement brought this project to a happy conclusion, and Jim Berner, Mark Kline, and Mark Combs, whose steady support through the low periods has meant more than they can know. And, of course, a special thanks to my wife, Carol, for her support, inspiration, and judicious editing, and my son, Ramesh, for putting up cheerfully with my absences. And, though I can't express my gratitude in words, to my teacher, Sri Easwaran, for the privilege of participating in this work.

Rick

RISE owes its life to everyone who has ever taken or taught the RISE program, and it belongs to those who make its practice a part of their lives. It has been the privilege of the authors to organize, interpret, integrate, and transcribe the experience of all those into the RISE Response.

I would like to thank personally: Eknath Easwaran, who gave us the gift of RISE; Bob E., one of the first RISE alumni, who showed us how to receive a small gift and give it back a thousandfold; and my wife, Jessica, whose advice, patience, love, and courage have made my part possible.

Foreword

by Sri Eknath Easwaran

Ever since I began teaching meditation to American audiences more than thirty years ago, I have believed that meditation on an inspirational passage could help people of all persuasions to lead a healthier, fuller, and more productive life. I am especially pleased that during the past six years the RISE program has amply demonstrated this in helping people to manage their illnesses, to find greater peace, and to enable them to lead more fulfilling lives.

It is my sincere hope that the publication of *The RISE Response* will enable the program to extend its reach to many more thousands in this country and even abroad who face the menace of HIV/AIDS, or who are trying to manage the challenges of other kinds of illness and disability, or who are looking for practical tools that can help them enrich their lives.

Blue Mountain Center of Meditation
Tomales, California
August 9, 1993

Foreword

by Sheldon Margen, M.D.

At the Sixth International AIDS Conference in San Francisco in 1990, the RISE Institute presented research, funded by the Centers for Disease Control, from a study of men coping with HIV illness. The study demonstrated a significant lowering of anxiety, depression, and hostility in those men who had participated in ten-week RISE courses, as well as a significant increase in their sense of well-being. These were impressive findings. In her closing statement at the plenary session of that conference, Dr. Anne Willoughby of the National Institutes of Health remarked that she hoped following conferences would "provide additional insight into...how sound programs of proven benefit like the RISE program may be implemented."

I agree heartily with Dr. Willoughby's assessment, and I hope this book will make the RISE program much better known among both the lay public and health professionals. I have followed the development of the RISE program since its beginning in 1987, when it worked almost exclusively with people coping with HIV illness, then watched it expand first to people living with other kinds of serious and chronic illnesses, and more recently, to helping otherwise healthy people cope with the insistent and sometimes deadly pressures of modern-day life. I was greatly pleased to learn of this publication of an expanded version of the course manual, for with it comes the promise that the program's tools will be available to many more individuals. I have read the manuscript with care to ensure the accuracy of its information and the soundness of its overall approach to self-care. Both as a physician and as a researcher in public health, I can recommend it unreservedly to anyone looking for systematic, self-empowering tools for coping with illness, or workplace stress, or for simply maintaining a healthier lifestyle.

You will find here a straightforward presentation of the RISE tools, as well as explanations for their uses in managing illness, enhancing lifestyle, and coping with the pressures and tensions of the workplace. The RISE program goes well beyond the margins of a simple self-care program for managing stress. It offers a comprehensive set of "life-management" tools with which any individual — diseased, threatened, or healthy — can reclaim some autonomy over his or her health in ways that are supportive, practical, spiritually nourishing, and — not to be undervalued — cost effective.

This book reflects the combined perspectives of a physician, a mental health nurse, and an educator, each of whom I have come to know on a personal basis. I can vouch for their professional skills and, perhaps more important, I know them to be grounded in their own practice of the RISE tools.

One further word, of special interest to me. You will notice that attention is paid in the program to the concept of support — here called "healthy ties." During several decades of work in public health, I have found no more powerful component for promoting general health than that of support — in the form of giving and receiving support from friends or members of a group, or even the less documented variety that can come from pursuing a common purpose with like-minded individuals. Any form of support you can find while learning these tools — participating in a RISE course or study group, going through the weekly self-study guide with a friend — will add immeasurably to their effectiveness.

Department of Public Health Nutrition
University of California, Berkeley

Stewards of the Self

Tim Flinders

"There isn't any magical element in RISE. There is no zap with a wand, and you're fixed. There are just solid, wonderful, productive changes, small victories. When a person takes control of his own destiny by changing and focusing and acting, he achieves these small victories." (Mort B.)*

"When I got to RISE I was mad at everybody, and feeling very sorry for myself. Every morning I would wake up thinking I cannot live another thirty years with these symptoms. After taking the course, I was able to get some . . . detachment . . . I guess, from what was going on in my body. I became more peaceful about what had happened to me. I'm not so angry now. The mantram and the meditation have helped me get through all of this. What more can I say?" (Cecily E.)

The room was warmer than we'd have liked — still ninety degrees at 7:30 in the evening — but it was also fuller than we'd anticipated. Twenty-four people had turned up for the first meeting of an eight-week midsummer RISE course. My brother Rick and I would be teaching the course, but since Madeline happened to be up from San Diego, she had come along to help with the orientation. At her suggestion, we gave latecomers a few more minutes to find the room and invited those who were already on hand to introduce themselves.

Shirley said she was a school teacher currently following a twelve-step recovery program. She had recently tested positive for HIV. Ed had coronary illness and required regular, usually

---

*For descriptions of the people whose quotes we use throughout the book, see "The Voices of RISE" on page 215.

1

painful, treatments to maintain his health status. Louis said that his stress levels at work in the county government office had become unmanageable, and Walt, a computer programmer, told us that his wife, a RISE alumna, had more or less insisted he take the course. "She says I'm too speeded up," he laughed. "She's probably right." Sharon was experiencing what she called a "spiritual vacuum" in her life. Like an increasing number of people coming to our courses, she was facing no immediate threat of illness, but was looking for spiritual light or a little peace, and a measure of command over her life.

Probably a fourth of the people there were dealing with HIV or AIDS. Roger had come from New York two years before, "withered," he said, by the losses he had suffered. He had stopped counting the friends he had already lost. Peter's hands opened out in an eloquent gesture of despair as he told us how devastating it had been for him to test positive for HIV. His partner, Robert, had taken a RISE course a few months before, though, and Peter was intrigued by the growing calmness he saw in Robert's eyes. Terry and Brent told similar stories, hinting at disasters borne. "I've been living with death for the past four years," Brent said quietly. "I need to start living with life again."

At 7:45, Liz and Ellen hurried into the room, apologizing for being late, hoping they hadn't missed anything. They were both intensive care nurses from the county hospital. Professional burn-out had brought them to RISE. They needed help coping with the unremitting stress and grief of their work.

Time was we might have felt diffident. This was such a diverse group of individuals, with so many different and pressing needs. But a few years' teaching RISE had shown us there was no room in these classes, and no reason, for diffidence.

The RISE tools, we explained now, were part of a spiritual path the three of us had been following for years under the direction of our meditation teacher Sri Eknath Easwaran. A former English professor, Easwaran had come from India as a Fulbright scholar in 1959 and had been teaching meditation in California since then. In numerous books, including his popular *Meditation* and *Dialogue with Death*, he had outlined a non-dogmatic, eight-point program of spiritual living that spoke directly to the pressures we faced in our professional lives and addressed the full range of human needs — physical, emotional, and spiritual.

In 1987, Sri Easwaran had asked us to adapt his program to a self-care, health education model for the thousands of people already coping with HIV illness. We jumped at the chance, glad to be able to "give back" a little and extend to others the enormous help we ourselves had already received from the tools. In what would become for us a wonderfully enriching collaboration, we joined our own backgrounds in medicine, psychology, and education with his thirty years of teaching meditation and developed a self-care program that could work for all people, regardless of the spiritual orientation they had — or didn't have.

Two pilot programs began in the fall of 1987 — one at Rick's hospital in Santa Rosa, and one at the Owen AIDS clinic at the University of California Medical School in San Diego under Madeline's direction. By 1989, eight-week RISE courses were being offered in a dozen cities in the western United States and Canada. In 1990, at the Sixth International AIDS conference, RISE presented research from a federally funded study showing that the program significantly improved the coping abilities of people living with HIV. And hundreds of alumni had reported coping substantially better with a variety of illnesses, disabilities, and conditions. (As of this writing, more than three thousand people have taken RISE courses.)

However...could it be effective for the two dozen people seated here together this sultry summer evening? Could the RISE tools help them steer through the relentless whitewater in their lives with more calm and clarity? We had good reason to think they could, and we said so. But we made it clear that only they could decide this and make it happen.

> *"In order to stay healthy, it's not enough just to take care of your body. You've got to do the physical work, the mental work, and the spiritual work, if you want to be well. So I take AZT for my body, and RISE for my mind and spirit."* (James R.)

"Well, what is the RISE Response?" Peter asked when we had finished. He had been watching his partner sit for the past several weeks, eyes closed, for fifteen or twenty minutes each day. Sometimes more. "What is he doing?"

Madeline answered: "The RISE Response is a way of training your mind — slowing it down and focusing it so that you can get yourself off automatic pilot and respond with more clarity and calmness to the challenges in your life." Most of us react to stress automatically, she explained. We become hostile or anxious before we know it. We light up the cigarette or reach for the beer without really thinking about what we're doing or whether it's in our best interest. Usually, she added flatly, it's not.

"The RISE tools can buy you time to think about what you're doing," she said. "Most responses are automatic: stimulus" — she held up one hand — "and response." The other hand came up; the palms were nearly touching.

"When things are happening this fast, there's no room for deliberation. We've reacted before we know it. The RISE tools create a small window of time between stimulus and response..." — slowly, emphatically, she moved her hands farther apart — "...and in this space you can make a conscious choice to react with greater calmness and clarity, more concentration and control, and finally (we call these the five Cs), greater compassion — for yourself and others."

She asked them to think for a moment about their lives. "How many of you have ever awakened in the middle of the night in the grip of a fear you couldn't get rid of... one you couldn't just tell your mind to stop thinking about?" Several hands went up.

"How many of you have found yourselves in a negative frame of mind — depression, anger, anxiety, say — that wouldn't let go of you; or driven by a physical urge for a cigarette, or alcohol, or sex, that seemed beyond your control?" Now a whole thicket of hands could be seen.

"Well," Madeline grinned, "Welcome to RISE!" Amid the laughter, she kept the questions coming. "How many of you are experiencing low-grade irritability? How many turn into couch potatoes when you're not at work? How many are always on the run, or alarmingly distractible? How many of you seem to change personalities when you get behind the wheel of a car and rant about the incompetence of other drivers?"

By now everyone had found reason to raise a hand and include themselves in the diagnosis. People often come to RISE courses, Madeline explained, oppressed by mood swings into fear or hostility they can't dispel. Or they're daunted by waves of hopelessness, a plummeting self-esteem, or the dread that their lives are out of control.

"The RISE tools take direct aim at these states of mind," she explained. "They help you interrupt negative feelings and attitudes before they become chronic or automatic." She told them that people come to RISE for a lot of reasons, but they usually share a desire for more control over what they think, feel, and do. "There's more to the RISE Response than this," she added, "We've developed a life-management program around it. But it's essentially using the tools to stay focused and in control in the face of stress."

Rick talked to them next about the increasing evidence of links between emotions, states of mind, and bodily health. None had been proven conclusively, he admitted — at least, not yet. But ample evidence existed to warrant acting as though better mental and emotional states could influence one's health. "The RISE tools can help you make the most of what you have," he concluded. "They can help you get access to what is already there."

Then I explained the structure of the course and introduced them to passage meditation. They took a few minutes to memorize a short inspirational passage and then tried a five-minute meditation. The room stilled, eyes closed, and breathing slowed down as they had their first RISE experience of battling the endless flow of distractions that fragment the mind and undermine our capacity to manage our lives....

Most of the group came back the next week, and there were a few new faces too. We began each class by asking them how things had gone during the week as they practiced the tool they had learned. They reported real leaps in self-awareness, surprising revelations about themselves and their minds. "I can't believe I'm so scattered!" Walt said, and Roger reflected: "It's a powerful discovery to know that you can change the way you think."

They told of new satisfactions as they slowed themselves down, brought more focus into their work or the way they managed their health. At the third class, Walt related an experience he'd had at work. The day had been hectic, he said. "I was using my mantram, and I actually stayed calm, which for me, is...well...unusual." Finally, his boss called him into his office and said, "You know, you've been really calm this last week. What are you taking?"

"I almost lost it there," Walt said. "But before I could say anything, he said, 'I want some of it!' "

The next week Ed told us that he had his first coronary procedure since he had started the course. "They give you some medication, which is supposed to numb the pain. But it doesn't work for me. This time I said the mantram, and it was much better. The pain doesn't go away, but you feel it less."

They reported difficulties, too, problems in finding time to meditate or a quiet place, and doubts about themselves. Shirley said she had run into a surprising degree of resistance to changing the way she did some things. And Brent, with a world-class sigh: "It's so hard to change."

They talked about how challenging it was to bring their attention back to their passage when it wandered. "I just don't have much tolerance for delayed gratification," Peter moaned one week with such candor we all had to laugh. *Who does?* He hadn't even started meditating, Peter confessed, and this was the fourth week of the course. Every night he was sure he would meditate in the morning, but somehow....

The next week Peter bounced into the room announcing that Robert, his partner, had started him meditating. He had done it every day.

"What did he tell you," I asked, hoping for a revelation.

"Well, actually...," Peter hesitated, his hands starting to flutter. "All he really told me was...*Just do it*."

We encouraged them not to pay much heed to how they felt at the time, but to look instead at the larger picture — at subtle changes in attitudes and behaviors. For instance, did they notice less helplessness? Were they aware of a growing equilibrium, fewer mood swings, less extreme reactions to stress, more sense of command or control in taking hold of their illness or the stress in their lives?

They all spoke of a greater awareness about themselves and about their thinking that they found powerful. And there was unanimity about a restored sense of possibilities....

Three months after the class ended, Rick saw Roger in the

hallway at Community Hospital. His lover was dying from a second bout of pneumocystis pneumonia. Rick wondered if there was anything he could do. "You've done more than you know," Roger said. "If it hadn't been for RISE, I don't know how I could survive this."

> *"I just couldn't seem to take charge of my life. I had systemic lupus and my stress level was at the max. I felt like I had no control whatsoever. At about week five or six into the program, things started to come together, I was able to focus my attention for the first time. I felt like I had some control. After three months I was finally able to let therapy go. I was gaining control over my life."* (Sandra H.)

Part One: The RISE Tools

The first five chapters of this book give instruction in the four tools. The term that best captures the spirit of the RISE tools is "self-stewardship." A steward is a caretaker, someone who manages another person's estate. The tools help you become a better self-caretaker, a more effective steward of all the resources that lie within, but are often out of your reach. They include:

- *physical resources* over which you have some control, such as diet, exercise, and relaxation;

- *emotional capacities* such as calm and equilibrium, the ability to manage negative states like depression or chronic anxiety, the clarity to respond more appropriately to stress;

- *mental capacities* like greater concentration, a more robust self-esteem, more control;

- *spiritual resources* like compassion, insight, and patience, a vigorous will to live, a sense of usefulness and purpose, greater inner peace.

The tools themselves are straightforward and fairly simple to learn — precision instruments with specific applications and outcomes. Passage meditation, for instance, has three specific objectives, (1) to slow down the thinking process, (2) to focus it, and (3) to transform your thinking, by concentrating your attention on self-selected inspirational passages from the world's spiritual traditions. In passage meditation, you repeat the words of the inspirational passage as slowly as you can, returning your attention to it each time your attention wanders. We've listed a wide selection of passages in Chapter Eighteen so that you can choose one from a tradition in which you feel at home. They're meant to appeal to a wide variety of tastes, from the religious and traditional to the lyrical, the intellectual, the pragmatic. Participants use the passage in their meditation as a focusing agent, drawing their attention through their distractions like a tow line through a troubled sea. Chapter Two gives detailed instructions.

Other tools include using a mantram as a rapid focusing device to interrupt automatic and obsessive behavior. It's easy to use, and doesn't require the discipline that meditation does. Participants tell us of using their mantram to sleep better, to manage old anxieties and fears, to overcome tensions at work, to break free from addictions. Slowing down and practicing one-pointed focus are tools that support training attention.

The tools are easy to learn, but a challenge to incorporate into a routine. Madeline has created an eight-week self-study guide to help get you started. You may wonder whether you need to take a course to learn the tools. The answer is no — many people have learned them on their own — but getting support from friends or a study circle can be helpful to your success. And it may be essential to maintaining your practice on a long-term basis. The RISE Institute sponsors a study circle network and instructional materials designed to support users of the tools, and you will find a detailed description in Chapter Seven.

Part Two: Choices

Once you have made the use of the tools routine, you will want to apply them to your specific needs. Part Two of _The RISE Response_ arranges these needs into four general areas, illness and disability, wellness, workplace concerns, and self-empowerment. You will probably find something of value in each, so I encourage you to read them all. Here are brief descriptions of each area.

1. Coping with Illness, Disability, and Stress

Illness and disability challenge your capacity to remain in control over your mental and emotional states. It's easy to become hostile or depressed or to feel helpless when you're faced with chronic discomfort or pain. Still, there are ways to remain more in charge of your reactions, and the tools have been shown to be effective in helping you do that.

In 1989, a federally funded study in Denver following a large cohort of people at risk for HIV, found that RISE participants in the cohort significantly improved their sense of well-being and significantly reduced their anxiety, hostility, and depression. These results held up when compared to comparable ten-week programs of traditional group therapy and conventional stress management. Rick presented these findings at the Sixth International AIDS Conference in 1990.[1]

Following that study, we looked at high-risk sexual behavior and again compared RISE participants in the cohort to participants in five comparable groups. At the Seventh International AIDS Conference in Italy, we reported that the study demonstrated a lowering of high-risk sexual behavior among RISE participants.[2] (Abstracts of both presentations are reproduced on pages 211–214.)

These results confirmed the growth we had seen occurring in our classes. They were particularly encouraging when placed alongside the growing evidence that improved coping abilities may well result in improved health, and even better immune functioning. I will not examine this evidence in detail here, since Rick does that in his essay on the mind-body connection. But I will summarize some of the more frequent findings.

A number of studies show that stress, anxiety, and bereavement are closely associated with impaired immune function.[3] Counting the T4 and T8 "natural killer" (NK) cells that identify and destroy invading viruses as a measure of immune function, several studies found that people suffering from depression or bereavement demonstrated a loss of T4 cells and, more significantly, an important ratio between T4 and T8 cells changed unfavorably.[4] In other studies, depression was linked to lowered immune function,[5] as well as stress and anxiety.[6]

Perhaps more important from our standpoint is that the ways we appraise and respond to stress appears to alter the ability of lymphocytes and antibodies to resist infection.[7] For those people using the tools to interrupt automatic stress reactions, these findings may have special significance.

Other research suggests that being hostile or giving up might weaken the immune system.[8] Loss of a sense of control in animals showed a lowering of immune functioning and increased likelihood of illness,[9] while pessimism in early adulthood appears to be a risk factor for poor health in middle and late adulthood.[10] On the other hand, studies at Stanford University showed that a strong sense of self-efficacy — a belief in your ability to exercise control over events in your life — "is the best and most consistent predictor of positive health outcomes in many different medical situations, including who will recover most successfully from a heart attack, who will be able to cope well with the pain of arthritis, and who will be able to make lifestyle changes (such as quitting smoking)."[11]

During the past two decades a body of evidence has emerged from which we were able to draw both inspiration and guidance. People like Herbert Benson, Joan Borysenko, and Philip Nuernberger in the East, and Robert Ornstein, Ken Pelletier, and Dean Ornish in California, to cite only a few, helped create a rich body of mind-body literature. Norman Cousins played a significant role in popularizing some of these concepts. For the first time, the National Institute of Mental Health is funding research into mind-body applications.

Still, no one as yet has been able to document a direct *causal* link between emotions and bodily health. The evidence has been built upon *associations* between mental states and immune function, rather than direct interactions. So until such evidence is forthcoming, we need to remain cautious about claims regarding emotions and physical health. But given the accumulated weight of the evidence, we certainly feel that it is in our best interests to act as though our attitudes and emotions can affect our health.

2. Wellness: Building a Hardy Lifestyle

The second area we explore in Part Two is lifestyle, especially diet, nutrition, and exercise. We try to empower participants to use the tools to make healthier choices and to contend with the addictive behaviors that threaten them. Over the years, we've watched participants use the tools to grapple successfully with addictions, make changes in their diets and fitness routines, become more productive in their work, and manage their stress better. Numerous studies have linked behavioral risk factors such as smoking, overconsumption of alcohol, high-fat diets, lack of exercise, and poor stress management to poor health.[12] Smoking is now considered a cofactor in HIV illness. Drugs and alcohol use speed up the rate of progression from HIV infection to AIDS.

Other studies have linked behavioral interventions with improvements in immune function.[13] Relaxation training, for instance, was associated with increased NK cell activity in older adults in one study.[14] In another, relaxation techniques were associated with immune function among metastatic cancer patients.[15] Yet another study demonstrated that a ten-week aerobic exercise program was associated with a significant increase in CD4 cell counts in HIV-affected individuals.[16]

A particularly significant study at Stanford showed that group therapy reduced anxiety, depression, and pain in a group of women with metastatic cancer at Stanford. A ten-year follow-up of the study showed that the women with the group intervention lived almost twice as long as did patients with no intervention. In other words, improvements in the quality of life for these women seemed to translate into longer lifespan, even though longevity was not the focus of the study.[17]

High-risk behaviors like smoking, inactivity, overeating, substance abuse, and unsafe sexual practices have a compulsive element that places them to some degree out of our control. It is this compulsive element, as much as the behaviors themselves, that the RISE Response is designed for.

3. Meeting the Challenges of the Workplace

At a time of rapid corporate downsizing, the environment of the workplace is undergoing dramatic changes and they are taking an increasing toll upon the mental and physical health of managers and workers alike. A large number of RISE participants have been managers or members of the workforce, and they've told us repeatedly how much the tools helped them come to grips with the insistent time pressures of work and the stressful interactions between colleagues, supervisors, clients, or employees.

And there is evidence to suggest that more appropriate psychological reactions to stress in the workplace can keep us healthier. In several studies during the mid-1980s, Suzanne Kobasa and Salvatore Maddi studied executive managers, bus drivers, telephone company employees, and others who work in stressful jobs, looking for evidence of coping styles and their relationship to health. Kobasa identified what she called three "hardiness traits" — a combination of "commitment, challenge, and control" — which seemed to decrease the illness-related effects of workplace stress on the executives.[18] The people in their studies with "hardy" personalities suffered from fewer illnesses. And the researchers concluded it was because they were able to respond to stressful events in ways that made them less stressful and less harmful to their health.

We look at this study in detail in Chapter Fifteen, so I won't go into detail here. But it raises a significant question for you. Can you learn the traits of hardiness? Can you enhance your own coping abilities and actually become psychologically hardier, more "stress-resistant"? Kobasa thinks so. "There are ways to change from helpless to hardy,"[19] she writes. And we have good reason to agree with her from our experience with RISE alumni. In fact, one way you can understand RISE is as an experiment to develop a hardier coping style that can help buffer you from the harmful effects of stress that are endemic today in the workplace.

> _"It's still a struggle. The stress doesn't go away and the issues in the environment don't disappear. I still have flare-ups. It happened a week ago, when another manager and I were sort of at each other's throats. But I noticed afterward that within twenty minutes, I'm humming, I'm singing to myself. It's sort of as if I'm able to let go. Something that might have simmered and escalated before is short-lived now, and I move right on. I feel like I have this secret from the RISE tools — I have a way to deal with whatever comes down the road." (Carl F.)_

4. "Spirituality and Self-Empowerment"

The acronym RISE stands for "Research and Instruction for Self-Empowerment." The final section of _The RISE Response_ looks at self-empowerment in its relation to spirituality and, in particular, to passage meditation.

The last section of Part Two of *The RISE Response* looks at the connection between spirituality and self-empowerment, especially in relation to passage meditation. These words have specific applications here, so I'll take a moment to clarify them.

If you look back at the English language a thousand years or so ago, you'll find that the word the Anglo-Saxons used for health was "wholle." In traditional cultures, "health" signified wholeness. In Chaucer's England, to be healthy was to be "wholle," in full flower, with all your resources fully engaged. English has changed greatly since Chaucer's time, but its native wisdom remains. Health is much more than the absence of illness. Full health still implies wholeness, and wholeness, with all your faculties in rich bloom, fully *empowered*, is the endpoint of the RISE Response.

The resourcefulness and creativity we have seen in course participants during the past five years have convinced us that we can all do much more than simply "get by." There is a far more fulfilling state that draws upon the spiritual core of the human personality. It is open to every person, call it wholeness, or high-level wellness, or, if you will, even "(w)holiness." This may be what Norman Cousins had in mind when he wrote that the difference between people was not between their ideologies or religion, but "between those who have a limited view of what a human being is and those who have an exalted view."

In developing RISE we proceed from an "exalted" view of the human being, with the assumption that there is much more to us than meets the eye. Each of us is greater than the sum of our biochemical parts, gifted with a reservoir of healing resources — insight, compassion, peace, resoluteness, equanimity, clarity, purpose — that lie largely untapped at the core of our personality. You can call this core "exalted" as does Cousins, or "sacred," as do the spiritual traditions of the world. In Chapter Seventeen, we refer to it as the "ample heart."

"What I liked most about RISE is that it can be spiritual, or it doesn't have to be. The tools can be used for whatever you need them for. If you want to go in the direction of spirituality, you can, but if you don't want to, the program will still work. You have that choice." (Sandra H.)

•

In any event, the recovery of those resources is the final aim of the RISE Response. The tools are meant to help you rediscover those resources and release them back into a healing confluence within your own life. How much healing can result from this discovery remains to be seen and, perhaps someday, fully documented. For now, I'll simply raise it as a possibility and leave it to a nineteenth-century Russian pilgrim to complete my thought:

> *And what depth and light there is in the mystery of a person coming to know that he has this power to plumb the depths of his own being, to see himself from within, to find delight in self-knowledge....*

A word about the writing. The chapters with bylines were written by the named author. The remaining chapters draw upon the experiences of each of us — Rick's work in the early 1980s with Alzheimer and hypertensive populations, Madeline's considerable work in mental health, stress management, and nursing education, and our shared efforts during the first two years of the program. But I did the actual writing for those chapters, since it seemed best to maintain a unified voice and style where possible. For better or worse, then, I take responsibility for the writing, although the book itself represents a true collaboration among the three of us, under the watchful editorial eye — and quickening vision — of our spiritual teacher, Sri Easwaran.

What RISE Is Not

I should probably say something here about what RISE is *not* since misconceptions have been commonplace:

RISE does not offer a cure for illness. It's not really about curing as much as it is about coping, managing better all your inner resources. As one facilitator has put it, RISE does not cure, but it heals. We encourage all participants living with illness or disability to continue the therapies they find valuable and to inform their physicians and therapists of their use of the RISE tools. We've always seen the therapeutic applications of the program working in partnership with conventional practices, not as an alternative to them.

RISE is not a belief system. The tools are spiritually based, they call upon the full range of human resources, but they require no special belief, except, perhaps, a belief in your own deepest capacities. We've often been surprised at the rich mixture of beliefs and attitudes people bring to the courses, crossing the entire spectrum of religious and spiritual understanding from the orthodox to the openly skeptical.

And one thing more... *RISE is not easy.* The tools are simple to grasp, but they require time and persistence to master.

I'll end here, and extend an invitation to you to join us as fellow travelers on this journey toward wholeness and health. The journey has already brought to many people a firmer grasp of themselves and their capacities. And it has brought many of them closer to the bedrock of their own deepest selves, more alert to their powers for recovery, and, hopefully, more whole.

For you, the pertinent question now is, how to begin? Don't feel you need to read the entire *RISE Response* before you begin using the tools. You could read Chapter One where you'd learn about the problem of the mind and the compulsive negative thinking that makes coping with illness and stress so difficult. Then go on to the next chapter and begin passage meditation. We always start course participants meditating with a minimum of preliminaries. They're not that complicated. You'll find some straightforward instructions for meditating on a passage and how to begin. Memorize a short passage, take a few minutes to give it a try, sample its effects.

First things first... and in half an hour from now you'd be "doing" RISE, battling the aimless flow of thoughts and impulses that fragment your mental focus. In the process, you'd learn more about how your mind gets trapped in compulsive thinking, and more about the meaning and power of the tools, than anything I can tell you here.

Or you can read the book in its entirety. Get a feel for where the program leads, and how the tools fit together in a piece. Then look at the self-study guide in Chapter Seven. Madeline has done a superb job of walking the beginner through the program, week by week, step by step. She answers many of the questions you're likely to have, and anticipates problems you may run into. Rick's essay will throw light on the central concerns that surround the issues of illness and self-care.

Then get started. The tools are not a panacea. You'll still have plenty to struggle with once you've completed the training. We're promising no miracles, here, not even a quick fix... *"just solid, wonderful, productive changes."* And I won't pretend that there is an easy way to get the tools integrated into your life. They take commitment and time.

But the tools work. And you can learn to adapt them to your own needs as have hundreds of people during the past few years. It will be challenging, but it's possible.

The best way to get started? I've taught RISE now to hundreds of people since 1987, but I've yet to hear better advice than what Robert told Peter during that first course... the words that got him meditating....

Just do it!

And my warmest wishes for your success.

"When I looked down is when he got me with the Gatorade bottle. And the first blow was bang, like that, I was out. The neurosurgeons had to dig three hundred pieces of my skull out of the top of the brain. While I was lying on the table, prior to surgery, I started coming back. I realized that I was very close to death. I lay there and thought, well, I'm not doing anything, I'll just meditate. And then I did.... I can't begin to say how long it took them to get things ready for surgery. But suddenly I was in absolute and complete peace with myself and with the universe. I was lying there and cracking jokes with the staff. They couldn't believe I was so at peace.

"I will tell you right now, I think RISE saved my life that night. I was so completely at peace that my body was able to attain a level that wasn't fraught with the symptoms of stress. I just didn't feel any stress. None whatsoever. That ability to be able to come down to my inner self, whatever that may be, caused me to survive. I can't put it on anything but the tools. I simply can't." (Mort B.)

Part ONE

THE RISE
PROGRAM

I. The Tools

Chapter One _____

The Problem of the Mind

"It's a powerful discovery to learn that you can change the way you think." (Roger S.)

Walk into Dr. William O.'s office on an afternoon and you'll probably find him scanning x-rays on his office wall screen, looking for trouble. He may inspect over a hundred x-rays in a day, sometimes pinched close to the screen, a jeweler worrying over flaws in a gem. He is searching for the minute gray etchings that signal lung disease.

The gray marks are caused by smoking. A radiologist specializing in lung disorders, Dr. O. spends much of his time in front of his wall screen trying to spot the telltale marks of lung tissue that has been damaged by cigarette smoke. You may see the doctor stare for minutes at a suspect gray spot back-lit on the wall screen; you may even see him scratch at the negative with his forefinger, unconsciously trying to flick away the twenty years of abuse it represents.

As the afternoon advances, Dr. O. will sometimes stop for a few minutes, sinking into his armchair for a brief respite, his hand reaching for one of the thirty-or-so cigarettes he will smoke during the day. He lights up, draws deeply, pulling the smoke down into his lungs and across the same mass of fragile tissue that lies scarred in gray on the x-ray above his head.

19

"I've tried to stop," the doctor explains when you ásk him why he smokes, "but so far it hasn't worked." Dr. O. knows all the risks surrounding smoking: he has stopped three times, but has not been able to stay clear of the habit. Somewhere between his more than ample knowledge of the subject and the many unwanted cigarettes he smokes each day, lies a flaw, and Dr. O. is acutely aware of it.

Self-Imposed Risks

And none of this should come as a surprise. The news has been around for years. Yet despite the statistics, millions of people cannot change their high-risk behavior. More than 150,000 fatalities occur each year from cigarette smoking, for instance, yet 51 million people still smoke.[1] Of the more than 200,000 "premature" deaths attributed each year to heart attacks and strokes, "at least" 90 percent are considered preventable.[2] Especially relevant is the alarming number of people at risk for HIV infection who are apparently relapsing into what amounts to life-threatening sexual practices.[3]

Dr. O. belongs to a large group of people whose lives in some way have gotten out of their control and have put their health status at risk. Driven by addictions or compulsive habits, they are victims of what the medical profession calls "self-imposed risks." These include patterns of living and thinking that may undermine their health. It is a baffling paradox — inflicting disease upon oneself — but not uncommon. Most people put themselves at risk with behaviors like smoking, a poor diet, lack of exercise, chronic hostility, hurry sickness, low self-esteem, poor stress management skills, unsafe sexual practices, drug or alcohol abuse.

The problem with most high-risk behaviors is that they lie outside the domain of conventional medical treatment. Their best cure is prevention — stopping, or not starting in the first place. These are rarely matters of physiology or anatomy, where conventional medicine excels. Surgery cannot remove the craving for nicotine. Drugs cannot make us exercise regularly or induce a sense of control or purpose in our lives. Only we can.

Dr. O. and millions like him know what they have to do to improve their health. They are at risk not because of insufficient knowledge, but because of insufficient command over their lives. They cannot make consistently healthy choices. The problem of high-risk living patterns — whether thoughts, attitudes, or behaviors — often gets down to a fairly straightforward matter: we cannot do what we need to do to ensure our health, and we cannot stop doing what we should not do.

Why is that?

The Force of Habit

We speak easily enough about the force of habit. How many of us, though, stop to wonder what gives a habit its force? How is it that a two-and-a-half-inch stick of tobacco can have such power over our behavior? During one recent year, for instance, more than a third of all smokers tried to stop, but failed.[4] We generally believe that compulsive physical behavior arises simply from the allure of something we like: see it, smell it, and we have to have it. It is a simplistic notion and an inaccurate one as well.

There is often much more to a physical craving than meets the eye. A compulsive drive is more of a process, really, than a single event, a linked chain of forces that have built up inside us over long periods of time. These forces run deeper than the urge for nicotine or sweets, drugs or compulsive sex. Most physical cravings answer to some hidden emotional need. Peel away the pure physical urge from a habit like smoking or drinking and you will often find a layer of emotional forces that fuel it. The physical urge for nicotine or cocaine is real enough. But a closer look at these cravings reveals an undergirding insecurity, perhaps, or stress, anxiety, even boredom. Your supervisor doesn't like your report so you take it out at home on the ice cream in the refrigerator; a tense phone call from home brings a cigarette to your lips. Physical activities, no doubt, but mentally charged and emotionally driven.

Compared to the relentless emotional drives underlying many cravings, the habit itself may represent only the tip of an iceberg. Deeper down may lie a field of emotional and mental forces driving us into compulsive behavior. The deep-seated drive that nudges Dr. O. toward a high-risk health status, for example, is not just the physical need to light up and inhale smoke. There simmers inside him a long-standing emotional need, expressed as the urge to smoke, that reaches out his hand and strikes the match.

Some physical cravings run even deeper than emotional needs, their tendrils trailing into the mind itself. The more we think about sweets or coffee, drugs or sex, the more we come to need them. Then the time arrives when we can hardly stop thinking about them. A habit has formed, an apparently physical habit, but with its source in the mind, its driving energy surging from the thinking process itself.

The Habit Cycle

Thoughts, feelings, urges, compulsive actions form a cluster of forces that drive us into compulsive behaviors. We call this cluster the "habit-cycle." It may begin with a thought triggered by an advertisement near the newspaper rack ("Napoleon Brandy!"), picks up force in our emotional field ("We had some last Christmas!") — and you find yourself at the cash register with a bottle of brandy when you had intended only to pick up a morning paper. You may register only the physical nudge for alcohol. But it was the combination of thought, memory, and physical desire that brought you home with a bottle under your arm that you hadn't gone out to buy.

The example may sound simplistic, but it reflects a familiar pattern for many people, where deeper emotional needs drive them into harmful behaviors. And deeper still, beneath the emotional layer even, rising from the hidden core of the mind itself, there is the tip-tap of one thought falling after another, nudging us on: eat this, drink that, smoke this, sniff that. The commands are insistent, deeply compelling: we react, often unconsciously, and eat, drink, swallow, or practice all manner of things we would like to resist, but cannot.

So it is with compulsive emotions like anger, hostility, fears, and anxieties that can be as tenacious as physical cravings. When in their grip, we can't say no to them, we can't simply push them out of mind. When a troubling dream leaves you in a panic in the middle of the night, can you tell your mind to drop the fear? Does it? Probably not. Course participants regularly report being oppressed by waves of hostility, anxiety, or helplessness that they can't rid themselves of.

To many of them, it is news that a combined assault of thoughts, feelings, and physical urges may confront them when they try to change their reactions or behaviors. It seems unfair! For them, developing the RISE Response really begins with the recognition that if they want to regain control over their more destructive moods and behaviors, they will have to grapple with the problem of the mind itself.

The Problem of the Mind

Well, we're asked, what is the problem with the mind? After all, our minds function well enough. We can balance our checkbooks and get to work on time. By conventional standards, anyway, we get by. But then there they are, the unwanted thoughts, feelings, and habits we wish would go away — the lingering anxieties, feelings of guilt or low self-esteem, too short a fuse, unwanted cravings, nameless fears....

The main problem of the mind is that it has too much speed and too little direction. Our thoughts do not normally follow the fixed, logical patterns we'd like to believe. They more often come in loops and whorls, sometimes careening in several directions at the same time. Follow your thoughts for a moment. Watch them while you're jogging, or brushing your teeth, or, now, while reading this book. Notice how easily they scatter into digressions that have nothing to do with your task at hand: snatches of an old Beatles tune might pop in, a conversation from the night before, the president's statement on the Middle East, the final scene from *Casablanca*. On it goes.

Now focus them. Try to fix your thoughts for just a minute on some detail before you — the color of the wallpaper, the texture of the paper in your hand. How long can you hold the thought before it skips away? A minute? (You're doing well.) Half a minute? Ten seconds?

How long was it before you found your mind raising irrelevant questions: "What was the color of that wallpaper? Did I remember to invite Charles?" Try to focus in spite of the distractions, and watch as your mind may snub even your best efforts to fix it on one thought. You can ask yourself, who is in charge here? And it may become apparent that no one is in charge — the mind has a mind of its own. You can tell your leg to move, and it will, your hand to scratch a certain itch, and it does. Why can't you tell your mind what to do? Why so little control?

> *"My mind's been going crazy trying to just focus on one thing in my everyday life. During the last week I stepped back a little from myself, let's say ten feet, and just watched my mind thinking about anything — this, that, here and there, everywhere! . . . It's not focused at all. My focusing is like zero right now. . . . The one thought that did come to my mind was, When did this happen to me? How did it happen?* (Helen P.)

The Acceleration Syndrome

Look around the world you live in. You'll see that two of the primary values that drive our modern culture are speed and multiple, simultaneous tasks — doing many things at the same time, and as quickly as we can manage. Propelled at warp speed, driven by our conditioning to do more and more in less time, we often move through our day on automatic pilot. We're rarely conscious of just what we are doing at any moment, or how we are doing it.

It's called the "acceleration syndrome." Pervasive and almost inescapable, it keeps many of us in a chronic state of automatic pilot, so that we seldom have the time or mental clarity to choose appropriately.

More often than not, we respond unconsciously to the stresses we encounter. We react without thinking, rarely making intentional choices. Add to this condition the pressures of a life-threatening condition and you intensify an already frenetic state of mind to the point where it's just about impossible to cope well. This is a common dilemma, and we all suffer from it. The constant pressure of too little time and too many demands leaves us vulnerable to all kinds of compulsive behavior, from obsessive moods to unsafe, even life-threatening behaviors.

Reflexive Thinking and Captured Attention

Obsessive moods or compulsive behaviors are a signal that your thinking is not under your control. ("If only I could stop thinking about it!") The helplessness you may feel in the face of a self-destructive mood may include a powerful compulsive element to it related to the way you think. Norman Cousins writes about two kinds of thinking. The first he calls "reflective" thinking, where we choose what we will think about and are more or less in control of our thoughts. Then there is "reflexive" thinking, far more common. Here our thoughts react to whatever internal or external stimuli happen by. We shouldn't confuse this with creative "free association," which a writer might choose to use as a source for ideas. In "reflexive" thinking we are not choosing at all. We're merely reacting to whatever catches our attention — sights, sounds, fears, regrets. In advanced stages, we may have little control at all over our thoughts.

Aimless, reflexive thinking is a major obstacle for making changes in our attitudes, moods, and behaviors. As our thinking becomes automatic, we can lose the ability to choose how we think, feel, and even act. Our attention is "captured" by the sights and sounds, the worries and interests that come our way, to use a phrase coined by economist E. F. Schumacher. So we drift. Finally, Schumacher adds, "I function very much like a machine: I am not doing things: they simply happen."[5] We can lose the capacity to make choices.

This describes the condition of many of us living in the grip of the acceleration syndrome. How did we get into this state? Is it because we're morally deficient? Weak? Not really. We're products of a relentless conditioning that shapes us in a hundred hidden ways to do more and more, faster and faster. We're taught to be like this. We're praised and rewarded when we're successful. We've *learned* it.

Retraining the Mind

And we can unlearn it. We've been conditioned to live this way, and the tools can break down this conditioning. They are designed to get us off of automatic pilot. They can slow down and refocus us by taking direct aim at the speeded up, multiple focused thought factory of the mind. But let us be clear. The "problem of the mind" does not imply any lack of mental capacity. Intelligent people are victims of compulsive attitudes and behavior as much as anyone. It is not the lack of mental energy that turns the mind toward unhealthy patterns, but the reverse: it is the mind's formidable powers — *out of control* — that cause the problems.

Learning the RISE Response, then, begins with the mind, with tools designed to help you train your attention and recapture its focus. This is basically a retraining of the mind and the way it thinks and influences our feelings and behaviors. You may find that in time you can begin to direct your attention where you want it to go, or away from where you don't want it to go. You can then choose more freely and with more judgment how you will think, respond, and live. This training brings a new freedom, and with it, a renewed sense of personal power. As Schumacher noted, "The difference between directed and captured attention is the same difference between doing things and letting things take their course, or between living and being lived."[6]

For all of that, it is still easier to read about training the mind than doing it. You need time and persistence and patience. And you need tools designed to slow down and refocus the thinking process. We'll introduce you to just such a set of tools in the next four chapters. They're accessible, straightforward, and proven.

"One of the things the program taught me was how much of what you do is nothing but a habit. And you can focus on that. You can change that habit. It is not mandatory that you get this habit and you have to live with it the rest of your life. You can change it."
(Carol C.)

Chapter Two _____

Passage Meditation

"I'm not my mind — it's a part of who I am. It's a part of me I want to learn to control, and now seems to be the time to learn that skill,. It's like exercise, building up the ability to control the mind." (Carl F.)

"I didn't know!" Michael reported to his small group during a recent class in San Francisco, *"I didn't think I was so ... so.... "*

"Distracted?" someone tried. He nodded. "Speeded-up?" Another nod.

We had heard it before. Michael's complaint went back to the beginning of the program. Participants often find themselves far more speeded up and less focused than they could have imagined. Cheryl, a recovering cancer patient, agreed. "I always thought I was a little hyper," she said, "but my gawd!"

They shouldn't feel alone, we told them. It's to be expected.

It may be that the greatest obstacle to working with the mind, in the beginning at least, is its speed. A fast mind, almost by definition, is distractible. So you need a way to slow down your thinking, reduce the flow of thoughts. Then you can begin to focus your attention where you want it to go. Slowing down the mind is an essential first step to recapturing attention.

Training the Mind

Passage meditation aims at slowing down and focusing the thinking process at the same time that it transforms your thinking. The method comes from the classical Indian tradition described in the book *Meditation* by Sri Eknath Easwaran; from his eight-point spiritual program we adapted the RISE tools.[1] You select an inspiring, "transformational" passage and memorize it. Then you repeat it silently, learning to focus more and more of your attention upon the words of the passage.

The method contains three main elements: slowing down the thinking process, focusing your attention, and transforming or reconditioning the thinking process itself. The theory is simple: the mind moves too fast, so slow it down; it lacks focus, so recapture its attention; it is influenced by what it thinks about, so choose wisely the material to which you will give your attention.

Here are the basic instructions for passage meditation as adapted from *Meditation.*

1. *The Passage:* Memorize an inspirational passage that appeals to you. It should be positive and practical, and contain what we call a "transformative charge." More on this later. (See the passages on page 33 and additional passages in Chapter Eighteen.)

2. *Posture:* Sit in a straight-backed chair or on the floor, and close your eyes. Keep your head, neck, and spinal column erect. It helps if you can set aside a small corner of a room to use for your meditation.

3. *Saying the Passage:* Start repeating the words of the passage, silently, in your mind. "Go through the words as slowly as you can," Sri Easwaran writes in his instructions, "letting each word drop singly into your consciousness. Do not follow any association of ideas, but keep to the words of the passage."[2]

Focus all your attention on the words. Try not to follow or dwell upon any thoughts or feelings that might come up, positive or otherwise. This includes images, associations, memories, even "creative" impulses.

Don't try to visualize. Simply focus all of your attention on the words of the passage. If you reach the end of the passage before your meditation period is over, repeat it, or start another passage you have memorized.

4. *Distractions:* When emotions, old anxieties, or ideas arise, do not resist them or give them your attention in any way. Instead, give your attention more to the words of the passage — "turn up its volume," as Louis, a facilitator, tells his study group. The more attention you give to the words, the less you give to the distractions. Sooner or later they will fade away. If your mind wanders completely away from the words, go back to the first line of the paragraph or verse and begin again.

HOW TO MEDITATE
ON AN INSPIRATIONAL PASSAGE

1. Memorize an inspirational passage.

2. Sit in a straight-backed chair or on the floor with your back, neck, and head straight.

3. With your eyes closed, repeat the words of the passage silently as slowly as you can.

4. Do not follow any associations or distractions, but concentrate on the words of the passage. When distractions come, do not resist them, but instead focus your attention more on the words of the passage.

5. When you finish the passage, start it again or begin a new one until your meditation period is over.

5. *Repeat the passage again* or start with a different passage. Keep meditating until your allotted time is over. Meditate each day. Many participants find that morning is the best time to meditate, since your mind hasn't had a chance to get too speeded up. But any time of the day will work. Start with as long a period as you can and try to build up over time until you are meditating thirty minutes. If you want to meditate longer than thirty minutes you should consult with an experienced meditation teacher.

This is the heart of the method of passage meditation. Read the directions carefully several times before you start, especially the directions for dealing with distractions.

How Passage Meditation Works

We said earlier that we needed a method of training attention that would both slow down the pace of our thoughts, and focus them. In *Meditation*, Sri Easwaran's directions compress into two sentences enough basic instruction to make significant inroads into lessening the speed and distractibility of your thoughts, while helping you to reshape your thinking and behavior patterns:

• *Go through the words of the passage as slowly as you can:* set a pace that slows down the impulse of the mind to speed up. But it shouldn't be so slow a pace that it leaves a gap between the words. Distractions can slip in! Note that you set your own pace, compatible with the speed of your thoughts.

You may begin meditating at a faster pace than you would like, if, like Michael and Cheryl, your thinking is especially speeded up. Don't get discouraged. If you meditate regularly, you will begin to slow down the words and reduce the pace of your thoughts. Repeating the passage slowly acts like a brake that gradually curbs the mind's speed until it comes down to an acceptable rate.

• *Keep to the words of the passage:* at the same time that you are slowing down the pace of your thoughts, you are narrowing the field of your attention. It is important that you give each word as much concentration as you can give it, "and let the words slip one after another into your consciousness like pearls falling into a clear pond."[3] Don't try to think about the meaning of the word: simply attend to it with concentration.

Other thoughts will compete for your attention. Let them. Old memories may arise or anxieties about the day. Neither resist nor give way to them. Focus more attention on the passage, gripping each word with it.

What happens to the distracting thought? Unattended, it is silenced and falls away: "When your attention rests completely on the passage," Sri Easwaran explains, "there can be no attention for anything else."[4]

Remember the formula: slow down and focus. The rhythm that the mind develops in meditation gradually influences the pace of your day. The focusing, at first difficult, can become effective enough so that the mind, as Schumacher writes, "maintains a silence when ordered to do so, and moves into action when given a specific task."[5]

The Passage

Slow down, focus, and...*transform*. By meditating on a self-selected passage, you can begin to recondition your thinking process in the image of a higher ideal. We recommend you choose meditation passages from traditional spiritual sources, passages handed down from men and women of exceptional inner insight. It does not matter from which tradition you choose your passages — the greater variety the better. Each tradition has something to recommend it. In Chapter Eighteen we have listed passages from a variety of spiritual traditions — Christian, Jewish, Buddhist, Indian, Sufi, Native American, Taoist.

What about contemporary sources, we're sometimes asked, poems, songs, affirmations? Do they make good passages for meditation? We don't recommend them. We have found that traditional sources — time valued, "consumer tested" — bring more depth, more of a transformative "charge" with them than passages written last week. One participant wanted to use a verse from a song. "I like Bob Dylan," he said.

So do we. But Mr. Dylan would probably be the first to tell you not to look to him for guidance in personal transformation. We come to resemble what we give our attention to. The passage "becomes imprinted on our consciousness," Sri Easwaran writes. "As we drive it deeper and deeper, the words of the passage come to life within us, transforming our thoughts, feelings, words, and deeds."[6]

If you have aversions to traditional religious language, you can select your passages from a variety of traditional sources that use no "religious" language at all. Buddhist sutras, Taoist texts, the Upanishads, and Native American prayers are some examples.

Your passage should appeal to you and contain language that speaks to your highest ideals. Be sure that it doesn't contain negative language, references to sin or guilt. The words of the passage enter your stream of consciousness in meditation. They will influence how you think about yourself. With well-selected passages, your meditation can become a process of intentional self-transformation, of "selected inner change." It can lend vigor and hope to your outlook on life, boost your self-esteem, and empower you to make wiser choices.

And notice that passage meditation is not in any way occult: its aims are practical and verifiable. We list a number of objective criteria in the Study Guide in Chapter Seven that you can use to evaluate your progress.

Visualization

So many of our course participants use visualization techniques as part of their self-care that we feel called upon to explain why we recommend that they do not substitute it for passage meditation. Visualization, or guided imagery, has become almost a standard intervention for a number of disease processes and is widely used by athletes, chess players, and mountain climbers to enhance their performance. It involves the cultivation of images in the mind's eye to improve self-esteem, desensitize fears, reduce the side effects of medications, enhance the therapeutic effects of drugs, increase immune efficiency, control pain, and curb compulsive behavior — with documented effects.

Central to the practice of visualization is the opening up of all the senses, where you try to visualize multiple images or mental scenarios with specific purposes, like Pac-man eating cancer cells, or relaxing journeys through mountain meadows. In this respect, visualization is at cross-purposes with passage meditation, since you are trying to *reduce* the amount of images in your mind rather than form new ones, while withdrawing your attention as much as possible from the sensory world. So the two techniques have substantial differences — again, in methods and aims — and should not be mixed.

In passage meditating you're trying to focus your attention on the passage to the exclusion of all other thoughts. You want to go beyond sensory images altogether. The passage is a focus for *reducing* your thoughts and images, not for stimulating new ones, no matter how ennobling or even useful they may seem. Passage meditation is meant to remove the congestion altogether and to improve your ability to concentrate. In fact, a number of course participants who use visualization as a therapeutic tools have reported that passage meditation improved their ability to visualize. The important point to remember is not to mix the two practices.

Passage meditation can be difficult work. It can feel tiresome at times. But this practice can bring measurable benefits in the long run. Each time you bring your attention back to the words of the passage you recondition your mental muscles, improve your concentration, deepen your awareness, strengthen your will.

Passages for Use in Meditation

INVOCATIONS

May quietness descend upon my limbs,
  My breath, my eyes, my ears.
May all my senses grow strong and clear.

Lead me from the unreal to the real.
  Lead me from darkness to light.
Lead me from death to immortality.

THE TWIN VERSES

All that we are is a result of what we have thought;
  We are formed and molded by our thoughts.
The man whose mind is shaped by selfless thoughts
  Gives joy whenever he speaks or acts.
    Joy follows him like a shadow
      That never leaves him.

TAO TE CHING

He who knows does not speak.
He who speaks does not know.
  Stop up the openings,
  Close down the doors,
  Rub off the sharp edges,
  Unravel all confusion.
  Harmonize the light,
  Give up contention.
This is called finding the unity of life.

Questions and Answers

Some of the more common questions asked during this stage of the program follow below, with our best attempt at answers:

- *I've been using another method of meditation for some time. Can I substitute it for meditating on a passage?*

If you want the benefits of RISE, you should try meditation according to the instructions we've given above. There are many forms of meditation, and each of them has its own tradition, style, method, aims, and value. Passage meditation aims at outcomes — slowing down, focusing, transforming the thinking process — that are closely linked to the specific training of attention that passage meditation brings. It shares elements with other forms of meditation, but it is probably unique in combining both a focusing and transforming element. Other forms of meditation, valuable though they may be, may not produce the outcomes we have documented in our participants.

Some participants want to continue previous practices while wanting to experiment fully with the RISE Response. We recommend they practice other methods at a different time than their passage meditation. It is important not to mix different forms of meditation together. We've no way to know what effects a combination may bring. Meditation acts powerfully on the mind. Mixing two separately developed methods of meditation may be like combining medications. They may cancel each other's effectiveness or even cause problems.

We ask only that you give this method a reasonable try, according to the instructions. Judge its effects in your own experience. Then decide for yourself whether this method speaks to your condition and aims.

- *Why do you suggest I concentrate on a passage in meditation and not on a mantram or on breathing?*

There are several reasons. First, as Westerners, our minds have been conditioned by language and linear thinking, so trying to focus on words may come easier to us than trying to concentration on a single syllable, say, or the breath, for thirty minutes at a time. It's something the mind is familiar with. It's hard enough asking the mind to concentrate after all these years

---

DIFFERENCES BETWEEN THE PASSAGE
AND THE MANTRAM IN RISE

- **The passage** should be at least a few lines long, perhaps even several verses long. Its content is inspirational. Different passages can be chosen to aim toward different outcomes, e.g., hopefulness, clarity, inner peace.

- **The mantram** is a word or short phrase. Once you select a mantram, you do not want to change it.

- **The passage** is used during your meditation period, for a specific time, while you're seated erect, eyes closed.

- **The mantram** is used at any time, anywhere, while walking, falling asleep, doing mechanical chores, or to interrupt stress reactions.

---

of letting it wander as it pleases. Giving it words to focus on meets it half way.

Second, the passage acts as more than just a focusing point; it contains inspirational content that you absorb as you meditate upon it. Remember that one objective of passage meditation is to transform your thinking process. The passage is central to this. In fact, meditating on traditional spiritual passages can open up the heart of these spiritual traditions to us and bring them into our lives in a way that our modern, critically trained minds can more easily tolerate.

Third, using words allows us to slow down the pace of our thoughts — another objective — since words have an easily measurable length and pace.

And last, as many course alumni who have used other methods of meditation tell us, it can be easier with a passage to know when you're *not* meditating. The passage is a visible marker of your attention. You're not so likely simply to wander in meditation, without realizing it, since you can usually tell when your attention has left the passage.

- *Can I write my own passage?*

We don't recommend it. If you want to learn mountain climbing, you would go to an experienced climber to train you. You wouldn't write your own manual. It's the same thing with meditation passages. Go to the people with experience in the field, the exceptional men and women in all the major traditional systems of meditation. Their writings come out of their personal experience, and that's what counts.

- *At what pace should I repeat the passage?*

As slowly as you can repeat it comfortably, without distractions entering in between the words. Short phrases, like "your peace" can be said as one word. You may have to experiment until you find the best pace for you.

- *How can I focus on a word and not think of its meaning?*

You probably can't, entirely, since the meaning of a word is inseparable from its sound. But don't *actively* think of the meaning, or reflect upon it. Simply say the word with concentration, and then go on to the next word.

- *What should I do if I experience colors or sounds during my meditation?*

People report a variety of sensations like seeing lights or feeling a tingling sensation. Our advice is to treat these experiences as distractions. Ignore them. Don't try to drive them away. Focus more attention on the words of the passage until you're not aware of anything else.

- *Sometimes I don't feel at all peaceful during my meditation. What's wrong?*

Probably nothing. You may be doing just fine, in fact. passage meditation is not necessarily a "feel good" method of meditation. It is meant to train your attention. Meditating on a passage with concentration will not necessarily make you feel blissful or even peaceful at the time you are meditating. You may feel peaceful at times. But more often than not your meditation will be a struggle with distractions. That's all right: you're meditating.

In any event, don't use how you feel as a criterion for judging your meditation. Feelings are too unreliable a measure of what is going on in meditation. Don't judge your meditation at all, not at least for the first few weeks. Just meditate.

> *"In the beginning, learning to meditate on a spiritual passage for a lot of us is very difficult because there's that confusion about religion. Yet it has nothing to do with religion. It is simply an exercise, the discipline of picking a passage that countless millions of people have repeated over the centuries. I ended up with the Twenty-third Psalm. Yet I have no religious affiliations. But the passage has kept me together through some pretty scary times. . . . 'I will fear no evil. . . .' I had to do it this morning, dealing with all this new stuff with IVs. It's just so automatic, it's just there. It's a wonderful gift."* (James R.)

Using a Mantram

"I've got a little car that doesn't go too fast so everyone passes me up. I was driving on the freeway the other day, and some-one almost pushed me off the road. I got very upset. But then I started with my mantram, and all of a sudden I found myself laughing...and I thought, 'This is it! This must be a benefit of RISE.' Because the mantram turned upset into laughter."

(Mark V.)

Training attention is the core of the RISE Response — slow-ing down, focusing, and transforming the way you think by meditating on a passage. But you meditate for only a certain time each day. And you do it according to a specific time, place, and posture. A mantram can be used at any time, anywhere, under any circumstances. It's a kind of rapid focusing tool. You can use a mantram to slow down, to refocus yourself, to regain your composure when you're stressed, to buy you time *before you react*. It's easy to use and doesn't require any discipline. Yet it has proven a powerful tool for many course partici-pants in dealing with the emotional stresses and challenges that accompany illness, the workplace, and much of modern life.

What a Mantram Is

A mantram is a word or short phrase; mantrams are found in most spiritual traditions. Users of a mantram, wanting to draw upon its healing and calming effect, repeat it silently in their minds as often as they can.[1] In the past decade, the mantram has been used in various health care programs, with documented medical and psychological benefits. Studies have shown that repeating a mantram reduces feelings of tension and anxiety and ameliorates "stress-related disorders."[2] Using a mantram has been shown "to produce a lowered state of physiological arousal"[3] and to be "effective in treating emotional disorders which are also characterized by physiological arousal."[4]

Dr. Herbert Benson of Harvard University demonstrated that repeating a mantram elicits a measurable calming effect, which he popularized as the "relaxation response." He argued that it acted as a balancing counterpart to the fight-flight response that stress arouses and that can result in organ damage when it becomes chronic.[5] Benson's studies showed that repeating a mantram over a twenty-minute period resulted in a lowering of heart rate, blood pressure, breathing rate, and oxygen consumption — all factors associated with a calmer state of mind.[6]In this state, brain waves shift to the more relaxed alpha rhythm, while blood flow to the muscles decreases and blood is sent to the brain and skin producing a feeling of "rested mental alertness."[7] A recent review of a large body of research concluded that the relaxation response can be helpful in reducing stress and controlling high blood pressure, as well as combating chronic pain."[8]

The Mantram in RISE

We use the mantram differently from most programs we're familiar with. It's a practical tool, used to interrupt the stress response at any time, anywhere we happen to be. We don't use the mantram to meditate on, not because it can't be useful for that, but because the passage contains more meaningful inspirational content to help transform the thinking process. (Many course alumni open their meditation by repeating their mantram a few times to relax, before they start the passage.) A mantram is deliberately short, no more than a few words at most, so that it can be accessed quickly, at *any* time, even in the grip of a strong emotion like anger or fear.

The mantram is a popular tool for many course participants. It's easier to practice than meditation and less cumbersome to incorporate into their already crowded lives. Many alumni have reported almost immediate benefits using a mantram, and sometimes they've been surprising. We've regularly heard that they're sleeping better, coping better with their pain and discomfort, or even managing their negative moods better.

Still, other people have had problems with the mantram, especially in the beginning. It looks too esoteric to them, or even simplistic. Repeating the same word over and over seems mechanical, they've told us, or just too "weird." We invite them to set aside their skepticism for awhile and give the mantram a try. They've nothing to lose, we argue—no harmful side effects, no great investment in time or money. And surprising results may follow.

Take Bob, for instance, a group facilitator. He reacted skeptically to the mantram initially. It wasn't his "cup of tea," he said. But he did try it out, and in fact used a mantram for a few months as an experiment. When he later tested HIV positive, he told us the mantram helped him recover from his depression. "The mantram was there when I needed it," he told us at a facilitator's session. "I was starting to cave in to the depression. And the mantram reminded me that I was quite alive."

Charles, an alumnus, told us he was about to change his mantram after a few weeks since it wasn't "taking" for him. Then a traumatic experience on the freeway left him on the verge of panic. He realized that his mantram was repeating itself and brought him a lucid calmness in which he was able to cope. "Needless to say," he told us, "I didn't change my mantram."

These are typical of the many "mantram stories" we've heard in courses from San Diego to Toronto. Stressed beyond their endurance, struggling out of their emotional depths, alumni have time and again told us how their mantram helped them through a crisis. Jim was on the forty-fourth floor of a high-rise in San Francisco when the 1989 Loma Prieta earthquake struck. "I learned a lot about the mantram," he told us.

It isn't a panacea. You still undergo the stress and pain that accompany life and illness. But using a mantram can help you keep your balance in difficult circumstances. It can reduce your mood swings to more manageable proportions. And it can bolster your confidence that you can handle the stresses that life and illness will bring.

"I used to be very fearful going into the shower, because when I had the panic disorder, it started in the shower. My heart would be pounding, and I thought I was going to have a heart attack. That was one of the first places I started using the mantram, in

the shower. Before going in, I would start my mantram, and as I used it more and more, I could take a shower without even thinking about the panic anymore. . . . Now I'm not as fearful as I was. I feel more in control, because of that." (Penny V.)

Other participants have used their mantrams to help cope with painful diagnostic procedures or the long periods in clinic waiting rooms. They've told us that before they took the course that these experiences would leave them drained. Repeating a mantram helped them remain calmer and more in control of their reactions. Bob told us that during a high fever repeating his mantram helped keep him alert in spite of the discomfort. Before, he could do nothing more than try to grin and bear the pain. Repeating a mantram has even helped some alumni to endure the suffering or even deaths of their friends and lovers. In any event, the mantram can work for you too. But you need to repeat it regularly for awhile before rendering a judgment.

Choosing a Mantram

Choose a mantram from the box on page 42. Give it a try for a few months. Then decide whether the mantram is a tool that speaks to your own condition. You should choose a mantram with care. Take into account your religious interests (or lack of them), your personal reaction to the mantram, and the practical significance of the words. We recommend you choose a mantram that has a literal meaning and comes from a traditional source. Such mantrams may carry a kind of transforming "charge" from having been repeated by millions of people over the centuries. And the meaning can help transform your thinking as it helps to refocus it. Its "charge" can help bring stability even in the face of the cataclysmic stress that sometimes accompanies serious illness.

In the accompanying box we've listed some of the most ancient and popular mantrams from the major spiritual traditions of the world. Don't let traditional language become a hurdle for you. The word "Lord" can be interpreted as a reference to a personal God, or it can simply stand for the deeper resources that lie in the depths of the human personality.

MANTRAMS

Christian

Jesus
Jesus Christ
Lord Jesus Christ
Hail Mary or *Ave Maria*
My God and My All   (Saint Francis of Assisi's mantram)
Maranatha   (Aramaic) Lord of the Heart. ("*Mar-uh-naw-taw*")
Kyrie Eleison   The Lord has risen. ("*Kir-ee-ay Ee-lay-ee-sone*")
Christe Eleison   Christ has risen. ("*Kreest-ay Ee-lay-ee-sone*")

Hindu/Indian

Rama   (Gandhi's mantram) Eternal joy within. ("*Rah-muh*")
Om Shanti   An invocation to eternal peace. ("*Ohm shawn-tee*")
Om Prema   A call for universal love. ("*Ohm pray-mah*")
Om Namah Shivaya   An invocation to beauty and fearlessness.
               ("*Ohm nah-mah shee-vy-yah*")
So Ham   I am that Self within. ("*So hum*")
Om Ram, Shri Ram, Jai,   An invocation to joy.
 Jai, Ram   ("*Ohm rahm, shree rahm, jay, jay, rahm*")

Buddhist

Om Mane Padme Hum   An invocation to the jewel (the Self) in the lotus
               of the heart. ("*Ohm mah-nee pod-may-hume*")
Namo Amida Butsu   I bow to the Buddha of Infinite Light.
               ("*Nah-mo ah-mee-dah boot-soo*")
Namo Butsaya   I bow to the Buddha. ("*Naw-moh boot-sie-yah*")

Jewish

Barukh Attah Adonoi   Blessed art Thou, O Lord.
               ("*Bah-ruke ah-tah ah-don-aye*")
Ribono Shel Olam   Lord of the Universe. ("*Ree-boh-noh shel ohlahm*")

Islamic/Arabic

Allah   Lord God, the One.
Bismallah Ir-Rahman   In the name of God, merciful, compassionate.
 Ir-Rahim   ("*Beese-mah-lah ir-rah-mun ir-rah-heem*")

Native American

O Wakan Tanka   Oh Great Spirit!

Using a Mantram

Select a mantram from the list. If one doesn't "jump out" at you, try "Rama" to start with. It's simple and means, literally, "joy." Then start repeating it whenever you get a chance. Look for the times during your day when you've no particular mental demands, such as walking, waiting for an appointment, or standing in line at the supermarket. You can repeat it while you're doing chores like washing dishes, vacuuming, or mowing the lawn. It can give your mind something to focus on. Practice is the key to making the mantram work. The more you repeat it, the more easily it will come to you in stressful moments.

Get creative. A little reflection will probably reveal a number of times during your day when you really have nothing to do but fill the time. That's when you want to practice repeating your mantram. It trains your mental focus while it makes the mantram a habit, ready to be used in times of stress.

The Mantram and Habits

We become most vulnerable to habits and addictions when we don't have anything particular to do. Boredom invites addictive behavior. With no task to occupy your attention, old habits pop out of your mental woodwork, like mice looking for cheese to nibble. Suddenly you remember the almost empty carton of ice cream in the freezer. Or you start to recall an old anxiety for no apparent reason. These are good times to use your mantram. Repeat it over and over. Go for a walk if you can. The mind needs a focus to direct its energy, and the mantram can provide this focus. It's surprising how much of the anxiety that haunts people at night comes from having nothing to think about. If your mind starts to drift toward an old fear as you're trying to get to sleep, give it the mantram to focus on.

You can use this same technique to deal with physical cravings. As you start to reach for the Danish you don't *really* want, change your field of attention. Say your mantram. You can actually distract your mind from the craving long enough that it may forget about it altogether. The mantram can help too, with even powerful compulsive cravings like the urge for drugs or alcohol or unsafe sex. A number of alumni used their mantrams to help them stop smoking or reduce their substance abuse. But the mantram will work for you in these circumstances only if you have been repeating it regularly.

The Mantram and Emotions

Louis, a landscaper and course facilitator, told a RISE class how the mantram helped him cope with just such a highly charged emotional circumstance. He received a phone call from a former client threatening a lawsuit over a matter for which Louis no longer bore responsibility. He knew this, but nonetheless felt his mind surging toward familiar emotional turmoil. He started to panic. Repeating his mantram, he told the caller he would get back to him later, and then headed out the door for a fast walk. He walked for almost an hour, he told us, repeating his mantram all the way, until he felt the tension loosen and some clarity return to his mind. Returning to his house, he called the former client, and peaceably worked out an arrangement that was agreeable to both. "I couldn't have done that before without freaking out completely," he told us, "and I probably would have freaked out the client too."

On a deeper level, the mantram can help cut the nexus that ties you to destructive emotional states. Haunting fears, chronic resentment, persistent feelings of hopelessness or low self-esteem, have a strong and sometimes overpowering mental component. They're difficult to stop thinking about once they start up. But you can use Louis's example and take the same kind of "emergency" action he did when you find yourself in the grip of a destructive mood. You probably won't have an hour to spare. But even a short, fast walk can help a lot to restore some clarity and to size up the situation and avoid the panic or hostility.

You need to walk fast, arms swinging, for a good twenty minutes and give all your attention to the mantram. The physical exertion of the walk deepens your breathing rhythm. And it helps release some of the pent-up energy of the emotion. The mantram focuses your attention away from the anxiety while it builds a soothing inner rhythm that can help to calm your mind. If it sounds simplistic, experiment. Give it a try. Many participants have started out as skeptics but then found that a mantram walk could help them in surprising ways to deal with some forms of emotional stress.

Getting to Sleep

One of the most effective times to repeat the mantram is when you are falling asleep. It requires turning your attention away from the TV or the novel you have been reading and trying to give it all to the mantram as you start to drop off. It is not as simple as it sounds. You have to be tenacious to keep the mantram going, especially as you get drowsy. But you can learn to fall asleep in the mantram, and you may find it keeps your mind calmer after you wake up. Course participants have regularly reported being able to sleep better, and several have reduced their sleeping medication or stopped it altogether (though we would not recommend this without consultation with your physician).

Other participants report difficulties during the middle of the night. An old fear or memory jogs them awake and they can't get back to sleep. "If only I could stop thinking about it," they tell us. But the more they try to drive the memory away, especially in the dead of night, the more attention they give it. So the fear swells, intensifies. It's like pumping air into a balloon! So instead of trying to push the fear out of your mind, repeat your mantram. Give all your attention to it, repeating "Rama, Rama" or "Jesus, Jesus." Just keep saying it, even though it makes you tired. (That's the point!) Fears, anxieties, old, haunting memories need attention, as plants need air and sunlight. Without it, even the most tenacious fears will start to wither. The attention you give to the mantram is borrowed from the fear and lessens its grip.

Repetition the Key

The key to the mantram's effectiveness is regular repetition. As the mantram is driven deeper into consciousness by repetition, it can help arouse dormant inner resources. Like many course alumni, you may find that using a mantram gives you access to greater calmness and clarity and to more command over your reactions, even during times of intense stress and high anxiety.

"I hardly slept at all for two years. Two years' worth of pills! Then no pills at all, and I would wake up upset with this fear of what's going to happen next. Now I can just lie down and go

---

USEFUL TIMES FOR
PRACTICING YOUR MANTRAM

- Waiting for a bus.
- Stalled in traffic.
- Waiting for a program to begin.
- Sitting in a reception room.
- Riding in a car or on the bus.
- Stopped at a red light.
- Waiting for service in a restaurant.
- Painting your room.
- Gardening.
- Waiting on hold on the phone.

---

right to sleep. If I do wake up with this fear in the middle of the night, I say the mantram and it's gone. The mantram has just been wonderful to help me get to sleep at night." (Cecily E.)

Questions and Answers

- *Is it all right to repeat the mantram while driving?*

We wouldn't recommend using the mantram while driving a car, at least not while driving fast. It would be better to focus all your attention on your driving. In a sense, one-pointed focus can have the same effect of keeping the mind centered as does repeating the mantram.

- *"I just didn't feel anything in my meditation this week,"* Kathy told us at a recent class. *"What am I doing wrong?"*

Nothing, it turned out, in Kathy's case. After questioning her, it was clear that she had been meditating according to the instructions and had been gamely fighting her distractions. What was "wrong" was her appraisal of her meditation. She was using subjective criteria ("It didn't feel right").

Now that you have been meditating for a few weeks, you may want to try to evaluate how your meditation is going. It is natural to think that if you feel "good" during or after your meditation it has been a good one. And if you don't feel good, the meditation has been a poor one.

Not necessarily so.

A good meditation may be one in which you have fought hard with the mind at a deeper level of consciousness, as was probably Kathy's case. It may have been a hard fight, and you may feel you lost. But the struggle itself makes it a productive meditation in the long run. It gives you just a little more leverage over the mind. Think of it as a good "workout" — a little tiring, sometimes difficult, but worthwhile in the long run.

We have listed a number of criteria in the self-study section with which you can begin to assess the quality of your meditation (see "Evaluating Your Meditation" on page 97).

- *Why am I so inconsistent?*

This is a recurring question in our classes. Why is it, participants ask, that one day we can be so consistent and full of resolution with regard to our habits, and then the next day act as though we had never heard of RISE?

This is natural and to be expected for a couple of reasons. First is the tenacity of habitual behavior itself. Habits are not easy to change. In Chapter One, we found that when we try to alter a compulsive physical habit we may encounter resistance from both the mind and body. As a result, our enthusiasm will naturally come and go.

Second, remember that it is the nature of the mind to waver and lose its focus, especially when its attention has never been trained. You need time and practice before you can expect your attention to become steady. But you can use your distractibility to your advantage in fighting a habit. When a craving for something unhealthy invades your thinking, tell your mind to wait half an hour. After that, you'll indulge it. Repeat your mantram and throw yourself into some useful activity. The chances are better than even that when the half hour is up, the mind will have moved on to something else.

Chapter Four

Slowing Down/Seeing Clearly

"When I started the program, the last thing I wanted to do was slow down. I thought I needed to run, run, run. I was trying to run away from my diagnosis. In slowing down, I learned that I didn't need to run. I don't mean you have to walk slower, and think slower. It's just taking a look at what you're doing. Now I love to be grounded." (Kyle B.)

Twenty years ago two San Francisco cardiologists announced their theory that the frantic pace of modern life was unhealthy, if not fatal, to many people. Doctors Meyer Friedman and Ray Rosenman studied the high-level executives who came to them with coronary problems and concluded that their high-pressured lifestyles — time-pressured, competitive, hostility-inducing — had a lot to do with their disease. In their landmark book on the subject, *Type A Behavior and Your Heart*, the doctors describe a number of high-risk behaviors that correlate with coronary problems. People are considered to be Type A if they:

- Try to achieve many poorly defined goals.

- Love competition.

- Crave recognition and advancement.

- Easily become angry.

- Are always in a hurry.

More recent research has generated controversy on which of the Type A traits is the most "toxic," with hostility showing the strongest evidence of causing harm (see Chapter Eleven).[1] But a consensus has emerged among most physicians that Type A behavior does place us at increased risk for coronary problems, even if the specific mechanisms are not fully understood.

One of the most prominent cofactors described by Friedman and Rosenman was a syndrome they called "hurry sickness."[2] They defined it as the compulsive drive to accomplish too much or to take part in too many events in the amount of time available. People afflicted with hurry sickness were driven by a heightened sense of time urgency, the doctors explained, and the sense that there was never enough time to get everything done. They kept accelerating their activities, and even reduced their interactions with other people in order to get more time. Eventually they came to view even the normal functions of life like meals, relationships, and recreation as obstructions or delays.

In her *Guide to Personal Health, New York Times* columnist Jane Brody vividly described the life of such a person (herself). She writes that she was,

> ...worried about every wasted moment, anxious about every missed train or bus, hostile in every traffic jam, unable to wait in any line. I pushed ahead of people without even seeing them...I regarded busy signals, overly protective secretaries, and slow moving salespeople as deliberate obstacles to my attempts to get more and more done in less and less time. Then one day I realized I was rushing my life away."[3]

You don't have to qualify as a certified Type A to be so accelerated as to inflict harmful levels of stress upon your mind and body or to make the hurried, automatic reactions to challenges that lead to poor choices. In fact, the compulsive Type As that Rosenman and Friedman describe are probably only at the extreme of a condition that affects most of us. As we wrote in Chapter One, speed is a way of life for people living in the industrial West. Hurrying, for most of us, is as natural a part of our lives as eating. It's a way of life.

In fact, we barely notice it. We can live a good part of each day in a race against an imaginary clock and think nothing of it. We get up in a rush, eat breakfast with a gulp (if we eat it at all), drive dangerously, work as though possessed. Then we're back home in a blur, racing toward the next morning's starting bell. Jeff, an alumnus, realized that he sat down at his desk each morning in what he called the "racing position." He sat there tensed, hunched slightly forward, hand poised above the phone for the call that would start him down the track.

Conscious, intentional choices are extremely difficult to make when you're in a hurry. The faster you move, the faster your mind goes and the less control you have over your thinking. Don't be surprised if you find that you're most likely to reach for the cigarette at times when you are rushed. Compulsive drives thrive on speed.

So it is that slowing ourselves down is essential to regaining control over our lives and the ways we think, feel, and act. And slowing down during the day helps to reinforce the training we give the mind during passage meditation. This coherence between the two tools is characteristic of the program, since the tools are designed to reinforce each other.

What Slowing Down Means

But misunderstandings can arise. Royce, a computer technician, worried aloud during a class that by slowing down he would become less productive and therefore less competitive in his work. It's a common concern among course participants — that they could lose their jobs if they "slowed down." They shared an unspoken assumption that one either moved fast or slow through life — no alternatives. It is a misconception. You can learn to move with deliberation, briskly when warranted, at no cost to efficiency or productivity.

Slowing down does not mean simply...*going*...*very*... *slowly*. It has more to do with your state of mind — how conscious you are, how aware — than it does with the actual acceleration of your body through space. Slowing down means moving with deliberation through your day, making conscious choices along the way rather than accelerating through it on "automatic pilot."

You can slow down and be productive. In fact, the deliberate person is often the most efficient and, in the long run, the most productive. He isn't wasting time correcting mistakes made in a rush; she isn't taking more time on a job because she didn't allow time to think it through. When you gain some control over your attention, you will find that you can move briskly and efficiently through the day without getting hurried or falling victim to "hurry sickness."

Slowing down does not mean that you have to convert your personality to a snail's or get a job as a fire lookout. It does not imply inactivity. Many of our alumni are highly successful people working in competitive environments. Some of them have reported that they find themselves more efficient now than before they learned the RISE Response. Mark, a financial advisor in the same class with Royce, found that by becoming more deliberate he was actually able to become more productive in his work. "I'm able to listen better to my clients," he told us. "And in my work, that improves results."

What is true in a work environment applies as well to managing illness. The stress of a life-threatening illness can plunge a person into a frenzy of activity, racing to try one intervention after another, in the hopes of stumbling over a cure. Sometimes they may not even allow an intervention the time to run its proper course before trying something else. It's common. Many participants have told us that they came to the course after trying dozens of treatments, often superficially. Learning the RISE Response convinced them of the value of focusing with deliberation on a few select treatments and giving them their full attention.

Slowing Down

There are many ways to begin. The best place to start is to look at your own patterns and identify those where you are most likely to get caught in the race. We have listed below some signs of developing hurry sickness in three major areas of activity:

Driving Patterns

Nothing brings out the speed demon in us as does getting behind the wheel of a car. A surprising amount of small group discussion in our courses involves driving. ("I seem to change into another person when I get in my car!") Nothing quite challenges our peace of mind as does the freeway system. You should ask yourself if:

- You habitually drive faster than you need to.

- You get angry at drivers who don't immediately move when the light turns green.

- You change lanes constantly to jockey for a few seconds' time.

- You rail frequently at the gross incompetence of other drivers.

- You can't stand drivers who insist on driving a little slower than (or at) the speed limit.

Eating Habits

Eating patterns have changed profoundly in this country during the last twenty years. Many meals are eaten out, if meals are eaten at all, reflecting the extraordinary acceleration of time urgency along the central nervous system of our culture. See if:

- You hardly ever take the time for meals anymore, and resort mostly to snacking.

- You frequently eat at your desk or while continuing to work.

- You eat standing up (often in front of the refrigerator).

- You prefer to eat alone and quickly, unless it is a working lunch.

- You take the time to eat deliberately, savoring your food and mealtime conversation.

Relationships

It is in our relationships — with a partner, with friends or family, at work — that time urgency takes its severest toll. For love can't be hurried; friendship and affection need time. It is probably not an accident that the recent decades of accelerated time urgency have also been marked by a palpable sense of increasing isolation. Check to see if:

- You don't seem to have time anymore for people, other than business interests or casual acquaintances.

- You carry on conversations with people while reading the paper, or watching TV, or thinking ahead to your next appointment.

- You feel inconvenienced when someone engages you in a conversation you didn't initiate.

- You interrupt the conversations of other people or finish their sentences for them.

There are others markers of encroaching "hurry sickness" too numerous to go into here. And no doubt you will have a few special patterns of your own. A careful examination of your most prominent patterns should turn up the major trouble spots and give you a starting point.

Slowing Down and Vitality

Few people connect that exhausted feeling at the end of the day with how speeded up they have been. If you find yourself exhausted when you get home after work, look carefully at your day: was it a true physical expenditure of energy that depleted your vitality, or was it the rushing around? Eileen, an alumnus and therapist, told her "RISE Again" support group that she found that after she started slowing herself down, she could have a demanding day with any number of clients and not feel exhausted at the end of it. She felt tired, well used, she said, but did not experience the physical and emotional drain she had been used to before trying to slow down.

Making a Friend of Time

Here are some ways you can begin to slow yourself down:

- *Set your priorities.* Decide what is important for you and arrange your time accordingly. Think in terms of quality, as Jane Brody counsels, not simply in terms of "quantity, number of clients or patients, number of committees on which you serve, number of accomplishments."[4]

- *Write down your priorities.* Make a list. It helps to remind yourself in the heat of action what you had decided upon in a more reflective mood. Stick to your list. But be realistic! Don't burden yourself with too much to accomplish in the time you have. Don't give yourself deadlines you can meet only with murderous Type A efforts. And accept the fact that despite your best efforts, some things may not get done. Life goes on.

- *Set a relaxed pace.* This may mean getting to bed earlier the night before, so that you can get up earlier in the morning. In fact, your day really begins with the time you go to bed, rather than when you get up. Have a leisurely breakfast, and allow enough time to drive at a reasonable speed to work.

- *Get to work early.* Then you can set a steady, unpressured pace throughout the day. Take short, periodic breaks during the day as you feel tension building up. Take a mantram walk at lunch. Try not to procrastinate. This only leaves more work for the end of the day and places you under added pressure.

- *Challenge old patterns.* You can put your watch in your pocket, for instance, if you find you look at it every thirty seconds. Let someone stand in line in front of you at the supermarket, or slip into your lane on the freeway. When a red light stops you in your tracks, smile and repeat your mantram.

- *Save time for people.* Take a little more time with secretaries and receptionists. Take a moment to ask about their families, pets, or hobbies. Tell the clerk at the bank to take his time, there's no hurry. Allow ample time for friends or family.

- *Set limits.* Decide what you expect of yourself in a given day or week. Be realistic, and stick within the limits you set, even if it means dropping something.

- *Slow down slowly.* Don't try to change everything at once. Select one pattern to alter, and try to gain a foothold there before moving on. Expect relapses into the old patterns since life around you will be pressuring you in a hundred different ways to *get moving!* Several alumni have reported success just trying to slow down for the first hour of their day. Then they gradually extended the period.

Chapter Five _____

One-Pointed Focus

*"When it came right down to it, I found that in my mind —
I describe it as a PBX operator — I'd been answering all these
phones, and all the lines had been coming through just fine. But
in the last few months, with the diagnosis and everything, I felt
like I had every line in the world coming in. I was overwhelmed.
I really didn't know which way to focus."* (Edward S.)

Is your thinking unfocused a good part of the time? More
than you would have thought? *Much* more? Welcome to RISE.
We hear this all the time. Paul, a San Diego alumnus, told us
he thought of himself as highly disciplined, both in his work
and life style. He was "shocked," he said, at how undisciplined
his thinking was. "I wouldn't have believed it before I started
to meditate," he told us. And most of the people in his small
group nodded in agreement.

Let us take another, more detailed look at the kind of "reflexive" thinking typical of most people today. It's the kind where
thoughts run at will, bursting at random like fireworks on the
Fourth of July. Here's what it can look like. You are writing a
letter to your sick aunt, and you start to tell her about your recent vacation to Mexico, the sunsets that dazzled you over the
Sea of Cortés? Then you remember the pizza that you had for
lunch. The anchovies, actually, which you regret. Why now? The
pizza has nothing to do with your Mexican trip. Even less to do
with your aunt. The thought simply stepped into your mind,
unbidden, an intruder.

You return to the sunset, but before you can get all the hues
worked out, you're suddenly aware of snatches of conversation
from yesterday's luncheon. They've come from nowhere, like
the pizza, and you find them an annoyance. You really want to
finish your letter, and you want to do it with a little flair. But the
distractions won't stop. Lunchtime conversations are followed

by the opening chords of Beethoven's Fifth, which you heard on the radio on your way home from work...then an idea on how to redecorate your bedroom...a recipe for asparagus à limón for tonight's party! The aunt doesn't stand a chance. You give up on the letter and go out for a snack.

It's a polite euphemism to call this "thinking." In a way, we're being thought by our thoughts. Yet it describes what most of us do, most of the time.

Polyphasic Thinking

In their research into Type A behaviors, Drs. Rosenman and Friedman identified another risk factor for coronary illness they called "polyphasic" or "many-pointed" thinking. It's typical of many Type As. Polyphasic thinkers try to occupy their minds with as many different thoughts and activities as they can *at the same time*. It's more "efficient," they believe. Dr. Friedman describes one patient of his who listened to the news on the radio and read his trade journals, *while he brushed his teeth*.

Many type As "double up" in their conversations, thinking or doing something else while they're pretending to listen. Dr. Friedman writes of a New York publisher who could be heard on the phone crinkling up a piece of paper while talking. "I wouldn't mind as much if I heard him doing it when I was speaking," a friend reported, "but he shuffles that paper even when he's talking to me!"[1]

"Reflexive" and "polyphasic" thinking are typical of a lot of us, and we don't have to be Type As. At best such thinking is an annoyance. When it becomes chronic, though, we become vulnerable to compulsive behavior that may be unhealthy. Attention disorders, for instance, have been correlated with poor coping behavior. A high prevalence of attention deficits has been found among alcoholic patients too.[2] Having poor control over attention when grieving is a negative factor in the coping abilities of widows.[3] Other studies have shown that disorders of attention play a role in bringing on senile dementia.[4]

Selective Attention

Both reflexive and polyphasic thinking can be modified by retraining the mind to become more "one-pointed." It requires learning to focus on one field of attention at a time. Psychologist William James became interested in one-pointed attention at the turn of the century, when he discovered its health giving effects. He called it "selective attention." Sports psychologists still use the term to describe the focused mental state that assists athletes striving toward peak performance. For James, one-pointed, "selective" attention was "the very root of judgment, character and will," and a powerful tool for reconditioning behavior.[5]

Increasing one-pointed attention can help you direct your attention away from unwanted thoughts and compulsive urges, toward more healthful thinking. One recent study even suggests that attention training ("mindfulness") can play a constructive role in preventing or alleviating dementia.[6]

Passage meditation is a powerful antidote to unfocused attention. Every time you bring your attention back to the words of the passage, you strengthen your concentration and focus. But even regular meditation needs something to reinforce it during the day if you are going to fully rebuild your attention.

We suggest you try the fourth tool, one-pointed focus. Basically it comes down to doing only one thing at a time. We'll repeat that, since it may fly in the face of every work-related training you've undergone: try whenever you can to do only one thing at a time. It means giving your complete attention to whatever you are doing at any given moment. You could be driving, studying, working, reading, even eating or watching a movie. Stay one-pointed. Don't listen to the radio while you're working on your proposal. Don't talk on the phone as you plan the menu for Thanksgiving. Try to do just one thing at a time, and give it your full attention.

This may strike you as odd, perhaps even job-threatening, advice if you work at a high-pressure job like Lynne, an administrative nurse in an intensive care unit of a major urban hospital. *"I remember taking the RISE program,"* she told us,

> *"and we were at the fourth week, 'one-pointed focus,' and here I was an intensive care nurse doing fifty things at a time. I got really worried. I'm like, 'Oh, my God, I can only do one thing at a time? I can't do that!' I was really worried. Then Warren said, 'No, it's okay, just take your time.' And it's true. It's really true. If you just slow down and focus on the one thing, you will get it done. And you get the bigger picture too."* (Lynne M.)

Becoming One-Pointed

It's not going to be easy to build one-pointed focus into your work pattern. Many jobs require that you perform several tasks at once. You will probably be struggling against the personal habits of decades. Even more daunting, you will run directly against the grain of modern life, which one writer recently called a conspiracy "against *a clean, one-pointed focus.*"[7] Much of life today urges us toward unfocused or multiple thinking. Look at the pace of television advertising, for instance. It's images last only milliseconds now. Or the background music *in elevators,* as though we'd collapse without violins to get us to the tenth floor.

So expect a battle then, and a protracted one. But you can get results, sometimes right away. And you've already begun the fight! The time you spend in passage meditation is basic training. You're schooling the mind in one-pointed focus. Now you try to extend that focus to your day, a little at a time, step by step. Start with your breakfast or your drive to work. Consciously try to stay as focused as you can, even for a short while. If you keep at it, you may find you've worked completely focused for an hour!

Here's how to get started:

While Eating

Don't eat and read. Try not to eat and watch TV at the same time. We know — it's a way of life for a lot of people. And it's common behavior for high-risk Type As to watch television, read a report, and eat at the same time. When you give your full attention to what you are eating, you gain in two ways: your attention benefits, and you may even find that the food tastes better.

While Driving

Try to drive without the radio on. It may sound like solitary confinement, true. But it certainly helps to train your attention. And you'd be surprised at how many alumni tell us that after a few weeks of practice, they actually find the car radio an unpleasant distraction. This is beneficial to the other drivers out there too, since a high percentage of driving accidents can be attributed to poor concentration.

While Working

We mentioned this already, but it's worth repeating. Try not to work with background music on. It may seem soothing, but it splits your attention. Even if you are not aware that the music is on, it may be a source of unconscious tension. Get absorbed in your work, which is perhaps the best way to train attention.

With Other People

Avoid "doubling up" (thinking about something else when you're talking with someone). Give them your undivided attention. You may find surprising results, like Michael, an alumnus from our first northern California class. He decided to give a salesman his undivided attention and ended up selling the salesman something from his shop! Your focused attention may result in more concentration from the other person too. Try it as an experiment. Your love and affection for friends and lovers are powerfully conveyed through the quality of your attention. Children especially respond to focused attention and seem to know instinctively when you're pretending.

While Being Entertained

Eat your popcorn *before* the movie starts. Look around at the next movie you go to and watch how unaware most people are of the popcorn they're eating as they watch the movie. Try not to snack while you are reading. Don't put on a tape or CD and then start mopping the floor. *Listen* to the music. Give it your full attention. You'll be surprised how much focused attention improves the quality of your enjoyment.

Slowing Down and One-Pointed Focus

There is a close connection between the third and fourth tools. In fact, it's probably not inaccurate to describe them as two sides of the same coin. You really cannot be one-pointed if you haven't slowed down. That is why we teach slowing down first. And, as we tried to make clear in Chapter Four, the essential quality of slowing down is not physical movement but deliberation, which is a function of one-pointed attention. They're inseparable, really. And together they can bring you a formidable capacity for making intentional choices and gaining command over what you think, feel, and do.

The Power of Attention

Not everyone in our culture is many-pointed or lacking in one-pointed focus. Watch a good artist at work in his studio. Visit a first-rate scientist in her laboratory. Follow a professional golfer during a tournament. In each instance you'll observe a powerfully focused attention. High achievement requires a capacity to concentrate. Sometimes it comes naturally, and sometimes it's been developed. But any high-performing individual — athlete, artist, executive, scientist, technician — has to be capable of sustained concentration. Professional athletes stand out because of the highly competitive environments in which they work. Watch the televised finals of a major tennis match or golf tournament and count the number of times the commentators use the word "concentration" — who has it, who's "lost" it. Athletes have long understood how crucial concentration is to peak performance.

Or follow the lives of some of our most prodigiously gifted individuals from different fields. You'll usually find an extraordinary capacity to lose themselves in their work. Albert Einstein could concentrate for weeks at a time upon a single idea, until he had worked his way to its core. He had the capacity, wrote C. P. Snow, to "meditate, day after day, night after night, week after week, with the kind of concentration which was like a man grasping an object in his fist, on the nature of the physical universe."[8]

Great art is a by-product of deep absorption. Listen to Leonard Bernstein speaking in an interview on conducting a symphony: "The only way of knowing whether I've done a really remarkable performance is when I lose myself completely and become the composer and have the feeling that I'm creating the piece, writing the piece on stage, just click, click, click, making it up as I go along.... And when it's over, I usually don't know where I am, what city, and it takes quite a while to get back. And then you hear the applause."[9]

Ernest Hemingway had the capacity to bring an extraordinary power of concentration to his writing: "Nowhere is the dedication he gives his art more evident than in the yellow-tiled bedroom where early in the morning Hemingway gets up to stand in absolute concentration in front of his reading board, moving only to shift weight from one foot to another, excited as a boy, fretful, slave of a self-imposed discipline which lasts until about noon."[10]

These individuals developed their concentration to such a degree that it released deeper gifts and enriched the quality of their work. Nor were they unique. A study of Nobel laureates, Pulitzer Prize winners, and other "eminent achievers" found that what distinguished them from less recognized colleagues in their respective fields was not stellar I.Q.'s (above average was more common), but a quality the researchers called "task commitment," the capacity to stay with one idea or project for an extended period of time.[11] They all had in common a highly developed capacity for sustained attention.

Power and Beauty

There is power in the fully concentrated mind, and there can be great beauty. Depths are touched, and the deeper reaches of the mind can begin to give forth light. Deep and prolonged concentration can suspend the writer or artist in time and space. It can free him or her from inner and outer distractions so that nothing exists at that moment but the task at hand. What distinguished Bernstein, Hemingway and Einstein from other artists and scientists of nearly equal gifts was a mental attention so fixed and penetrating that it touched and released the full range of their talents.

Teaching RISE the past five years has convinced us that focused attention can perform something of the same function for more ordinary folk lie us. It can harness our own deeper resources, help us take more control of our lives, deepen our faith in ourselves, help us make changes in our attitudes or behavior. A powerful, focused attention is within the reach of anyone, and we can use the power of its integrating energy for our growth. This does not mean that we will all become Einsteins or Hemingways or even Boris Beckers. But that is not the point. What is important is that each of us become more fully ourselves, with all our depths sounded, and with the full range of our inner resources brought forth to a healing harmony.

> *"I never understood it to be an advantage to be able to do just one thing at a time. I grew up believing the more things you could juggle at once, the more of an achievement it was. And I learned through RISE that being able to become focused is invaluable. I've used it not only on the job, but in my treatment situations. I can earn a living, and I can manage to bring all of my treatments into focus and to stay focused on one thing at a time. And that is the gift that the RISE tools gave me."* (James R.)

Questions and Answers

- *I am in charge of a busy office and I often have several demands to deal with at one time. How can I stay one-pointed and keep my job?*

Many alumni have expressed this concern. It arises from the misconception that one-pointedness means staying focused on one thing for *long* periods of time. When you're faced with multiple demands, you can take each one in stride. Give one your full attention, even if only for a few minutes or even seconds, and then shift your attention to the next task. It's important that you keep your attention focused on the task before you, as long as it's before you, no matter how briefly that may be. You might in fact attend briefly to ten tasks in ten minutes. What you want to avoid is doing two of the tasks at the same time.

- *People keep interrupting me when I am trying to be one-pointed with another person. What should I do?*

You can motion the interrupting party away with a hand gesture that says quietly, but firmly, "Not now. I'll be with you when we are finished." Interestingly, some alumni have found that when they are one-pointed with people, others seem to take notice and do not interrupt them as much.

II. Support

Chapter Six _____

Healthy Ties

"When stressful situations come up, I start using my mantram. It's sort of changed how I deal with people. I work with a person who has tantrums and outbursts, and before RISE I would get real upset, and yell and scream back at him. Now I don't get crazy anymore, I don't yell. I'm just able to deal with it. I don't know what else to attribute it to, other than finally getting focused and starting to pay attention to what I need to do to make my life less stressful." (Sandra H.)

Roseto was a small community of largely Italian-American families in Pennsylvania that caused a stir among epidemiologists during the 1960s. It was discovered that the death rate from heart attacks there was one-half that of the United States as a whole.[1] Even older Rosetans who had suffered heart attacks had a low mortality rate. The researchers wanted to know why. They studied the community and looked for low levels of major risk factors that would explain the mortality rates.[2]

They didn't find them. Rosetans smoked, lived sedentary lives, ate an Italian-American diet rich in fats. Most were overweight. In fact, Rosetans turned out to have "terrible habits." The researchers found high levels of all the major risk factors for heart disease.

What explained the low death rate?

Strong ties. "Unlike most communities," one researcher concluded, Roseto was "cohesive and mutually supportive with strong family and community ties."[3] The extended family "was alive and well," the mobility rate was low, and there was a "great deal of closeness" among the families. The researchers concluded that what protected Rosetans from their high-risk habits was their close knit, supportive social fabric. Other data supported their conclusion: Rosetans who moved away from the community saw their rate of heart disease rates reach predicted levels.[4]

Social Support: The Great Buffer

Traditional wisdom long held that a close network of social ties is good for us. Now medical and epidemiological evidence has begun to confirm it. Several recent studies have shown that a strong network of supportive social ties contributes to improved resistance to heart disease, hypertension, and depression, and to improved immune function. One stress researcher calls social support "the great stress buffer."[5] A recent study of more than ten thousand Israeli men at high risk for heart disease found that risk factors like hypertension and high cholesterol could actually be "counteracted" when the individual believed he had his spouse's support. Such men also were two times less likely to develop angina pectoris.[6] Even people with Type A behavior have been found to have less arterial blockage as a result of social support.[7]

When Support Breaks Down

One ominous living pattern emerging today is the growing sense of isolation people experience. The dissolution of extended families and community life and the spread of a depersonalizing technology have made people more isolated from each other than ever before.

Persuasive evidence now suggests that individuals who feel socially isolated and unsupported become more vulnerable to disease. Studies have repeatedly shown that feeling unsupported is associated with decreased longevity and poorer heart function and immune response. In a recent study of almost five thousand people in California, researchers found that people without spouses, who had few friends or relatives, and who shunned community organizations "were more than twice as likely to die during that time than people who had these social relationships."[8] Another study found that English civil servants with the highest rate of death from coronary heart disease were those who had less contact with neighbors, relatives, or friends.[9] A poor sense of support was shown to deplete the immune resistance of students at Princeton. A study of undergraduates there showed that students with low social support had lower levels of an important immune system protein than students with high support.[10]

Loneliness and Hardiness

In the introduction we briefly discussed Kobasa's notion of the "hardy" personality. Traits like commitment, control, and challenge seem to act as buffers against high stress, forming a "stress-resistant personality." But these traits do not thrive in isolation. A chronic sense of loneliness and social isolation can impair hardiness. "The lonely adult," one researcher writes, "may have problems sustaining the attitudes of hardiness."[11] The continuing feeling of isolation can undermine the sense of control in life, turning it into one of helplessness or hopelessness. Commitment — an attitude of involvement in whatever is happening — is the opposite of alienation,[12] which is perhaps the most prominent characteristic of the socially isolated or chronically lonely person.

Recent studies have documented the effects that social isolation and loneliness have on our ability to withstand disease. Higher rates of tuberculosis have been found among "isolated and marginal" people with little social support, even when they lived in affluent neighborhoods.[13] Another study that analyzed the mental and physical health data of a group of Harvard alumni over a period of thirty years, concluded: "Lonely men often became chronically ill by the time they reached their fifties."[14]

Self-Involvement

We all have a tendency to become absorbed in ourselves and our problems. It's natural. But coupled with the increasing de-personalization of life, self-absorption can reach a point where people become so fixed upon their personal needs that they become indifferent to the needs of others. Traditional wisdom has long told us that a total disregard for other people can be harmful to the spirit. Now medical research is showing that such chronic or obsessive "self-absorption" can be hazardous to health as well.

One recent study of more than three thousand people, for instance, measured "self-involvement," defined as the number of times participants referred to themselves during interviews. The researchers found that the "self-involvement" score was a better predictor of who would later have a heart attack than all other risk factors for heart disease, including age, blood pressure, cholesterol levels, smoking, and Type A behavior. Counting the number of "self-references," the words "I," "me," "my," or "mine," the researchers concluded that "self-reference frequency was the strongest predictor of mortality among all the measured risk factors."[15]

Using the same "self-referencing" measure, another study at the University of California at San Francisco Medical School found that "compared with patients who rarely referred to themselves, those who used frequent self-references had more extensively blocked arteries."[16] One researcher concluded: "Self-involvement leads to a feeling of isolation and incompleteness, promoting Type A behavior, hostility and the incapacity to give and receive social support."[17]

Altruism: When Giving Is Receiving

You can increase your social support and reduce your tendencies to become overly self-involved by involving yourself in caring for other people. It can be through an institution or in less formal, more intimate ways. Helping friends, neighbors, and colleagues will not only increase your network of social contacts. The act of caring may well have a beneficial and therapeutic effect on your health.

Current medical research supports this, demonstrating that

caring for others can become in itself a healing force, *"a potent mediator of bodily responses."*[18] In what has been described as "an explosion of new research [into] the benefits of altruism,"[19] researchers from several fields are finding that helping other people has measurable therapeutic value. In a major ten-year study of 2,700 people, University of Michigan researchers found "that doing regular volunteer work, more than any other activity, dramatically increased life expectancy."[20] Men who did no volunteer work were two-and-a-half times as likely to die during the study as were men who volunteered at least once a week.[21] "People need other people for their health's sake," one recent survey concluded.[22]

Caring is such a potent "mediator" that it may not even require a human being at the other end in order to bring benefits. In one study of coronary patients, for instance, those who owned pets had half the mortality rate of those who did not.[23] In another study, researchers gave plants to nursing home residents to tend and care for and provided suggestions for taking more responsibility for themselves. The study found that the death rate of those with plants was half that of a control group that was not given plants to care for or suggestions for self-responsibility.[24] The study was repeated giving patients parakeets to care for, and then pet dogs. Those caring for dogs had longer life spans than those with parakeets. Although the patients tending only plants didn't live as long as the other groups, they still outlived patients who had nothing to care for but themselves.[25]

Caring and Hardiness

In our weekly courses we strongly urge participants to become involved in some form of support work for other people. In fact, giving and receiving support may be considered the fifth RISE tool. Caregiving can become an antidote to loneliness, isolation, or a lack of meaning. It serves as a buffer against stress, particularly in helping to restore a "hardy" sense of control. Alcoholics Anonymous has long taught that helping other people overcome their addictions to alcohol makes it easier to overcome one's own addiction. AA recognizes that "taking the helpful role creates a feeling of inner strength that can help overcome their own problem."[26]

It is important that the care you give be appropriate and as skilled as possible. Try to get some training if you can. Most communities have support networks that provide training in the essentials of care giving, working hotlines, counseling, facilitating support groups and other useful skills. Good intentions should be matched with reasonable skills, with what Stewart Brandt has called "skilled compassion." The benefits of such caring and support flow in both directions, between client and caregiver. We've always known that it was healthful to receive support, and now we are learning that it is healthful to give too. In more ways than he could have imagined, St. Francis's words have proven true: "it is in giving that we receive."

One significant example of this is in the story of Norman, an alumnus and facilitator in Canada. Norman's HIV diagnosis left him devastated. But he found a support group through a local AIDS network, joined a RISE course, and has facilitated study groups. When we asked how his service had affected him, he told us: "It's changed my life. My friends tell me how much I've changed. I'm less driven, more open — happier, I guess. I never thought I'd get over the shock of the HIV diagnosis, and now I'm immersed in AIDS work."

Study Circles

We also recommend that alumni get together regularly for periodic support. The research on lifestyle change is clear about the need for continued, ongoing group support to maintain such changes. The tools are difficult enough to learn. Practicing them alone increases the difficulty. Getting together regularly to meditate and to discuss the other tools and their applications is a sound way to support other alumni while strengthening your own practice. Group meditation can be a more powerful experience than meditating alone. And it can help you become more regular in your meditation.

We recently developed a network of RISE study circles to support alumni, users of the Starter Kit, and, more recently, readers of *The RISE Response* who have learned the tools from the book. Chapter Seven gives detailed instructions on forming and facilitating a study circle. The RISE Institute offers audio cassette tapes as well, which can be used by study circles as focus points. For information you should contact the Programs Division at the address listed on page 232.

We all need all the help we can get. RISE study circles and RISE Again support groups provide a way to receive regular peer support, to give help, and, in doing so, to receive it.

The Therapeutic Value of Personal Relationships

During the past few years, a body of evidence has developed supporting the view that rich, enduring personal relationships are health-giving and can enhance stress resistance. One study of men who had lost their jobs because of factory shutdowns, for instance, showed a correlation between their personal relationships and their resistance to stress during the layoff. Those who saw themselves as receiving support from partners, relatives or friends experienced "lower levels of cholesterol, fewer illness symptoms and less depression" than those men who saw themselves as having little support.[27]

In a study of married women at Ohio State University College of Medicine, those who perceived their relationships as supportive had less depression and loneliness as well as better immune defenses than married women who did not feel supported. The study found that the amount of support a person perceived in her relationship was "significantly associated with immune functioning, including percent of helper T-cells and ratio of helper to suppressor lymphocytes."[28] But the study also emphasized that it was the quality of the support that made the difference.[29]

Other studies have shown that a few deep personal relationships are preferable, from a health standpoint, to many casual ones. One researcher writes, "It may be more important to have at least one person with whom we can share open and honest thoughts and feelings, than it is to have a whole network of more superficial relationships."[30] In a study at the University of New Mexico, researchers found that among 256 healthy elderly people, those with "confiding relationships had significantly higher indices of immune function, lower levels of serum cholesterol and uric acid," factors which have been associated with heart disease.[31]

> *"In my relationships I could be a shrew. I could be awful to live with. And now, it's interesting, because the mantram does buy me time — that little window of time where I can pause, and just kind of run it through my head a few times before I bite someone's head off. I can stop and say, 'Okay, be reasonable here, this is not something to get upset about. Don't put your energy into it.' "*
>
> (Sandra H.)

"Hardy" Relations

Enduring relationships do not come easily. They require patience, understanding, and determination. You have to learn how to accommodate differences and to withstand the predictable ups and downs of intimate relations. But they are well worth the time and effort. "It's only through our relations with others," one stress researcher writes, "that we develop the outlook of hardiness and come to believe in our own capabilities and inner goodness."[32]

Here are some suggestions for building more lasting relationships:

Slow Down. Relationships take time, quality time that is unhurried and attentive. It is difficult, perhaps impossible, to be sensitive to another person when you are in a hurry. When pressed for time, you can easily be inconsiderate or offensive and not even be aware of it.

Develop One-Pointed Attention. Respect and sensitivity are conveyed powerfully to another person through the quality of attention. A fixed, powerful focus on another person can be reassuring. It demonstrates that your affection is more than superficial. And trained attention can help withstand the wandering of desire outside a committed romantic relationship. As the excitement of the initial physical attraction fades over time, your attention can begin to wander elsewhere, drawing you to the brief, superficial relationships you may be trying to avoid. With one-pointed attention, you can call your attention back with more freedom and command.

Focused attention helps fix love and affection at a deeper level in consciousness, below the level of physical attraction. This can help build and sustain the supportive, "confiding relationship" that buffers against stress.

Live with Differences. Differences are going to arise even in the soundest relationship. But they do not need to disrupt it. When conflicts appear, you can take steps to help prevent a rupture. Here are some suggestions:

Show respect. You can express your differences and still show respect. You don't have to idealize the other person, but you don't have to stand in judgment either. What offends people is lack of respect. You may be following all the proper protocols: "Please have a chair. Would you like something cool to drink?" But if you're thinking inside, "I am right. You're wrong!" it's going to get communicated.

Don't View the Other Person as an Adversary. Try not to draw battle lines that force you and your partner into opposing camps. Even serious differences do not have to cause a stand-off if you can view them as a mutual problem to be resolved for the good of the relationship itself. Look at the disruption as the problem: that's the adversary.

Listen. Listening with one-pointed focus conveys respect. It shows you care for the other person, even though you may not agree. It's not unusual to want to have the last word. But it's divisive, especially if you're thinking of your retort while the other person is still talking.

Bring your attention to bear on what the other person is saying, even during an argument. It's not easy. But just trying to listen signals the other person that you still have respect and affection, even though you may feel hurt. This in itself can help heal the estrangement.

Don't Look Back. Quarrels sometimes get protracted because we can't help looking into the past, dragging out old skeletons from the closet. If you hear yourself reaching back to an old hurt, bring your attention into the present moment. Use your mantram as a rapid focusing tool. Don't let the past control your present.

Take the Long View. Ask yourself during a quarrel, is this going to matter a few years from now? Is it important enough to destroy the relationship over it? Keep your perspective. Remind yourself that the relationship itself may be far more significant than the matter in dispute.

Likes and Dislikes

One way to help relationships endure is to develop a more agile sense of self, one that avoids rigid, unbending tastes and preferences and includes a willingness to forego smaller satisfactions for the sake of the relationship. Personal tastes can take on the status of inviolable rights. "I have to have Perrier!" "I can't stand cats!" Differences become exaggerated rather than minimized, protracted instead of transformed. They can become barriers to the growth of the relationship. When neither person makes his or her needs more pliant, even trifling matters can create "irreconcilable differences." The relationship founders unnecessarily.

Purpose

Having a purpose in life larger than your private concerns minimizes the harmful effects of self-involvement. It can also guard against the stress that comes from alienation and meaninglessness. You can become more vulnerable to addictions when you do not have a meaningful pursuit in life. Boredom, inertia, and languor are invitations to old cravings. The restless mind gravitates easily to old, habituated ways of thinking.

You need only scan the daily headlines to find a larger purpose. There is plenty of work that needs doing. Working for a selfless cause, helping to rebuild communities or to save the environment, giving time, energy, and resources to reduce suffering and distress are all ways to expand social contacts and concerns. But be careful of overinvolvement and burn-out. Pace yourself. A deep and abiding purpose can bring added motivation to practice the tools and master the RISE Response. For when your life counts to people around you, your own health matters more. Purpose, intention, an eye for the needs of others, a gaze that reaches beyond our own private needs: these can bring into play the deeper resources of the healing system and, at the same time, bring greater satisfaction and fulfillment into our lives.

Doing RISE:
A Weekly Study Guide

Madeline Gershwin, R.N., M.A.

The quickest way to begin the practice of the RISE tools is ... to *begin* — plunge right in on your own and start meditating. Follow the eight-week study guide until you feel comfortable with the tools. It will be a challenge, but if you're a natural self-starter you can work your way through the weekly plans, and in a few weeks you should have a fair idea of just how these tools can make a powerful difference in your life.

Creating a Supportive Climate

Of course, we're not all self-starters — and change is difficult, especially when we are trying to change the way we think. If it's at all possible, find a friend to learn the tools with you. Our experience suggests strongly that a critical factor in building these tools into your life is finding support from others who are trying to do the same thing. Even independent-minded self-starters can benefit greatly from some form of mutual support. The recovery movement has amply demonstrated the "strength in numbers" notion, putting it to work to help thousands of people break free from addictions in their twelve-step meetings. As you read in the previous chapter, support — receiving and giving it — is a powerful therapeutic tool.

This isn't to say that you cannot learn the RISE Response on you own. Certainly you can, and many have. It's just that it is difficult to make significant changes in isolation, and it's especially challenging to maintain these changes over time without some form of continuing support. Fitness trainers have learned, for example, that people are more regular in their exercise programs if they have a workout partner. We are social creatures for the most part and seem to perform best in a social context.

Making lifestyle changes is a tremendous challenge for the majority of us. We are swimming against a powerful current in trying to put these tools to work in our lives. I do not mean to discourage you here, but rather validate the experience many people have described during our courses. You can do this; it *is* possible. Any support you can receive will simply increase your capacity to make this work.

"Partner RISE"

So we strongly recommend that you try to find at least one other person to learn the tools with — a RISE "partner" with whom you can work your way through the weekly study guide as a kind of learning team. Ask your partner to read *The RISE Response,* and then arrange to meet weekly for awhile to share your experiences and to meditate together. You might want to purchase a RISE Starter Kit, which includes a set of tapes I've made to accompany this study guide.

Study Circles

We have developed a network of study circles and some audio instructional materials to help people learn the tools together. Write to the RISE Institute to find out if an authorized study circle exists in your area. Or you could form your own study circle and join the network. Once you contact the Programs Division (see page 232), we will send you a packet of materials for starting and facilitating a study circle. Again, you might want to purchase the instructional tapes that are designed to help study circles learn the tools together. You might be able to find a few people at work, at your church, or at your social club who would be willing to give it a try with you.

"RISE Again" Support Groups

Once you have gained some facility with the tools, you will probably want to experiment with them in some area of personal choice described in Part Two of *The RISE Response* — illness or disability, wellness, workplace concerns, self-empowerment. In areas where courses have been active, ongoing support groups called "RISE Again" have formed to provide long-term support for practicing the tools and applying them to everyday challenges. You could join one in your area, or simply turn you study circle into a "RISE Again" support group once you've finished with the introductory study guide.

With the help of numerous alumni, the Programs Division of the RISE Institute has developed a set of guidelines for "RISE Again" support groups, which give detailed instructions in their structure and content to ensure that the meetings remain focused on RISE concerns — that is, on applying the tools to challenges of life and work. "RISE Again" is intended to help you make the transition from the natural starting point marked by questions like, Should I meditate? and Does this really work? to the determined conviction to become the person you most want to be. Write to the Programs Division for these guidelines.

Using this Study Guide

Whether you're on your own or in a study circle, you can get started, book in hand, right now. The eight-week study guide that follows is designed to walk you week-by-week, tool-by-tool, step-by-step, through the program. At the end of the eight weeks, you will have a solid notion of what the tools are and how they can help you manage better the challenges in your life. I've distilled the most common concerns that surface in the courses and allowed two weeks for each tool, but don't feel bound by this schedule. You might want to proceed more quickly or more slowly. Find a pace that fits your schedule. Don't crowd yourself so that your RISE work becomes an imposition. On the other hand, don't space this out too long, or you'll risk losing your momentum.

Weekly Plans

Each weekly plan follows the same format with specific suggestions for meditation and the mantram, a weekly "experiment" and "weekly focus" activity, followed by my suggestions in the weekly review material. The activities are recommended for your convenience, and you shouldn't feel that you have to perform them all in order to master the RISE Response. I have drawn them from several years of teaching RISE classes, and they reflect the concerns and anticipate the questions that arise during the early stages of a typical course.

Bear in mind that training attention through meditation on an inspirational passage is the essential tool of the program. The sooner you can begin using this tool on a daily basis, the better your chances for realizing the documented benefits of RISE. The most important thing to consider during these first few weeks is how to establish a regular practice of meditating on a passage, while trying to slow down your pace and increase your concentration during your normal activities.

It isn't how often you read _The RISE Response_ or how much you think about doing the experiments. It is the practice of the tools that generates the response. So always give practice your priority, especially with meditation.

Making Changes

The most difficult issue you're likely to face is changing yourself. By and large our culture encourages and applauds us for taking on challenges that are external — climbing mountains, exploring outer space, producing great works — problems "out there" in the visible world of space. We are not generally encouraged by the culture to value inner explorations like taking on the challenge of mastering ourselves. It is a conditioning process we need to recognize and overcome if we are going to begin to tap our deepest resources. The RISE tools can help you do just that, as they build a bridge from psychological empowerment to spiritual unfoldment.

Change is not easy, and there are sound reasons. Change is resisted in nature, so it is naturally stressful for any organism to undergo change, even in spite of our intention. Yet we know that we can change. Homo sapiens is distinguished from the lower evolutionary species by its capacity to override conditioning.

The Internal Self-Critic

Somewhere between the human urge to adapt to new demands and our natural resistance to change, lies what I see as a major obstacle to growth. Continuous, carping self-criticism and its partner, self-doubt, may do more to hinder self-empowerment than anything else I've seen in my thirty-year career as a mental health professional. This internal self-critic has enormous reserves of energy that supposedly protect the "self" by trying to keep it unchanged and unchallenged. Unfortunately, energy that we use for this "defense" is not available for growth.

I am not talking here about conscience, the capacity to make objective, even critical, assessments of our behavior. A healthy capacity for intentional, reflective self-assessment shouldn't be confused with the internal critic, which is a conditioned response, not reflective, but *reflexive*. It continually offers unexamined (and unsought) comments on our self-worth, creating a constant assault on our self-esteem; it blames, compares, sets unrealistic expectations, magnifies our limitations, and minimizes our strengths.

We need to learn to deal with its ancient baggage of shoulds, oughts, and musts that generate a chronic sense of always having done something wrong: guilty, until proven innocent! The internal self-critic often masquerades as conscience, with the result that guilt becomes a habit that is more an attack on the self than a restorative self-assessment.

Such guilt does not help you grow. True self-empowerment draws upon a set of checks and balances that is neither too flexible nor too rigid and leads to visible, positive outcomes. Joan Borysenko's book *Guilt Is the Teacher, Love Is the Lesson* offers a thorough discussion of the subject. But enough said about the self-critic. It's time to begin. Good luck, or better yet, *bon voyage!*

WEEK ONE
Starting to Meditate

Reading

Take a few days to reread the introduction and the first two chapters of *The RISE Response*.

Experiment

Meditation. This practice forms the foundation of the RISE Response and is the constant thread woven through all the other experiments during a course. Reread the instructions in

Chapter Two on how to meditate (pages 28–29). Below is a checklist to help you get started. You might make a copy of the short version of the instructions in the box on page 29 and look at it just before you meditate.

Checklist. Select a passage that is meaningful to you from the selections on page 33 and in Chapter Eighteen. You might find it helpful to write down the passage and take it with you to memorize in spare moments. Keep it next to you for awhile while meditating, in case you forget.

- *Place:* Try to put aside a corner of a room where you can meditate each day. It is better to keep it just for meditation. Is it reasonably quiet? If traffic noises or barking dogs become a problem, you might consider a pair of ear plugs.

- *Posture:* Remember to keep your back and neck straight. You might check once or twice during your meditation to see if they are straight. But don't make them rigid.

- *Distractions:* Expect them. Don't fight them. Just concentrate more on the passage.

Don't get discouraged if your entire meditation some days consists of nothing but fighting distractions. In fact, they might have been very productive.

Try to meditate each day if you can. Being regular is more effective than doing longer periods of meditation irregularly. If you have been thinking about starting, but haven't been able to, you may be waiting for "the right time" or "the right place."

Be aware that the perfect time, the ideal place are probably going to elude you. And it may be that no passage will seem exactly "right." This is a common resistance at the beginning. The best plan is to ignore the time and place and start by meditating for as long as you comfortably can with the goal of reaching thirty minutes. Some participants report that even ten minutes can feel like an hour in the beginning. So start with what feels comfortable, fifteen minutes, ten, even five, with the idea that you will gradually increase the time as the weeks go by. If you find that thirty minutes is not enough, you should get personal instruction from an experienced teacher of meditation before you extend the period.

Some people take easily to meditation. But many more find it difficult even to choose a passage. Be patient with yourself, but firm. Set a realistic goal for the week and stick to it. It is better to meditate every day for short periods than for thirty minutes twice a week.

Choosing a Meditation Passage. In Chapter Two we talked at some length about our selection of passages. We have selected a broad spectrum of inspirational passages used by people of different cultures over the centuries. These passages are "consumer tested" and have come to us from inspired men and women who have mastered the mind and plumbed the depths of self-discovery. We can have confidence in their words.

If you are participating in a study circle, it would be beneficial to come to the first meeting prepared with the Week One activities. Thereafter, Week Two activities would be discussed in meeting two, Week Three in meeting three, etc.

"When RISE came along, I focused on my selection of a passage so that it fit in with my own belief system, my being a part of everything. The choice of a passage is a personal choice. A mantram can be tailor-made for people from different backgrounds, from different belief systems. Even from the days of my first involvement with RISE, my choice of a passage had to do with where I fit in with the scheme of things." (Carl F.)

WEEK TWO
Meditation Continued

Reading

Go over the instructions for meditation on pages 28–29. Follow the checkpoints below to make sure you are meditating according to the guidelines.

Meditation

Check the following:

- Do you have the passage memorized well enough to remember it when you sit down to meditate?

- Have you found a quiet place to meditate?

- Try meditating at a different time this week. See if it makes any difference in the quality of your meditation.

- What resistances to meditating have you encountered in yourself?

Experiment

Choose an unimportant moment during the day to observe what you are thinking about. How many different thoughts flow through your mind? How much time do you stay with a single thought?

Weekly Focus

Continue to observe your thoughts at various times during the week. Observe the quality of your concentration:

- when someone is talking to you

- when you are particularly bored

- when you are nervous or tense

- when you feel especially relaxed

- when you are excited

Also observe:

- When is your concentration the best?

- When is your concentration the worst?

Weekly Review: Your First Week of Meditation

What did you notice in your meditation? If you're like most beginners, you may have developed an amazing number of itches or even a new acuity in your hearing. You may hear sounds that you never knew were there before: traffic noise, dogs barking, the garbage trucks that seem suddenly to appear when you sit down to meditate. You're suddenly aware that the children living down the block are playing a familiar game. And why is it, you've been asking yourself, that the birds seem to have become louder and more persistent since you started meditating? Perhaps your mouth becomes parched and you can think of nothing but a glass of water.

These represent common experiences in the early stages of learning to meditate. Give yourself all the margin you need in the beginning so that you can get started. Scratch the itch, if you have to; keep a glass of water next to you in case you're overwhelmed with thirst. Get some earplugs if the kids or garbage trucks just won't cooperate. This isn't cheating. The time will come when your concentration gets so complete that you no longer hear the garbage truck or the basketball game. But that's a way off. Now your first priority is to get through your period of meditation, whatever it takes!

If the passage gives you trouble and keeps slipping from your mind, keep a copy next to you and glance at it when you need to refresh your memory. Wear your glasses if you need them.

Follow this rule as a general strategy in the beginning: make the adjustments you need to get started, but get started. Don't expect perfection.

In Chapter Two we discussed several common problems and misconceptions that arise with regard to passage meditation and other forms. These are persistent enough that I'll take a moment now to address them again.

Religious Aversions

Even the most neutral of passages in Chapter Eighteen is drawn from one of the world's spiritual traditions. If you have an aversion to organized religion, you may find this an obstacle. In that case, use a passage that doesn't come from an organized religion, like the Native American or Taoist. You should be able to find something from those traditions that won't offend your sensibilities.

But you should also consider that your aversion may be a kind of bondage that keeps you prisoner to a fixed and rigid response. You undoubtedly have good reasons for feeling as you do about religious traditions, and we certainly won't try to dissuade you from them. But don't necessarily rule out entirely more traditional passages. Do your best to select a passage according to our guidelines. And you may even find in time, as many of our participants have, that your aversion was not as deep-seated as you thought.

Affirmations

Enough of our course participants have suggested that affirmations are good substitutes for an inspirational passage that

I want to explain why we don't recommend them. Generally speaking, an affirmation is a positive statement designed to counteract negative thinking (e.g., "I'm O.K."). Affirmations tend to speak specifically to psychological states, but don't address root sources of conflict. Compared to the deep self-empowerment that passage meditation offers, affirmations represent a surface approach, something like the difference between light dusting and deep cleaning. Continue to use your affirmations as you have. But when trying passage meditation, select one of the time-honored, transformative passages from Chapter Eighteen.

Other Meditation Techniques

Many course participants have experimented with other techniques of meditation. Some of them regularly practice other forms and ask us if they can substitute their current practice for meditation on a passage. We strongly recommend they do not substitute other methods of meditation for meditating on an inspirational passage, if they really want to do RISE. We are not in any way implying that other forms of meditation are not valid or useful; they just are not RISE meditation.

RISE aims at very specific and measurable outcomes, and it relies upon passage meditation to achieve those outcomes. If you want the documented benefits of RISE, you should give this method a try for a reasonable amount of time. Then decide for yourself about its usefulness.

Mantram Meditation. Some of the course participants first learned to meditate using Transcendental Meditation (TM), which is a mantram meditation, and they feel very attached to their mantrams. If that's your experience, then by all means continue to use your TM mantram according to the suggestions we give for using a mantram. You might even consider adding the word "Rama" to your TM mantram because you will probably be using it in new ways. But in meditation, if you want to do RISE, you will need to use a passage instead of your mantram as the focusing point for your mind. You might begin your meditation by repeating your mantram for a minute or two to relax yourself; then begin to repeat the words of your passage as slowly as you can. Passage meditation is meant to transform the content of your thinking, and only a passage contains images and concepts that can do that.

Visualization. In Chapter Two we explained the differences between visualization and meditating on an inspirational passage. We recommend to RISE course participants who practice visualization exercises for therapeutic or performance reasons that they visualize at a separate time of day from their passage meditation. This will maintain the integrity of both techniques and may in fact enhance the effects of your visualizing, since passage meditation will improve your ability to focus your attention on particular images.

Breathing Meditation. Concentrating on the breath and breathing techniques called *pranayama* are common forms of meditative practice and, like other forms, should not be mixed with meditation on a passage. In fact, we would caution you against attempting sophisticated breathing techniques because they are extremely powerful, potentially mind-altering techniques that can lead to serious problems if used without skilled guidance. Both techniques were developed in traditional, simple settings where students practiced under the direct guidance of an experienced teacher, in environments close to nature. Life was unhurried, with minimal external distractions, and the breathing exercises were incorporated within a strict discipline of diet, exercise, and study. Transported to our modern, time-pressured, frenetic, overly stimulated world, these techniques can pose serious hazards. We do not recommend them.

Simple deep-breathing exercises, however — "diaphragmatic breathing" — are harmless, and are in fact an essential component of calmness and relaxation. Some of our course participants have reported that they hold their breaths while concentrating on their passage or try to coordinate the words of the passage with their breathing. Neither is correct nor necessary. You can take a few deep, slow breaths as you begin to meditate and then focus your attention fully on the words of the passage. You will notice that as your concentration on the words deepens, your breathing automatically slows and deepens.

Lying Down. Some people have asked us if it's all right to lie down while meditating. We don't advise it since it invites falling asleep. If you're physically able, sit up. If you're bedridden, you may need to bolster yourself with pillows. Make yourself comfortable, but sit up with your spinal column erect. It will enhance your alertness.

> *"I had never meditated before. I thought it was a joke, people closing their eyes, meditating. My stepmother over the years had gone through meditation and yoga, and I thought it was one of those hocus pocus type things. And lo and behold, I'm now one of them! It's an amazing situation, when you close your eyes and meditate on a passage. I've upped my time to thirty minutes. I've graduated and am going to get my thirty-minute degree!"*
>
> (Doug C.)

WEEK THREE
Choosing a Mantram

Reading

Read Chapter Three of *The RISE Response.*

Meditation

Meditate at least ten minutes this week, longer if you are able. Just at the point you feel you are "done," sit quietly for a minute longer. This exercise can help train your capacity to sit for longer periods of meditation.

Experiment

Choose a mantram this week from page 42. You may try out two or three different mantrams "for size" over the next week or two, but then choose one and try to stick with it.

The Passage and the Mantram. Make sure that you understand the difference between repeating a mantram and using a passage in meditation:

- The passage should be at least a few lines long.

- The mantram may be just a word or short phrase;

- The passage is used during your meditation period, while you are seated, eyes closed. When your attention wanders from it, you return it to the passage.

- The mantram can be used at any time of the day or night, whenever you have an opportunity: while doing a mechanical chore, while falling asleep, when you feel anxiety, anger, or fear coming on.

Weekly Focus

Begin to repeat your mantram during the day as often as you can. Try using it while waiting in line or for an appointment, or when you're washing the dishes or the car. If you get the opportunity, try taking a "mantram walk" as described on page 44. A beach is ideal, or a path, but a sidewalk will do just as well. Walk at as brisk a pace as you can so that your breathing deepens. This is not meant to be a stroll. Keep saying your mantram for the whole time you are walking.

Keeping a Journal

You might try to start a journal this week. A RISE journal is not so much a personal diary of events as it is a log of your observations of your practices and experiments during the week. Your journal entries do not have to be lengthy, but your journal keeping can become a useful tool for helping you to become regular in your practice.

There are two parts to keeping a journal:

1. *The Practice Log:* to track progress in developing skills. Each day make a brief note about the following:

   - How long you meditated and which passage(s) you used.

   - Any difficulties you may have had, i.e., distractions, interferences, etc. But do not record observations during your meditation. *The journal is an exercise to be done apart from your meditation.*

   - Any changes you may have noticed in your daily habits (slowing down, concentration, diet, etc.).

   - The results of the weekly experiments and weekly focus exercises.

   - Your successes — the times you found yourself slowing down or showing a little more patience.

2. *Personal Reflections:* to promote the development of self-observation skills. Use the journal to reflect upon situations, relationships, events, circumstances, ideas, or feelings that seem significant to you. Patterns may begin to emerge and your increased awareness of them may help you make more informed choices in your life.

Weekly Review

Now that you've meditated for a few weeks, you may find that there are days when you can't remain concentrated at all. Don't worry. It happens even to veteran mediators, and it's part of the cyclic churning of the mind. Gradually you'll adjust to these ups and downs and recognize that however your mind seems — calm, agitated, frightful — the mood won't last. The best reaction is no reaction, really, other than making sure that you put in your time in meditation and give as much attention as you can to the words of the passage.

Falling Asleep

Some people report about this time that they have trouble staying awake during their meditation. In one sense, that's a good sign, because it a signal that your nervous system is relaxing a little. Concentration itself is relaxing, and one sign that you are concentrating in your meditation is that you get drowsy. Still, sleep is not the desired outcome. So have a cup of tea or coffee before you start meditating, or take a walk, or do some stretching exercises, yoga postures, or calisthenics.

> "The thing that made me commit to RISE was the fact that we are shown in a real basic way the strength, the power of the mind. And getting hooked up with my own power, the energy, the vitality — knowing you can deal with a lot of stuff, as opposed to feeling helpless." (Terry A.)

WEEK FOUR
Using a Mantram

Reading

Reread "Useful Times for Using Your Mantram" in the box on page 46.

Meditation

Try to increase your meditation by five minutes. You may want to try it first just on the weekend when you have more time.

Checkpoints.

- Do you have the passage memorized well enough to remember it?

- Do you need to memorize more so that the passage does not get stale?

Mantram

If you haven't chosen a mantram yet, try to do so this week. Start repeating it when you find you have some spare moments with nothing to occupy your mind.

Experiment

Try to remember to repeat your mantram when waiting in lines or while stopped in traffic. This helps to avoid getting annoyed while it also helps to make the mantram a habit.

Weekly Focus: Awareness

By this time you may be experiencing some discomfort with yourself. Are you finding yourself more speeded up than you thought? More distractible? Don't get discouraged. Your meditation is making you more aware of your states of mind, and this can cause some discomfort. Change and growth are always a little painful. But awareness is part of the program. Without it, you can't grow. In your journal, note:

- What have you noticed about the flow of your thoughts since starting the self-study course?

- Does the pace of your thoughts change when you become anxious, excited, afraid?

Weekly Review: The Mantram

The mantram is the most immediately practical of the RISE tools and the source of the most dramatic RISE experiences. It has no toxic side effects and it doesn't cost anything. There is a wonderful explanation of how the mantram works that I've borrowed from Sri Easwaran's *The Unstruck Bell* (Petaluma, Calif.:

Nilgiri Press, 1993). In it he writes about how Indian villagers keep their elephants from damaging their neighbors' stalls. The elephant's trunk is very powerful and inclined to wander. As it walks through the narrow village bazaar, its trunk may snatch a coconut from a vendor's stall, or pull down a bunch of bananas and swallow it in one bite. But the experienced villager simply gives the elephant a stick to carry in its trunk. Now it has something to take hold of and the wandering stops. The vendors relax, and everyone, including the elephant, is satisfied.

A mantram is a stick for the wandering mind. When it wanders into anxieties or resentments, you can give it the mantram to repeat and draw its attention away from the unwanted thoughts. I call it an RFT, a rapid focusing tool — it's instantaneous and easy to use.

For some people, choosing a mantram is easy; it practically chooses them. They read the list and one jumps out at them and "feels right." If that's your experience, fine. But some people find that they can't find the right mantram. They read down the list and nothing catches their interest. I myself had that problem. Although I can't imagine my life now without my mantram, I confess that at first I thought I would never find the right one. But it was really a case of resistance. The best thing to do is to simply choose a mantram that may seem less than perfect and experiment with it for awhile.

WEEK FIVE
Slowing Down

Reading

Read Chapter Four of *The RISE Response.*

Meditation

Try to add a minute a day to your meditation and extend it to fifteen minutes daily if you haven't already done so. If you find you cannot meditate for fifteen minutes, then have a second brief meditation at a different time.

Experiment: Slowing Down

Look at your daily life and try to observe where you come under time pressure:

- *At meals:* breakfast, lunch, dinner, snacks. When do you rush, when relax?

- *While driving:* Do you leave yourself enough time? Do you rush when you really don't need to?

- *With people:* How does hurrying affect your relationships?

- *At work:* Which situations or people tend to speed you up?

Be sure you understand the difference between going slow and what we mean by "slowing down" (see page 50, "What Slowing Down Means").

Weekly Focus

Set specific course goals for yourself. Choose from the list below, or decide on a goal for yourself. Jot your goals down in your journal.

- establish the daily practice of meditation

- solve a specific emotional problem

- improve your dietary habits

- establish a good program of physical exercise

- increase your volunteer time

- drop an unhealthy habit, such as smoking or alcohol

Weekly Review

By the fifth week of a RISE course, participants often talk about new awarenesses they've had about themselves; and you may have had similar experiences. Perhaps you've noticed that you're not getting as angry during a predictable stressful moment at work. Or someone has complimented you on how calm you seem. Or your supervisor asks you why you seem so focused. Course participants regularly report these developments during the first few weeks of the course, and it's difficult for them to tie these successes to the RISE tools, because they seem indirect, subtle. We remind them that these kinds of indirect, observable, *objective* experiences are exactly the kind of changes in attitudes and behavior they can expect from using the tools.

Or...you seem to have gotten worse since you started meditating. You're more speeded up now, more distracted than before; you seem to get angry more often, or you are more impatient. It's not unusual about this time for course participants to complain that they've lost ground since they started using the RISE tools. *What's wrong?* they ask.

Nothing's wrong, really. Awareness cuts both ways: you see yourself more clearly, both the good and the not so good. By slowing down and improving your attention, you become more aware of the way you are and how you respond to challenges. In fact, greater self-awareness is an indication of growth, though it can be painful. But just becoming more aware of how you move through your day or how short your fuse can be is a significant step forward in making substantial change. You should regard it as a measure of your meditation.

Journal Keeping

One of the ways to capitalize on this new awareness is to choose an area to concentrate your attention on, and collect information about yourself. You might look at an aspect of your work, at a relationship, your diet. Remember that you are not going to make judgments about your behavior, but merely observe it. Write down your observations in your journal. It can be helpful, later on, to measure your progress against an observable behavior.

If you haven't started a journal yet, I encourage you to do so. If you don't like to write, try using a tape recorder. Some people don't keep a journal for the same reason they have a hard time getting started with meditation. They set a standard of perfection that is impossible for them to meet. If the concept of keeping a journal puts you off, just think about taking notes to remind yourself about the tools. These notes can prove helpful later on to measure your growth. But if keeping a journal is something you simply choose not to do, that's fine. Don't burden yourself with "shoulds" or "ought tos" that may only sabotage your other efforts.

> *"I was coming home from LA, and my jeep stalled when I got to Irvine. I mean right in the middle of the freeway! The mantram kicked in right away and I pushed the car to the side of the road, and I'm calm. Some guy picks me up and drives me to the jeep dealer. I rent a car and drive on home, no sweat. Can you believe*

it? The old me would have been freaked out, obsessed, panicked! But I just got through that, no sweat!" (Edward S.)

WEEK SIX
Slowing Down Continued

Meditation

Try to meditate every day this week. If you can't get it in during the morning, meditate in the evening, before dinner, or before you go to sleep.

Experiment

Choose a day during the week to focus on slowing down:

- Go to bed early so that you can get up early.

- Eat your meals slowly and chew your food thoroughly.

- Drive moderately. Try not to get impatient with slower drivers.

- Try to be deliberate at work and not let yourself get speeded up.

- Take time with people. (Tell the grocery clerk to take his time.)

Weekly Focus

Log in your journal some of the observations you made when you tried to slow down.

- Did you encounter resistance? When?

- Did you notice any differences in your work?

- Did you concentrate better?

- Did you notice any differences in the people you encountered?

- Were you able to slow down your driving?

In your journal, log the times of day when you find yourself getting especially hurried. Note any occurrences, people, or other stresses that seem especially to get you speeded up.

On Meditation

If you have not yet tried meditation, may I make another plea that you have a go at it? You could simply read a passage for ten minutes and then close your eyes and try to remember the words of the passage you just read. It is a way to get started if you find yourself particularly resistant to meditation. Remember, there are benefits to RISE even if you just acquaint yourself with the concepts and tools. But let's be honest — the real benefits come only with sustained practice over time. And passage meditation creates the foundation for the increased awareness necessary to move from unconscious, automatic operation, to strategic choices in our lives. After thirty years as a mental health professional, I have found no better tools for increasing self-awareness and personal empowerment than the form of passage meditation developed by my own teacher, Sri Easwaran.

If you have been meditating, try to increase your time by a few minutes. If you've been regular in your practice, you may have found that the rhythm of your passage has slowed down as you recite it to yourself. Many participants report around this time that they are less distracted by the ordinary sounds around them, while new and unfamiliar sounds keep turning up to distract them!

You may still find your passage adequate as a focusing tool, and its meaning still significant to you. Or you may feel that it's becoming a little automatic and so familiar that you can repeat the words of the passage while you think about other things at the same time.

It's probably time to think about finding a new passage. Remember that the object of passage meditation is to train attention to stay focused under your conscious direction and to renew our commitment to the challenge that it represents. If repeating the passage has become automatic, then it is losing its power to focus your conscious attention. A new passage can help.

But don't feel you have to get the whole thing memorized before you use it. Take it a verse at a time, or even a line at a time. You can gradually add it to your repertoire, and eventually you'll have two passages you can use in a sequence. The mind loves variety. Where love is, there follows attention.

Slowing Down

How did your experiments with slowing down go? Some people actually report that they feel anxious when they try to slow down. Some even report feeling guilty. We all know that slowing down is good for health. This is certainly not the first book to recommend it. And still, we get anxious at the thought.

It's the culture's paradigm at work here. We're so in its grip — doing more in less time — that when we try to slow down, we become conflicted. We feel delinquent. You are feeling the full weight of the culture upon you, including your own deep conditioning urging you on:...*faster...more!*

Think for a moment about your last vacation, in the mountains or at the seashore. Do you remember how aware you became of the difference between your state of mind and body on vacation and your normal pace back home? Did you think how wonderful life would be if you could feel as calm at work as you did under the pines? And you probably dismissed the idea as unrealistic because "real life" can't be like that.

Why not? It's a state of mind we're talking about, not the view from Diamond Head or the breeze along Lake Como. Why *can't* we live our lives at home and work with a calm, quiet poise? You can decide to slow down and focus; you can learn to recapture the clarity you felt in the Sierras and make it yours.

I don't want to imply that it is easy, but it is possible to bring to your work a far greater measure of deliberation and poise than we are used to. Many of our course participants have high-pressure jobs that require they move quickly — ICU nurses, emergency room physicians, fire fighters, ambulance drivers to name a few. Certainly these require speedy action, but they also are improved by clear and focused thinking. To slow down, you may remember, is to become deliberate, to *see* with clarity, not simply to go more slowly.

From the acceleration syndrome, then, to a measured calm ...how do you do that? The only certain method we know of is to practice slowing down, whenever you can think about it. And be gradual in your approach. Don't decide to slow down your whole life by the end of the week. Instead, choose one area of your life, like driving, and start there. Drive fifty-five on the way to work. See how it feels. After a few days, start driving more slowly on the way back home. Remember to be gentle with yourself. Start to slow down today or tomorrow morning...but start slowly.

WEEK SEVEN
One-Pointed Focus

Reading

Read Chapter Five of *The RISE Response.*

Meditation

Try to increase your meditation a minute a day until you are meditating for twenty minutes. If you are unable to meditate on a passage for that long, repeat your mantram to help you sit quietly until the twenty minutes are up. If you have not been able to start meditating, don't give up on yourself. Have compassion and repeat your mantram as often as you can. This can help prepare your mind for meditation.

The Mantram

Use your mantram at every possible opportunity. Remember that it is a powerful tool for interrupting negative thought patterns.

Weekly Focus

In your journal, note the challenges and consequences you encountered when practicing one-pointed attention.

- What forms did your resistance take?

- Note the times when you are most concentrated. Are there special conditions that help your concentration?

- Try to become more aware of how integrated the basic tools are. Observe how slowing down and one-pointed attention interact with and support meditation and the mantram, and vice versa. Notice, for instance, how your morning meditation affects your concentration during the day, or how getting speeded up affects your meditation.

Experiment

During the next week choose *one* of the following experiments with one-pointed focus:

- *Driving:* Give your attention to the act of driving. Turn off the radio or cassette and avoid conversation about important or emotionally charged issues with your passengers.

- *Entertainment:* Split attention prevents relaxation and uses energy. When you listen to music, listen with your complete attention. When you are reading, do it without background music. When watching TV or while at the movies, eat before or after the show.

- *In relationships:* Practice giving your complete attention to the person you are talking with. When interruptions or distractions occur, give more of your attention to that person.

- *Meal Preparation:* Use this time as an opportunity to focus your attention on the task at hand. Whether you're sautéing onions or setting the table, bring your attention back to your task if it wanders.

- *Mealtime:* Practice giving one-pointed focus to what you are eating. Try eating without the TV or background music and simply concentrate on your meal. This does not mean you shouldn't converse. Sharing a meal is part of healthful eating, but there is a learned skill in balancing conversation and giving attention to what you are eating.

- *Projects:* Choose something you have postponed for some time because it is difficult or distasteful. It should be relatively simple and not too time-consuming. Don't sabotage yourself by choosing a task requiring several hours. Give your undivided attention to it. When your mind gets restless and wants to drop it, give more and more of your attention to the task.

Use your experiment this week as an opportunity to observe the power of trained attention.

Weekly Review

Passage meditation is the foundation of the RISE Response, even if you're irregular about it or can sit for only ten minutes at a time. It buffers you for the day, sets the tone for your emotional responses, and increases your sense of empowerment.

If you have been meditating for the past few weeks, think about ways you can refine your practice. Try to make it as regular as, say, brushing your teeth or having breakfast. If you meditate ten minutes, three times a week, try to make it every day. Or increase the time period by five or ten minutes.

If you are still trying to "fit it in," examine your priorities. You might remember the discussion in Chapter One about the force of habit and about how powerful our conditioning is. Learning to meditate regularly will mean building a new habit, but once it is formed, it becomes a part of your conditioning. Then the force of habit works for you, in self-selected ways, rather than undermining your health. The more regular you can make your meditation, the sooner it will acquire the force of habit.

WEEK EIGHT
RISE High Day and Evaluating Your Meditation

Experiment

Now that you have completed the study guide, you might look at these suggested goals for the next few months. Be realistic about your expectations, and don't set yourself up for failure by overcommitting yourself. You could decide to:

- Get your daily meditation up to thirty minutes.

- Stop or reduce an addiction such as smoking, recreational drugs, or alcohol consumption. (It you attempt any of these, don't try to make any other major changes.)

- Make a dietary change toward whole foods, with less fat, sugar, and salt, and more fiber (see Chapter Thirteen).

- Get more exercise (see Chapter Thirteen).

- Improve your stress management skills (see Chapters Ten and Fifteen).

- Get more involved with others.

- Form a RISE study circle with others in your area who are using the tools. (For information on how to form study circles, write to The RISE Institute, Programs Division, 4362 Bonita Road, Suite 404, Bonita, CA 91902–01421.)

Weekly Focus

Plan for a day this week on which you will try to make special use of your tools. Call it RISE High Day.

- Plan to meditate for thirty minutes. Get up early so you can get in your meditation, some exercise perhaps, and a nutritious, unrushed breakfast. Then get on with the work of the day without being pushed for time.

- Take a mantram walk sometime during the day. Make it as fast as you can, and repeat the mantram while you walk. You might plan to take it on a beach or in the woods.

- Try to stay as one-pointed as you can throughout the day. Focus on the people you are with and their special characteristics and needs. When you find yourself getting distracted, use the mantram to recall your attention. Watch for signs of stress and use the mantram to help manage your emotional reactions to stress.

- At night, meditate again if you can fit it in. When you go to bed, see if you can repeat the mantram until you fall asleep.

Weekly Review: Evaluating Your Meditation

By now you may have wondered whether your meditation was going well and may have been inclined to evaluate it according to how it "felt." This is a natural impulse, but it's problematic. How we feel, what seems to be a good meditation, what we "think" about it are unreliable measures, since our feelings and thoughts are part of the mental processes we are trying to train.

If how you "feel" or "think" about your meditation are not reliable standards, how then can you evaluate it? We advise you to look at your behavior rather than your feelings in trying to judge the quality of your meditation. Remember, passage meditation is not meant to be a "feel good" experience. It aims at training your attention, and this often involves a struggle against distractions that may not feel especially pleasant — Although a deep, concentrated meditation can certainly leave you feeling profoundly rested. The time to evaluate your meditation is not while you meditate, or even just afterward, but as you go through your day.

Perhaps you've noticed, for instance, that you're more patient, less reactive, calmer. Experiences that used to upset you greatly don't upset you as much now, or your recovery time is less. You can use these kinds of objective criteria to evaluate your meditation. You have to learn to observe yourself with some detachment and your journal can be a useful tool to keep track of your observations. You can look for improvements in the following areas:

- *Concentration* Your concentration should improve, especially at work. You should be able to work with concentration for longer periods than before you started mediating. If you find yourself getting so absorbed in your work that you forget the time, your meditation is going well.

- *Awareness:* Are you more aware of the times when you get speeded up? Are you more conscious of the times when your mind is distracted? It is not uncommon for our course participants to feel that they have become more speeded up or distracted since they began meditating. They usually haven't. Their increased awareness had made them more conscious of their reactions.

- *Equilibrium:* Are you able to recover your equilibrium more quickly in a crisis? This is a clear sign of progress in meditation. It does not mean you won't be shaken by emotional turmoil, or that you won't continue to feel deeply. On the contrary, you may find that you feel even more intensely than before. But you can "right" yourself more easily. And you are less likely to "lose it" altogether in moments of high stress.

- *Will:* Is your will increasing, even a little? Can you say "no more" easily when you need to? Can you make a resolution and stick to it better than before? These are solid indicators of progress in training attention.

- *Depressions:* Are your "lows" less low now that you are meditating? Are they of shorter duration? Some depressions act like a fixation of sorts in which the mind has got stuck. With your attention trained, you can pull your mind more easily out of such "ruts." But depressions also have physiological correlates, treatable by medication. You should consult with your physician if you suffer from depression, *and do not terminate any medication without medical consultation.*

• *Patience:* If you find yourself more patient, especially around people who easily annoy you, your meditation is going well. And you may begin to feel more patient with yourself.

Progress in any one of these areas indicates that your meditation is deepening and that your deeper resources are coming more and more into your hands. But don't worry too much about how you are doing, as long as your meditation is regular. Too much concern over your progress can even inhibit it. The important thing is to meditate, regularly, every day, following the instructions given in Chapter Two.

With this week's lesson, you've completed your introduction to the RISE tools. It's an introduction to a life of greater intention, more choices, and the gradual discovery of deeper resources lying within. It's a tremendous challenge — we know that — but profoundly worthwhile. So if you have found it difficult to get underway, don't give up on yourself. Stay with it. Even a few minutes of daily practice will begin to pay dividends as you develop the increasing capacity to take charge of your states of mind, to respond to illness with greater detachment and clarity, and to become more fully empowered.

You now have the basics. Work with them; polish and refine them over the next few weeks. In time, you'll begin to see from your own experience how the tools can work at deeper levels than you thought possible, how they can draw up resources from within that you didn't know you had. If you're determined you want to live in charge of yourself within a culture that doesn't make it easy, you'll need the support of like-minded people. Share this with a friend if you haven't already or write to the RISE Institute for some of our support or follow-up tapes.

Be determined. Be patient and compassionate. The journey has just begun, and the road ahead can be fascinating and richly rewarding. I am pleased to have been able to come this far with you.

"The RISE program has taught me that I need myself. That no one's really going to take care of me any better than God and myself. And how do you do that? You need to be able to focus. To be aware and to be conscious of what is good for you. It's just

been fantastic. The program doesn't end in eight weeks. That is just the beginning. I'm up to thirty minutes meditation now, and I wouldn't leave the house in the mornings without meditating. It is as important to me as taking my shower and eating my breakfast. It is a part of me now." (Carol C.)

Part TWO

CHOICES

I. Coping with Illness, Disability, and Stress

HIV/AIDS, RISE, and the Mind-Body Connection: Bringing It All Back Home

Rick Flinders, M.D.

On October 11, 1987, a massive quilt of more than two thousand separate patches was spread across the steps of the capitol in Washington, D.C., covering the entire Capitol mall. Each patch had been made individually by friends and families of the thousands of victims who had already died of AIDS. Young men in their prime were dying in the nations ICUs, on respirators from which they could not be weaned, from pneumonias caused by normally harmless viruses. One to three million North Americans were living with a quiet but deadly virus for which there was no cure.

For the earliest victims of the illness, there seemed to be little care either, in both the literal and figurative sense. An AIDS diagnosis brought with it the specter of terminal illness, but one that did not guarantee the usual sympathy and support afforded most dying patients. A Person with AIDS (PWA) could

103

encounter isolation rather than support, rejection rather than sympathy. Instead of being rallied around by friends and community, the PWA encountered loss of employment and income, termination of insurance benefits, withdrawal of associates, and more. At a time when dying should have been met with catharsis and release, the PWA was far too often left to struggle in isolation, often with the added imposition of guilt.

No one who has been a physician to someone with AIDS can have escaped the magnitude of the personal tragedy of this disease. A colleague of mine with a large AIDS practice confided that the majority of deaths in his practice were under the age of fifty. "Instead of informing children of the deaths of their parents," he pointed out, "I'm more often informing parents of the deaths of their children."

The same evening that the AIDS quilt went on display in Washington, the first RISE course got underway on the country's opposite coast in a community hospital north of San Francisco. And on one of the patches in the quilt was a light blue T-shirt with the name "David" painstakingly embroidered across its front. David had signed up for that first course, but had died before it could get started. I had, however, given him some basic instructions in the tools, so that he became the first "self-study" graduate of RISE.

I had talked with David several times on the phone, but I hadn't met him until July when his own doctor graduated from our residency program and placed him in my care. Even then, it was clear that David was preparing himself for death, speaking already of durable power of attorney, last will, position on conditions of hospitalization, no life-sustaining heroics. . . . To know David was to know that he was organized. The other impression he left with everyone who met him was a marked gentleness, which combined with a strong and exuberant spirit that came through his soft voice and sharp wit.

He'd had Kaposi's sarcoma (KS) for two years when I met him, but hadn't really been very sick until that spring, with pneumonias — first pneumocystis pneumonia (PCP), then recurrent and resistant staph. AZT-induced anemia and progressive KS, treated with radiation and chemotherapy, had robbed him of much of his color, and the beginnings of an increasingly severe peripheral neuropathy had begun to take his strength. All his medications gave him unwanted side effects. He was already nearly immobilized when we discovered the first signs of toxoplasmosis on a brain scan, and he reluctantly agreed to let me treat it as long as it didn't require him to enter the hospital. A consulting neurologist said it was one of the worst cases of AIDS myelopathy he had seen.

When I made my first house call that final week, David was bedridden, at home, and resolved not to enter any more hospitals. His mother and best friend were in constant attendance. They surrounded him with the flowers he loved to grow himself and read to him from the passages and poems he loved most. He was taking fifty-two pills per day, and when I suggested he would need four more medications, he could barely conceal a laugh. Instead, he suggested we get rid of everything except for treatment of his pain and discomfort. I asked him if he realized what that meant. His reply was as clear and confident and certain as any words I've heard spoken: "I'm ready to go."

I don't know whether it was the words themselves or the way they were spoken, but they seemed to come from some deep place inside of him to land in some deep place inside me. It was as if he had set off some distant alarm to awaken and remind me of our common journey. After all, our own mortality is no less certain: our round-trip passage through life is equally guaranteed. And if the only real difference between our conditions was that decade or two or three that I might be granted, then how precious each day of life must be. I felt a little shaken and was a little lost in my thoughts when his next words reached me: "Thanks for being here, for caring, for RISE." A long silence passed before I could find any words of my own, words that belonged to all of us who had worked in RISE: "Thank *you*, David."

I feel privileged for the moments I've spent at the bedside of a patient who struggled with life and death before my eyes. While I speak of the isolation some patients feel, I've been equally moved at the outpouring shown others by friends and lovers, lessons for all of us who have a conventional view of what defines a family. There is really nothing very different about AIDS from any other life-threatening or chronic illness except that the scale and intensity of the human drama seems magnified and compressed a hundredfold. In some cases, it seemed that the emotional tumult of an entire lifetime was compressed into a couple of months or years.

For anyone who has been a physician or caregiver during the first decade of AIDS, there is another personal memorial quilt that each of us carries inside — the patchwork of our own recollections of the ones with AIDS whom we've personally accompanied and who have already come and gone. Each with a name and a face and a history, and probably a family with whom we have spent anxious hours dealing with a private hell or heaven on earth. Eventually, in the immediacy felt from this interior tapestry of our own, an inevitable, breath-catching moment comes to us all, and the awful enormity of that larger quilt becomes, at once, utterly real and incomprehensible.

I can't presume to understand the scale of suffering endured by members of the HIV community — victims, relatives, lovers, and friends. It is a private sorrow on a scale only they can fully bear witness to. But it has been my privilege during the past five years, both as a physician and as a RISE trainer, to witness on more than one occasion, a courage, equanimity, strength, and radiant peace — as David demonstrated that morning — such as to shatter any preconceived notions I might have had about the scope and possibility of the human spirit. Clearly, there exists in the depth of the human personality a capacity for strength, compassion, clarity, and inner healing that goes beyond anything I was taught about in my own medical training.

Call it "the will to live," since we have no truly adequate medical term by which to name it. Nonetheless, it is real, it is healing, and it *persists* — as David and so many others have repeatedly demonstrated — even in the face the suffering and indignity that often accompany the final stages of AIDS. If anything from the AIDS catastrophe can in some small way honor the suffering of so many, perhaps it will be a renewed effort on the part of all of us — laypersons and health professionals alike — to make this healing force more manifest in our lives and, eventually, in our conventional models of health and treatment.

Something like this seems already to have begun along the periphery of the medical world. During the past decade there have been what could be called the first stirrings of what may yet become a substantial movement. It would be premature to set too much hope upon what has been learned so far about the interrelationships of the body and mental states, but the details and some of the background bear reporting.

In the summer of 1964 Norman Cousins, the longtime editor of the *Saturday Review* lay in the intensive care unit of a hospital in New York City, in something close to a coma after a lifetime of virtually perfect health. He had been diagnosed with an illness that inflames the blood vessels of the central nervous system and was considered terminal at the time. Lying in the bed, unable to move without severe pain, Cousins asked his physician how long he had to live. "We don't have a cure for this condition," he said. "It's advanced to the nervous system — you probably have less than six months to live."

As the world came to know through Cousins's account of his successful battle with the disease in *The Anatomy of an Illness as Perceived by the Patient* (New York: W. W. Norton, 1979), Cousins decided to put himself under his own care. He describes how he released himself from the hospital, checked into a hotel room, gave himself massive doses of vitamin C, and had his wife bring him movies of Charlie Chaplin and the Three Stooges to make himself laugh. Two minutes of gut-level laughter from a Chaplin film gave him more pain relief, he said, than the 15 mg of morphine sulphate he had been prescribed, probably the most powerful painkiller we have available. Eventually, he not only cured himself, but lived for another twenty-seven years. Due to the popularity and groundbreaking nature of his book, he spent his last decade on the faculty of the medical school at UCLA. From there he became an internationally known advocate for a medical model that included the non-physiological "realities" of mind and spirit in its model of human health. During the past decade, he did much to bring the notion of mind-body wellness back into the mainstream of medical science.

Still, of all the regimens Cousins experimented with in treating himself during his illness, it was arguably his indomitable will to live that may have finally brought him through. In all of his books, he writes passionately of the will to live as a physiologic reality with "real," therapeutic characteristics. Anyone who has cared for patients in life-and-death situations knows that the will to live is probably the single most powerful healing force they deal with. And probably the least understood. Yet without the will to live, even the most advanced technological modern treatment can't bring a patient around.

But the most significant point Cousins made over the past decade of his life is that we do not need to wait for a life-threatening illness or the deathbed to manifest the will to live. In fact, I'd hypothesize that the will to live may be the inner resources you are tapping into during your meditation each day. Every time you try to gain control of your attention, to use it as an instrument of your own healing, you are tapping the will to live.

However you may choose to regard Cousins's experience and its significance, it suggests that there is a capacity within the human organism to heal itself, and that by tapping into this resource one may be able to influence the quality of one's life, if not the quantity as well. Actually, the idea is not new, though it was largely neglected for the better part of this century by modern medicine. In fact, the idea that mental and emotional well-being may play a role in physical health is as old as medicine itself. Hippocratic medicine in ancient Greece, from which our Western models derive, was steeped in the underlying harmony of soma and psyche, a balanced vitality of mind and body.

What *is* new in our time is the specialized and technologically based medical system we take for granted in the 1990s: the miracle vaccines and organ transplants, cardio-pulmonary resuscitation, bypasses, CAT scans, and magnetic resonance imaging. It is a wonderfully potent array of diagnostic and treatment tools. But its extreme reliance upon technology and its rigid separation of mind and body have left it curiously unhelpful in treating many of the predominant illnesses of our times.

Despite the tremendous medical advances of this century — and they are indeed impressive, staggering really — people seem more distressed and "dis-eased" than ever before. Depression, boredom, loneliness, alienation all became endemic during the past few decades, and modern medicine, with all its breathtaking achievements, was surprisingly ineffective.

The failures were not in the technology or methodology, per se, but in the failure of modern health care to maintain an appropriate balance and perspective. Surely there is a rightful place for powerful pharmacological or surgical or technical interventions. But their indiscriminate use overran what had been a humane and compassionate model of medicine and replaced it with an impersonal, mechanistic model that has proved unable to meet many basic human needs. The coldness of modern medicine was a failure *in the application,* not in the methodology itself.

In RISE, then, we've tried to help restore a balance by helping patients and practitioners alike to recover some of the healing resources that we believe lie within the human personality. We deplore the depersonalization and overspecialization that has overtaken modern medicine, but we chose to work within the mainstream, hoping to help restore a greater balance to its methods and tools. We've never sought to become an alternative to conventional treatment, but an adjunct, a complement to a comprehensive program of overall health management. In this regard, we feel that RISE is consistent with the best of traditional therapies and may well enhance their effectiveness by bringing the patient more actively into the picture. The wholeness it encourages with its self-stewarding tools can perhaps help bring the healthcare professions to a fuller view of the patient.

So we've held RISE accountable to the same criteria of evaluation that governs standard research. We've been systematic in our collection of data from the beginning, so that we can make responsible conclusions about its outcomes. If our view of the human being as a creature of significant inner healing resources is correct, then it should be verifiable in the daily laboratory of human experience and within a model that is consistent with the methods and accumulated knowledge of medical science as it struggles to understand and document the mysterious and profound interactions between mind and body.

What are some of these interactions, and what do we know about them?

Scientific Roots and the Mind-Body Connection

In the early 1960s Dr. George Solomon first postulated that mind-body research might be fruitfully investigated from the combined perspectives of three separate disciplines, immunology, endocrinology, and neuroscience. He didn't realize at the time that he was giving birth to a new scientific discipline, which would come to be known as psychoneuroimmunology or PNI, for short. It represents now one of the most active and rapidly evolving fields among all the biological sciences. No longer arguing over its existence, scientists now debate its validity. Is it on the edge of the psycho-biologic frontier or merely another temporary foray on the radical fringe?

The interrelationship between body and mind, soma and psyche, is as old as medicine itself. All traditional medical systems were grounded in the belief of an underlying harmony of soma and psyche and the desirability of a balanced vitality between body and mind. Two thousand years ago, the Greek physician Galen observed that melancholia contributed to breast cancer. Closer to home, health and wholeness have been linked in traditional Western systems until just relatively recently. In this century, no less a figure than Walter Cannon was connecting emotions and the immune system as early as the first decade of this century. He noted, for example, that rage and fear could stimulate a 10–15 percent increase of red blood cells through the activity of the spleen, an organ that plays a major role in activating immune function. Cannon documented cases of young aboriginal Australians who had died following a shaman's curse. He was able to demonstrate that among otherwise healthy young men, an individual who came under the curse of a recognized shaman (effectively equivalent to social and spiritual banishment) could languish and even die, in some cases quite suddenly. Cannon's autopsies of some of these young men revealed an adrenal exhaustion caused by panic, demonstrating that even a young person in good health could be literally killed by fear.

Later in the century another classically trained physiologist, Dr. Hans Selye, illuminated the autonomic nervous system. As we've described in Chapter Nine, Dr. Selye showed how in times of persistent stress, our emotional states can result in chronic illness, impaired resistance, and disabling states of anxiety and depression. Following Selye during the 1970s and 1980s was a large number of investigators who studied the effects of numerous alternative, "holistic," and behavioral approaches to health. These included the study of Eastern spiritual techniques like yoga postures, various forms of meditation, and the therapeutic use of the mantram, all of which helped lay the groundwork for our own work in RISE. We feel very much indebted to such forerunners as Herbert Benson, Joan Borysenko, Philip Nuernberger, Robert Ornstein, Ken Pelletier, and Dean Ornish, to name only a few of the more popular researchers who have helped create a rich collection of mind-body literature.

During this period, research into such unconventional approaches as biofeedback, visualization, acupuncture, and Benson's relaxation response have proved powerful enough to find their way close to the heart of the medical mainstream. During the same period, the writings of people like Suzanne Kobasa, Deepak Chopra, Stephen Locke, and, of course, Cousins himself, popularized the legitimate and potentially powerful healing role of patients' attitudes and sense of control. The general effect of this work was to cast in more scientific terms the notion that our emotions and mental attitudes can influence our physical well-being, and perhaps profoundly so.

Mental States and the Immune System

One of the most significant developments in mind-body studies during the past two decades has been the development of psychoneuroimmunology. PNI researchers have focused on the immune system as the bridge between mind and body, and their evidence is often compelling. But it must be weighed carefully with regard to the health claims that can be drawn from it.

In the past decade, PNI researchers have produced a substantial body of evidence that largely confirms (1) that the mind and body are not separate entities, but a fluid continuum in constant interaction, with consequences that are both psychological and physiological; and, (2) that how we think and feel is registered in our endocrinal and central nervous systems, resulting in neural and biochemical events that may profoundly influence immunity and healing.[1] But does it really matter, as far as our health is concerned? Do these measurable effects have any clinical relevance to the sickness or health of real people?[2] Let's look at the more recent evidence, with an eye toward what might be subtitled "clinical PNI."

Medical students make especially eager experimental animals and, for studies of anxiety-related states, few subjects can compare with their anxiety to compete. Kiecolt-Glaser and Glaser studied a group of fifty such students, measuring several markers of immune function one month before final examinations, and then again one day before and one month after the exams. To no one's surprise, psychological measures showed that the students' anxiety levels rose sharply as the exams approached. What was surprising was that the gains in anxiety were associated with reductions in the total numbers of T4 lymphocytes and their ability to respond to invading proteins.[3]

In another experiment, the same team looked at similar measures of immune cells and their function in a large group of bereaved spouses.[4] They wanted to see if what was true in extreme anxiety (taking exams) would also be true in a state of bereavement. Both numbers and function of T lymphocytes were reduced, compared to a control group of paired spouses. In the bereaved group, the recovery of their immune function occurred between six to twelve months from the time of their initial bereavement, which corresponds to clinically observable signs of normal human grieving. In a study of grief-stricken women who had recently lost husbands, other researchers demonstrated a significant reduction of natural killer cell activity.[5] The same study looked at another group of women with husbands living in terminal conditions who demonstrated similar reductions.

Depression has been commonly linked to suppressed immune function. In one study, patients hospitalized with major depression were shown to have a 50 percent reduction of natural killer cell activity. The reduction was significantly associated with their depression, while their ages, alcohol consumption, or tobacco smoking were not.[6] Researchers at Mt. Sinai School of Medicine in New York showed in a series of studies that depression was associated with unfavorable changes in the immune system.[7] A study of people with genital herpes at the University of California School of Medicine in San Francisco found that depression, stress, anxiety, hostility, and fatigue are "significant predictors of poorer functioning of suppressor T cells."[8]

With regard to HIV illness and psychosocial factors specifically, the research over the past few years was summarized by a group of researchers at a symposium of the American Association for the Advancement of Science. Their tentative conclusions were that the "mental attitudes of AIDS patients may affect the progress of their disease"; that "the mental outlook of sufferers seemed to be related to the activity of their immune systems"; and that "the period between infection with HIV and the onset of the disease's symptoms might be substantially lengthened by healthy psychological factors."[9] The researchers noted that their conclusions were based on studies of relatively small groups of people, and that "there was no statistical proof that positive attitudes could prolong the lives of AIDS patients." The nature of the links between mind and body, they concluded, remain "highly uncertain."

Certain ways of coping, e.g., being hostile or giving up, appear to weaken the immune system and increase the risk of illness. Positive correlations between an individual's sense of control over events and health have been found by investigators in various fields.[10] One study of gay men infected with HIV showed that "good coping strategies not only reduced the perception of stress in some patients but improved the functioning of 'natural killer' cells used by the immune system to fight disease."[11] On the cellular level, studies show that the ability of lymphocytes and antibodies to resist infection can be influenced by the way we appraise stress and react to it.[12]

Negative mental attitudes are associated with decreased health too.[13] One recent study looked at questionnaires filled out by graduates of Harvard University classes of 1942–44 at age twenty-five and compared them with health profiles of the same students when they had reached middle age. They found that what they called a "pessimistic explanatory style" at the age of twenty-five was a reliable predictor of poor health at ages forty-five through sixty, even when physical and mental health factors were controlled. Pessimism in early adulthood, they concluded, appears to be a risk factor for poor health in middle and late adulthood.[14]

What about interventions that use mind-body concepts and tools? Some studies have shown that psychosocial interventions, such as relaxation techniques, support groups, and exercise training can effect immune parameters.[15] Relaxation training increased NK cell activity in older adults in one study,[16] and in another, relaxation techniques affected immune function among a group of metastatic cancer patients.[17] Researchers at UCLA examined the effects of a psychosocial intervention on eighty patients with malignant melanoma and found that statistically significant immune cell changes correlated significantly with reductions in depression, confusion, and mood disturbance.[18] Another study demonstrated that a ten-week aerobic exercise training program led to a significant increase in CD4 cell counts in HIV-affected individuals.[19]

In a groundbreaking study at Stanford in 1981, Dr. David Spiegel used psychosocial interventions like group therapy to reduce anxiety, depression, and pain in a group of eighty-six women with metastatic breast cancer. More significantly, although increased life-span was not an intended outcome of the study, a ten-year follow-up study found that women in the intervention group survived a mean of 36.6 months, while a control group who received no intervention survived a mean of 18.9 months.[20]

What can we say, then, about the extent to which our emotions influence our health? The answer is, frankly, unclear and threatens to remain unclear for a long time to come. For it remains a major scientific hurdle to translate what laboratory markers of immune function actually mean in the cause and recovery from clinical illness. And further, the existence of many variables makes it still more difficult to attribute results to a single cause.

The immune system is immensely complicated, and many of its functions are poorly understood. It is not surprising that immune research produces conflicting results. For example, in a recent study, Kiecolt-Glaser and Glaser found little or no effect of depression on immune function or clinical course of illness. Instead, they found a much greater influence exerted by the strength or absence of relationships and supportive social ties.[21]

Does this mean that mind-body research is not worth our time? Certainly not. It means only that the answers are not as easy to come by as we might have thought. Certainly, psychosocial interventions improve the quality of life. This is unarguable. They can provide the means to cope with the enormous stresses of living with life-threatening conditions like AIDS and HIV illness. And quality of life improvements may well turn out to have profound implications on the length of life as well. You may recall that in the Stanford study of cancer patients, a psychosocial intervention seems to have helped lengthen life-span, even though increased longevity was not its intention. The ninety-eight women in the study met to support each other, to improve the quality of the time they had left to them, and in the process lived longer than other women who had no such intervention.[22] So it may be that, by focusing on improving the quality of life, we may well even lengthen it. Whether these factors can also lead to improved immune function remains unknown, but the possibility is promising.

It is in this context of a cautious but reasonable hope that we have formed the working hypothesis that guides our work in RISE. Our hypothesis is twofold, that:

1. The immune system is not simply a hardwired complex of rigidly prescribed biochemical reactions. It is a complex network of forces that includes significant cortical and psychological input from the mind and emotions.

2. This cross-section of physiological, emotional, and mental forces we call the healing system makes the human organism a powerful source for healing itself.

Stated more clinically, we feel that improving an individual's ability to respond to the stresses of illness and life may well improve the quality of life, as well as the physiological environment in which the immune system functions. We are moving here along a delicate line between science and scientific speculation, between direct observation and plausible hope. We want to strike what Norman Cousins described as "a sensible balance between psychological factors and biologic factors in the understanding and management of disease."[23]

In working toward this balance, we have to proceed with equal doses of hope and caution. We've seen the darker side of unrealistic expectations — the disappointment that follows when participants in psychosocial interventions fail to gain health outcomes they've come to expect from incautious claims. But conventional attitudes that deny psychological influences altogether also deny the very real physiological benefits patients may receive from activating the healing resources they find within themselves.

If our hypothesis is correct, and if improved psychological states and reduced risk behaviors can indeed influence health factors, then this should be verifiable in the daily laboratory of human experience. And it should be measurable in ways consistent with the methods of medical science. This is why we developed RISE within the contemporary model, as a clinically based complement to standard treatment.

We have collected data for five years now, looking at both psychological and behavioral outcomes, and we've found some interesting and significant results. At the Sixth International Conference on AIDS in San Francisco, we reported on psychological outcomes associated with participating in RISE.[24] The data came from the Denver Gay Men's Cohort, which is run under the auspices of the Centers for Disease Control and the Denver Department of Public Health. In that study RISE participants showed more psychological improvements after participation in the program than participants in four other programs. Improvements were significant in such areas as lessened depression, lower hostility, less paranoid ideation, and increased sense of well-being. We later replicated these findings in RISE programs in California.

At the Seventh International Conference on AIDS in Florence, Italy, we reported that significantly lowered levels of risky sexual practices were associated with participating in taking RISE. This study was also conducted under CDC auspices and also compared RISE against several other programs.[25] Given time and sufficient resources, we'd like to investigate whether using the RISE tools reduces length or severity of illness, reduces the time and costs of medical care, or can produce measurable improvements in quality of life and longevity. Perhaps, in time, we'll be able to add our own verifiable contributions to resolving the debate of how much and in what ways our emotions and attitudes can influence medical outcomes like longevity or immune function. Both RISE and PNI share timely and fruitful beginnings. And chances are that for PNI, as for RISE and all those looking for a more fully integrated approach to health and healing, the best may be yet to come.

Understanding Stress

"When I got the test results back and they showed I was HIV positive, I became suicidal. Thank God RISE was there. It helped me restructure my life, gain control over it. If it hadn't been for RISE, through stress alone I'd probably be gone now. It gave me tools that allow me to control my future. No matter what happens to my life now, it'll be a lot richer." (Rick E.)

During most of the fall and winter of 1869, the philosopher William James was bedridden with an aching back and a case of frayed nerves. As the Massachusetts winter darkened, so did his mood. In February, he writes, he "touched bottom." One evening James walked into his darkened dressing room and was gripped by an unspeakable fear, "as if it came out of the darkness, a horrible fear of my own existence." A vision took hold of him:

> the image of an epileptic patient whom I had seen in the asylum, a black-haired youth with greenish skin, entirely idiotic, who used to sit all day on one of the benches... moving nothing but his black eyes and looking absolutely non-human.[1]

James became obsessed with the idea that he could easily become that image himself. "Something gave way in me," he wrote, and he became "a mass of quivering fear.... The universe was changed for me altogether, and for months I was unable to go into the dark alone."[2]

James brooded, thought about suicide, awaited the gathering madness. But he did not kill himself, nor did he go mad. By the fall of 1873, James was out of the woods, a well man, and the dark mood did not visit him again. He went on to an illustrious career as the "father" of American psychology. The clarity and

117

wit of his writings belie the image of a man who tottered for months at the edge of insanity.

Selective Attention

How did James get well? Medical science had little to offer victims of severe depression in 1869, and James, who had a medical degree, knew this. If we take him at his word, James brought himself back to health under his own steam. Using a process he later called "selective attention," he refused to allow his mind's irrational fears to lead him — think him, as it were — into insanity.[3] Each time the vision of his impending madness invaded his thoughts, James chose not to think about it. Instead he turned his mind's attention to thoughts other than those of approaching madness.

James's condition suggests what would be called today a "stress-related" disorder. His response anticipated by a hundred years one of the more significant recent developments in the modern struggle against stress. Simply stated, James discovered that he had a choice.

Stress and Disease

A broad medical consensus now confirms that stress is not simply a psychological phenomenon that results only in emotional disturbances. Stress is a physiological phenomenon with medical consequences, causing debilitation, organ damage, even death. Chronic stress, poorly managed, can inhibit immune function and leave one vulnerable to viral and bacterial infection.[4] Three significant points need to be understood in developing an adequate reaction to stress: (1) it needs to be taken seriously by anyone living in the industrialized world; (2) it is an unavoidable consequence of our times; and (3) it need not damage health.

How Stress Harms

Stress causes bodily harm through two contrasting processes within the central nervous system: arousal and inhibition. The earliest research into stress focused on arousal. This is the "fight or flight" response that orders the body's defense mechanisms to protect it from a perceived threat. Dr. Hans Selye was one of the first to explain the mechanism of arousal and how it can impair health. He demonstrated that the "fight/flight" syndrome is a defense mechanism of the autonomic nervous system that was carried over from when human beings lived with natural threats like human-eating animals.

In arousal, the sympathetic nervous system prepares the body to meet a threat or to flee from it: the heart rate is increased, blood pressure goes up, digestion shuts down, the blood gets ready to clot, and the individual is brought to a heightened state of awareness to deal with the threat. When the animal retreats and the threat is diminished, and the body returns to a healthy equilibrium. The "fight/flight" mechanism was a significant adaptation that helped early human beings survive in a hostile physical environment.

Everything has changed since then except the mechanism itself. Human-eating animals don't pose a threat to most people. Still, major sources of stress abound in industrialized societies: noise, urban violence, time pressures, economic distress, constant change, psychological tensions. They are less directly threatening than a hungry tiger, but far more pervasive. In fact, the stresses of modern life may be more threatening to us in the long run than predatory animals. Unlike the occasional tiger, they never go away.

As far as your nervous system can register, there is little difference between the growl of a tiger and the snarl of an employer. They both raise a perceived "threat." Your supervisor gets angry at you or puts you under intense time pressure, and the stress mechanism triggers the "arousal" response. Your adrenal glands flood your system with stress hormones, just as they would were a tiger to appear at your door. But your supervisor isn't going to go away. The time pressure is a constant. As a result, your nervous system remains chronically aroused, for long periods. It rarely returns to a healthy state of rest. It's as though a tiger were permanently lodged just outside your office, waiting to pounce.

It is this prolonged state of arousal that causes damage to the body. Selye's research showed that chronically high levels of stress hormones in the system lead to a lowering of bodily resistance to organ damage and eventually to disease.[5] Chronic hostility, for instance, causes an excessive secretion of stress hormones and contributes to hypertension, arteriosclerosis, and heart attack.[6] Chronic hormonal build-ups also impair immune functioning.[7]

Inhibition

Early stress research focused on the "fight/flight" arousal mechanism of the sympathetic nervous system. More recent research has begun to describe the debilitating role of the parasympathetic nervous system, which causes an almost opposite, inhibiting reaction to stress, the "possum" syndrome. In inhibition, the perceived "threat" results in a withdrawal of awareness instead of heightened perception. It causes a reduction rather than an increase in heart rate and blood pressure, decreased breathing capacity, and increased digestive activity.

Inhibition is an effective survival response. You "tune out," possum like, until the danger passes. But chronic inhibition can lead to withdrawal, depression, passivity, helplessness, and even disease and organ damage. Chronic inhibition has been associated with severe depression, cancer, and respiratory problems like asthma. Feeling chronically helpless, for instance, can make an individual more vulnerable to infections and some cancers.[8]

Imbalance

Other researchers have speculated that an imbalance between the sympathetic and parasympathetic systems, where one predominates, may itself result in disease and debilitation.[9] They theorize that the constant onslaught of modern stresses keep the body prepared for "threats" that may not exist. Our nervous systems remain almost permanently imbalanced as a result, leaving little opportunity to return to a normal state of balance, clearing the system of potentially dangerous stress hormones.

The Stress Revolution

The stress research of the past two decades caused a revolution in the way we look at health and disease in an industrialized society. But it unfortunately created a perception of stress as an unavoidable, relentless killer stalking the corridors of modern life. Short of moving to a tropical island, the popular conception went, there was not much you could do to avoid its ravages. "Ask most people what they think about stress," one researcher writes, "and they're certain to tell you something bad. Stress makes you sick. It wrecks the immune system, gives people heart attacks, raises the risk of cancer. Stress runs like a truck over its helpless victims."[10]

More recent research has changed the perception of stress as unavoidably damaging. It suggests that stress, though unavoidable, need not be harmful to health. Some researchers even argue that certain "hardy" personality types actually thrive on stress. You may even know one or two of them.

> *"I'm in a very stressful business, manufacturer's rep in the light fixtures business, wholesale. It's continual stress. Over the years, I've let it get to me. But now I don't get excitable any longer. When customers start yelling at me, I say a couple of mantrams and move on. I don't let the little things bother me as much any more."* (Doug C.)

Perception and Stress: What You See Is What You Get

The stress mechanism responds to perceived threats, regardless of whether a threat is actually present. In fact, many researchers feel that perceptions themselves are what trigger the stress reaction. If you believe you are being threatened, your nervous system will react accordingly. The tiger you "see" in the dark may turn out to be a harmless dog, but your nervous system still floods your body with stress hormones.

The implications are significant, and actually promising. They suggest that if you do not feel threatened during a stressful event, your nervous system will not order the body into a stress response. This suggests that you have some control. You can't control the stresses around you, but you can have a say as to how much they will affect you. Selye believed that the nervous system was beyond conscious control, that we were slaves of its automatic reactions. Recent research challenges this. It is finding that our perceptions, beliefs, and attitudes can play a critical role in determining how much stress will actually affect our bodies and health.

Recent studies of Harvard and Princeton undergraduates, for instance, showed that even normally stressful events like final examinations result in stress only when students' attitudes predisposed them to view the exams as stressful.[11] "It is not just what happens to you that's important," one researcher writes, "but how you handle it.... If you try to master stresses instead of feeling helpless and overwhelmed by them, they don't have to be bad for your health."[12]

Other researchers studied personality traits that may enable an individual to cope better with stress. Suzanne Kobasa and Salvatore Maddi found that certain "resistance resources" seemed to buffer individuals from the harmful effects of stress.[13] We talk more about this study in Chapter Fifteen.

Other Models of Stress

Most stress research during the 1960s and 1970s focused on Selye's model of arousal. In the past ten years, though, other models have emerged that look at stress differently and lead to differing emphases in stress management. Below we describe in more detail two particularly significant models.

The Holistic Model of Stress

The holistic model views stress as an imbalance in the nervous system caused by our reactions to circumstances, events, situations, and people (relationships) in our lives. This imbalance affects every organ system of the body, including immune function. When it is sustained or becomes chronic, it causes daily wear and tear on the body resulting in dysfunction and/or debilitation. As more evidence accumulates in support of this view, increasing numbers of researchers like Nuernberger, Pelletier, Ornstein, and Borysenko write of the importance of effective lifestyle management to maintain balance, in the interest of health and well-being. (See "Helpful Reading" below.)

The Perception Model

The perception of stress as an inevitable health risk has been reversed during the past decade. Stress is now viewed as essentially a physiological reaction to mental and emotional activities. "How aversive or damaging an event is," one researcher writes summarizing the evidence, "depends on how we choose to take it — which means that we can control its effects on our bodies and health by our attitudes and beliefs."[14]

We have choices, then, as William James wrote a century ago. We may not be able to control the stressors that modern life confronts us with. Time acceleration, hurry, and urban congestion are facts of life that will not go away. But we can determine how much they will affect our health by our attitudes and by the calm and mental clarity we can manage in appraising them. Further, by making appropriate choices in the way we live, we may be able to move from "helpless" to "hardy," toward a lifestyle that is more "stress-resistant" and healthier.

Simply understanding that we have choices is not enough to build resistance. We need tools to manage our emotional responses with more awareness and command. Without these, free-floating hostility will still secrete norepinephrine into our blood supply; a feeling of helplessness will continue to suppress the activity of our natural killer cells — no matter how aware we are of our choices. We need tools that can return us to a calming state of mind that will inhibit the flow of stress hormones and give us the clarity we need make healthy choices. This is where tools like the mantram and one-pointed focusing are especially useful.

In the next two chapters we talk in detail about how to use the RISE Response to respond to perhaps the most challenging forms of stress that illness and disability can confront us with — the deep and troubling emotional states of anger, fear, depression, helplessness, guilt, and low self-esteem. In Chapter Fifteen, we describe in detail the RISE stress management program or, as we phrase it, *beyond* stress management.

> "My T-cell count was around 300, so I really freaked out. I was really scared; I had a lot of fear. So I started to make some changes and started doing RISE. And I wasn't being so stressed out anymore. When stressful situations came up, I would start using my mantram and, you know, it sort of changed how I dealt with people." (Chris O.)

Suggested Further Reading

Baldwin, Bruce A., Ph.D. *It's All in Your Head*. Wilmington, N.C.: Direction Dynamics, 1985.

Borysenko, Joan, Ph.D. *Minding the Body, Mending the Mind*. Menlo Park, Calif.: Addison-Wesley, 1987.

Justice, Blair, Ph.D. *Who Gets Sick?* Houston: Peak Press, 1987.

Ornstein, Robert, Ph.D., and Paul Ehrlich. *New World, New Mind*. New York: Doubleday, 1989.

Ornstein, Robert, Ph.D., and David Sobel, M.D. *The Healing Brain*. New York: Simon and Schuster, 1987.

Pelletier, Kenneth, Ph.D. *Holistic Medicine*. New York: Dell, 1979.

———. *Mind as Healer, Mind as Slayer*. New York: Dell, 1977.

Selye, Hans. *Stress without Distress*. New York: J. B. Lippincott, 1974.

Managing Emotional Stress

"My big bad habit was taking out my hostility on other drivers, getting into traffic situations where I could see that I was going to get stuck behind this guy and get angry and hit my horn, and get myself all worked up. And it didn't involve that person at all. The hostility or anger I was carrying around behind the wheel of a car ... I was a just a wreck. And I learned, well I'm going to sit at this red light and say my mantram. And it was perfect."

(Carol C.)

As we discussed in the previous chapter, emotional stress is not simply a psychological phenomenon. It is a physiological phenomenon with real dangers. In fact, stress-related disorders can be particularly dangerous because early medical examinations may not reveal the pathological changes they cause. By the time these changes can be seen medically, the damage to tissues and organs may have become extensive. Although medication can help relieve the symptoms of stress-related disorders, medication cannot cure stress. Its causes lie in our lifestyle, perceptions, and attitudes, how we view ourselves and the circumstances in which we live our lives.

Most stress-inducing emotional reactions — hostility, fear, helplessness, anxiety, guilt — can be viewed as habits, automatic patterns of behavior that have been learned over a long period of time. Because of that, they can be unlearned or modified to protect you from harmful stress reactions. But they can be as resistant to change as any physical addiction. Anger, in fact, may well be addictive.[1] Changing emotional habits may require much the same dogged approach it takes to change a physical habit.

125

Managing Negative Emotions

We consider an emotion to be "negative" when it begins to have a corrosive effect on our vitality — like a resentment that continues to simmer, deep-running hostilities that consume vital energy like a blast furnace, chronic self-pity, jealousy, or uncontrolled outbursts of rage. Changing ingrained, corrosive emotional habits is hard to do, but you have already begun practicing for it. You can use the RISE Response to begin to change the way you respond to emotional stress. But be cautious here, and don't set yourself up for disappointment with unrealistic expectations. Don't expect dramatic transformations in your emotional responses. Strong emotional reactions run deep, so don't expect dramatic, overnight transformations. Look for subtle signs of progress. Many course participants have told us they only realized *after the fact* that they hadn't got as angry as they would have a few weeks before, or that they didn't stay angry as long as they would have before they started using the tools. You have to be alert to your emotional patterns in order to understand the changes that may well be taking place in subtle but very real ways.

Let's look now at some of the more obvious emotional patterns that commonly affect all of us, but do so almost routinely when we are coping with a serious or chronic illness or disability.

Depression

Depression afflicts millions of people in this country every year. It's becoming as common as the flu. And recently researchers have begun to suspect that depression may well have an affect upon the immune system, lowering its resistance and perhaps making us more vulnerable in the process. Several studies of people who had lost spouses showed significant effects on immune function, which continued up to fourteen months following a death.[2] Researchers at the Boston University School of Medicine reported lowered immune function, including natural killer cell (NK) activity, among depressed or anxious people.[3] Another study of first-year medical students at Ohio State University found that those who had the highest loneliness scores and highest stress had the lowest levels of natural killer cells when under the stress of examinations. Students who scored the lowest on loneliness and stress scores also had the highest levels of NK cells.[4]

We need to distinguish between a clinically diagnosed depression, which may require medical treatment, and the symptom of depression people commonly feel as a reaction to loss. Feeling "down" or feeling "blue" are common symptoms that are generally transient and do not require medical intervention. They should not be confused with the psychiatric disorder of depression, which may result from a genetic predisposition or from conditioned, distorted ways of looking at stressful situation — or a combination of both.[5] People suffering from clinical depression should seek medical treatment and should consider both physiological and behavioral factors in getting it treated.

Research has shown that a combination of cognitive interventions (such as RISE) and antidepressant medications is the most effective treatment for depressions that have not responded to drug treatment.[6] If you suffer from prolonged or severe depressions, you should consult with a primary care physician or therapist. As a further precaution, we recommend that if you have been diagnosed as clinically depressed or are taking antidepressant medication, you should not meditate unless you are combining meditation with the diet and exercise regimens recommended in Chapter Thirteen. Meditation draws you inward. If you are not getting adequate physical exercise and turning your attention outward through some kind of social interaction, meditation could have the effect of prolonging your depression. You can use the mantram in place of meditation.

Regardless of their cause, depressions can consume large amounts of vitality. Dwelling on your problem can lead to an obsession that prolongs the depression, draining you further, leaving you feeling listless and fatigued. One useful self-intervention is to try to avoid obsessing over problems surrounding the depression. This is easier said than done, but you have a useful tool in your trained attention. You can withdraw your attention when you find yourself obsessing and abort the negative thinking that prolongs the depression and its debilitating effects.

This does not mean that you should in any way pretend the

depression is not real or deny its significance. Depressions are certainly real and they can be accompanied by profound physiological effects. But they contain a strong mental component that can be modified by your response. Using the mantram is one alternative to dwelling upon yourself when you find you are obsessing. Numerous studies have demonstrated that the repetition of the mantram can elicit a state of greater mental alertness and well-being.[7]

Another useful intervention is to keep as busy as your energy allows. It is tempting to withdraw as a depression progresses, but withdrawal can exacerbate its negative effects. Stay physically active. Better yet, volunteer your time to a cause. Give someone a hand. Helping someone can refocus your attention and take your mind off your own difficulties. Such support, as we explained in Chapter Six, can become a vitalizing and health-giving experience.

Resentment

Resentments thrive on attention as plants thrive on sunlight. They cannot exist without it. Dwelling on a resentment feeds and nourishes it like a high protein diet.

What can you do, then, if you find that you are prone to resentment? *Withdraw your attention.*

If you have started to practice the RISE Response, then you've been developing the skill of withdrawing your attention, both in your meditation and by using your mantram. You've begun to learn how to redirect attention from mental distractions in meditation. You can use that same capacity to withdraw your attention, at will, when a resentment forms. Use your mantram: it's hard to keep a resentment nourished at the same time you're repeating the mantram. Or focus your attention on some work at hand.

Helplessness

Probably no attitude is as damaging to health and immune function as the belief that we are helpless victims of our fate and can do nothing to improve it. It's an understandable reaction, given the overwhelming pressures of coping with life-threatening illness in today's impersonal medical world. But it is counterproductive and potentially dangerous. Helplessness has been strongly implicated in health disorders as leaving us more susceptible to illness in general and cancer in particular.[8] Studies have shown that people who are inclined toward "giving up" have higher levels of cortisol and a greater risk of cancer from suppression of natural killer cells in the immune system.[9] Indeed, giving up itself can be a cause of death.

In one recent study of women in the early stages of breast cancer, those who reacted to their diagnosis with extreme distress and helplessness had significantly reduced activity of natural killer cells in their immune systems.[10] On the other hand, the determination not to give up has been reported as a critical factor in survival among cancer patients[11] and victims of heart attack.[12]

Numerous animal studies have shown that an inadequate sense of control actually registers in the pituitary-adrenal cortical system, triggering a flow of cortisol and other hormones that tend to suppress immunity to disease.[13] Laboratory animals placed in uncontrollable situations suffer a decrease in the activity of their natural killer cells.[14]

In RISE we operate on the assumption that if a sense of helplessness can impair immune function, then its opposite — a sense of control and "self-efficacy" — should result in beneficial physiological effects.

One way you can guard against depression is by keeping your mind from becoming too excited. It may seem paradoxical to link excitement with depression but they both cause stress. Excitement is certainly more pleasurable, but the source of that pleasure is the rush of adrenaline it forces into the system causing a momentary "high." Even that can become addictive. "Adrenaline junkies" come to need the high of excitement to feel productive and functional. This is particularly common among high-stress occupations like ICU workers.

From the physiological standpoint, excitement is as stressful to the healing system as a setback or disappointment. On stress scales, getting married is rated almost as stressful as becoming separated.[15] Marital reconciliation causes as much stress as getting fired from a job.[16] People who are chronically excited can become prone to depression, perhaps because prolonged excitement drains vitality. "Up" one day, "down" the next — it's a familiar syndrome to many people. And what is true of the natural world is true also of the mind: what goes up eventually has to come down.

It may be helpful to view excitement as one end of an emotional continuum, the other end of which is depression. Therefore, keeping the mind on an even keel during exciting moments may help protect you against the depressed aftermath. The mantram can be a useful tool to help keep the mind even when you feel it getting overexcited. This can help restore equilibrium and interrupt the stress response that excitement arouses.

Guilt

We view guilt as a waste of time and vitality. It is a defense mechanism that binds up a lot of useful energy and may in fact inhibit growth. Guilt is a habit. And it can be as obsessive and demanding a habit as a physical addiction. If you've done something you feel guilty about, learn from the experience, understand its causes and consequences, find out how you can avoid a repeat performance. Decide you're not going to go down that particular road again. Then forget about it. Get on with your life.

And remember Gershwin's Law: "As with the nation, so with the individual." Energy that is tied up in defense is not available for growth. Guilt may be viewed as a kind of frozen asset. And you can start "liquefying" by developing some compassion and tolerance for your own frailties. As you become more accepting of yourself, you'll free up the "frozen" energy of guilt to become more tolerant of others. Everybody wins.

If you've got a guilt habit, you can begin to undo it with the mantram. Use it to break the nexus with those past experiences that are preying on your conscience. When guilty thinking starts, replace it with the mantram until it passes. Take a walk. Or move your attention to a task, something that can take your mind off the guilt-producing thought. It is easy to forget that the past does not exist anymore, unless you feed it with your attention.

Low Self-Esteem

Guilt is often associated with low self-esteem. One of the outcomes of meditating on an inspirational passage may be an improvement in self-image. You can choose passages that affirm your self-worth and give expression to the "exalted" part of human nature. Many of the passages in Chapter Eighteen include reminders that we are all gifted with an innate spiritual core and have the potential to realize that giftedness.

Remember that spiritually speaking you have deeper resources to draw upon, inner resources of insight, creativity, love, compassion, and energy. Each passage meditation inches you just a little closer to those resources. No matter how limited, flawed, or hopeless you may feel right now, your deeper core remains unaffected. "Accepting that the core of your own being is as precious and wonderful as that of any other person," writes cell biologist Joan Borysenko, "is the greatest gift you can ever give yourself."[17] The more you can become aware of that deepest Self, the higher your "self-assessment" will naturally climb. Day by day, with regular practice, meditation can bring you closer to this Self.

Fear

Fear requires a thought, the idea of threat. A useful intervention is to treat fear as a product of your thinking. By removing the thought you can interrupt its emotional effects (as James confirmed). Repeating your mantram can divert your attention away from fearful thoughts, especially the ones that assault you in the middle of the night. But for the mantram to work then, it has to be repeated at other times during the day.

Try not to dwell on a fear when it comes up in your mind. Fear thrives on attention, so don't nourish it with yours. Move your attention away from the thought with the mantram or with some compelling activity. Keep busy.

A Word of Caution

We are not suggesting in any way that you repress or avoid powerful negative emotions. The RISE Response can help you cope with strong emotions with more clarity and awareness.

But you still have to deal with them. If you can do so calmly and with intention, you can minimize their effects on your healing system. Repressing powerful emotions only makes matters worse. Instead, by training your attention, you can learn to make conscious, strategic responses to moments of intense stress that better conserve your vitality and protect your health.

> *"I will tell you right now, I think RISE saved my life that night. I was so completely at peace that my body was able to attain a level that wasn't fraught with the symptoms of stress. I just didn't feel any stress. None whatsoever. That ability to be able to come down to my inner self, whatever that may be, caused me to survive. I can't put it on anything but the tools. I simply can't."* (Mort B.)

Further Reading

Farquhar, John, M.D. *The American Way of Life Need Not Be Hazardous to Your Health: Coping with Life's Seven Major Risk Factors.* Menlo Park, Calif.: Addison-Wesley Publishing Company, 1987. This includes an excellent and comprehensive chapter on stress management, which is a good supplement to our guidelines given in Chapter Fifteen.

Kabat-Zinn, Ph.D. *Full Catastrophe Living: Using the Wisdom of Your Body and Mind to Face Stress, Pain, and Illness.* New York: Delta, 1990.

Nuernberger, Phil, Ph.D. *Freedom from Stress: A Holistic Approach.* Honesdale, Pa.: Himalayan International Institute Press, 1981. This is a well-written and comprehensive discussion of stress, habits, and attention.

Chapter Eleven

The Problem of Anger

"When I started RISE I was handling hundreds of packages a minute on this conveyor belt. If someone farther back on the belt messed up, all the packages would be coming down the belt at once. I'd just start screaming. But once I started using my mantram, I'd see this coming and I'd say, "Oh, well, here's my mantram, no more screaming." And that was it. The job was not able to trigger my anger anymore." (Terry A.)

We set aside an entire chapter on anger because it has emerged in the research of the past decade as potentially the most damaging of emotional reactions. The research is extensive and compelling and certainly provokes at least a conscious reconsideration of our own attitudes toward anger and how best to manage it in our own lives.

In their landmark study of Type A behavior and heart disease, Drs. Rosenman and Friedman identified "free-floating hostility" as one of the chief characteristics of the coronary-prone Type A personality. They defined it as "a permanently indwelling anger that shows itself with ever greater frequency in reaction to increasingly trivial happenings."[1] In working with thousands of recovering coronary patients in the San Francisco Recurrent Coronary Prevention Project (RCPP), Friedman and his associates found that free-floating hostility appeared to be the factor most closely associated with a second heart attack or sudden death.[2]

More recent studies of Type A behavior corroborated and refined these findings about anger and hostility, while focusing attention upon it even more than Rosenman and Friedman did.[3] Dr. Redford Williams at Duke University and others have produced research demonstrating that the hostility cofactor may well form the "toxic core" of Type A behavior — that is, the aspect that inflicts the most damage.

In his book on the subject, *The Trusting Heart* (New York: Times Books, 1989), Dr. Williams describes how he looked at data from personality studies done in the 1950s that measured a "hostility score" in populations of factory workers and medical students. Comparing the subjects' hostility score with follow-up medical histories, Dr. Williams and others found that the workers who scored high in hostility eventually suffered one-and-a-half times more heart attacks than lower scoring subjects on the test. The medical students, now doctors, were four to five times more likely to develop heart disease than their non-hostile peers.[4] More recent studies like the Multiple Risk Factor Intervention Trial (MR. FIT) during the 1970s confirmed these findings when hostility scores were taken into consideration: men scoring high on the hostility component of the Type A structured interview were about twice as likely to develop coronary heart disease during the follow-up period as those with low hostility levels.[5]

According to Dr. Williams, no other single risk factor for coronary illness — diet, hypertension, smoking, exercise — predicted as accurately which subjects in the original studies would have heart problems. His subsequent laboratory research confirmed what the epidemiological evidence suggested: that hostile people were a population at high risk for coronary illness, because they got angry more frequently and their bodies stayed angry longer, leaving their nervous systems impacted by harmful stress hormones for extended periods.

After further research, Dr. Williams now defines the hostility component of Type A behavior as "a cynical mistrust of others that leads to the frequent experience of anger, which in turn is overtly expressed to those around one."[6]

Breaking the Hostility Habit

In order to help Type A men change their hostility patterns, Dr. Friedman's RCPP developed a number of strategies to identify the pattern and to change it which he describes in his most recent book, *Treating Type A Behavior and Your Heart*. His study of one thousand male heart attack victims, all identified as Type A, involved a treatment program designed to reduce both time urgency and free-floating hostility. The results showed that men in the study decreased their Type A behavior by a substantial degree, and, more significant, there was a reduction in the rate of recurrent heart problems.[7] We describe below some of these strategies.

The RCPP has developed a number of signs by which you can detect if you have free-floating hostility. Among them:

- You become irritated or angry at the relatively minor mistakes of the people around you.

- You find that you regularly examine a situation in order to find something that is wrong.

- You are unable to laugh at things your friends laugh at.

- You think that most people cannot be trusted, or that everyone has a selfish motive.

- You tend to regard people (even one person) with contempt.[8]

Like all emotions, chronic hostility is a habit and you are not going to get on top of it easily or soon. But properly understood and managed, hostility can become less of an impairment to your health and relationships. Two misconceptions that Dr. Friedman found common among his Type A subjects and that tend to perpetuate hostility need to be examined.

I need a certain amount of hostility to get ahead in the world. Far from contributing to success, the tendencies to become easily irritated, aggravated, or angry over trivial matters have more likely been responsible for disrupting relations with colleagues and associates as well as partners, family members, and friends.

I can't do anything about my hostility. Especially hostile Type As can become addicted to the "struggle hormone" norepinephrine, making them unconsciously resist changing while seeking out situations where anger will be elicited and the hormone secreted.[9]

To reduce the severity of their free-floating hostility, the RCPP recommends that their patients try some of the following strategies:

1. Find new ways to give and to receive love.

2. Employ understanding, compassion, and forgiveness when dealing with others.

3. Search for more joy and beauty in life.

4. Stop using obscenities (a trait of particularly hostile Type As).

5. Determine when they are most likely to become hostile and what circumstances are most likely to trigger their hostility.

6. Announce to their friends and loved ones that they are going to try to change.

7. Express their appreciation of others and encourage them.

8. Learn to accept more of life's uncertainties.[10]

Managing Anger

Anger is basically a defense mechanism, a function of the primitive fight/flight response we described in Chapter Nine. It is one of the ways the "self" seeks to protect itself when feeling vulnerable. When you get angry, your blood pressure and heart rate rise, and your breathing becomes rapid and shallow just as in "arousal." Anger is a natural force within the human personality and is neither "good" nor "bad" in itself. But it is powerful enough to cause measurably harmful physiological effects if not managed properly.

Denying or suppressing anger has been shown to be damaging, while unexpressed feelings tend to get expressed "sideways," as it were, in inappropriate ways. More to the point, feelings that are denied or suppressed cannot be dealt with, resolved, and transformed. One common psychological technique is to encourage people to express their anger while using soft bats or other tools to provoke a feeling of aggression and relieve the emotion in a "safe" way. While this may relieve the emotion temporarily, it does little to develop the capacity to choose appropriate responses when in the grip of a powerful emotion.

It is important to find constructive ways to deal with anger rather than simply suppressing it or inviting a rage at every provocation. The most useful ways to express anger are those that most closely respond to the circumstances in which it arose. This means gaining enough composure and clarity to interpret the issues surrounding the anger so that you can make an appropriate assessment. You should ask yourself, what reaction best fits the circumstances — respond immediately and forcefully, wait a while, ignore things for the time being?

You may not always find the perfect response. Circumstances may be complex and emotionally challenging to see clearly. But you can avoid the automatic reactions that will further cloud the situation and leave the significant issues unresolved. Reasoned, clearly communicated responses charged by deep feeling always stand the chance of being more effective than automatic reactions.

Anger and the Response

Finding appropriate ways to manage anger depends largely upon how well you are able to avoid uncontrolled reactions. If your reactions to anger turn automatically to compulsive outbursts or rigid denial, you'll leave yourself vulnerable to stress-related illness. But if you can learn to interrupt your automatic reactions using the RISE Response, you may be able to buy yourself some time. You can look more clearly at the circumstances surrounding the anger and choose a response that is more appropriate and perhaps more vitalizing.

When you feel yourself getting angry, try to recall the following strategies:

Don't react violently. Especially avoid flying into a rage. That depletes your vitality and makes it difficult to understand the circumstances at hand.

Discharge the energy. Anger is a powerful force and needs to be expended. Take a fast mantram walk if you can. Or do something physical to help discharge the energy build-up and help interrupt the stress response that anger triggers. While anger increases the breathing and heart rate, repeating your mantram, especially with physical movement, can interrupt the reaction without suppressing it and evoke the "relaxation response" that counteracts the release of stress hormones.

Take time to cool off. Wait until you have achieved some calm and clarity before trying to discuss the issues. It is virtually impossible to be discerning or even reasonable when you're enraged, so your efforts at resolution at this time are not likely to be effective.

Stay one-pointed. Even if you can't take a walk or are too engaged in work to repeat your mantram, you can try to become one-pointed in the task before you. This can help bring the mind to a calmer state, which in itself can evoke the physiological benefits of the relaxation response.[11]

Respond appropriately. Having gained some clarity, try to come to some understanding of the sources of your anger and begin to resolve them appropriately. Are they your own problems, someone else's, a combination of both? Ignoring, avoiding, or denying these issues prevents their resolution and invites a recurrence.

If you find that you can't resolve the external sources of your anger (the medical system, society, your job, your physical condition) then remind yourself that they do not have to impact upon your peace of mind. The RISE Response is especially suited to help you manage this.

Remember: You cannot control all the sources of stress in your life. Some things are going to provoke your anger and you may not be able to do anything about them. But you can control how they will affect your health.

> *"I remember people telling me that I lost my temper real quickly. I didn't realize I was doing some of these things, losing my temper, and being real sharp and saying mean, hurtful things to people. That doesn't happen as often anymore. I don't get upset, or when I do, the recovery time is much shorter. I realize what I am doing. Since then a lot of people have noticed a change in me."* (Chris O.)

Harnessing the Power of Anger

As we said, hostility and anger are sources of great energy. When hostility is left to simmer or explode, much of this energy is wasted. Like fuel, hostility can be put to work. Injustice or cruelty, for instance, should rightly provoke anger. But it can be harnessed into creative action, rather than dissipated in outbursts. Its energy can be recaptured and used intentionally in worthwhile causes.

One example of this "creative" application of anger can be found in the life of Mahatma Gandhi. By his own admission, this gentle, peace-loving "apostle of non-violence" was driven by a deep and abiding anger at the injustices of colonial tyranny and racism. But he harnessed his anger in non-violent action instead of suppressing it (as had many of his fellow Indians) or letting it explode in violent outbursts. In Gandhi's own words: "I have learnt through bitter experience the one supreme lesson to conserve my anger, and as heat conserved is transmuted into energy, even so our anger controlled can be transmuted into a power which can move the world."[12]

The Type A+ Personality

Type As generally have more raw aggression than others. Gandhi, by his own admission, had enough ambition, passion, drive, and anger to qualify as a high-powered, coronary-prone Type A personality. But he worked hard to transform this energy. In fact, he used versions of the same self-stewarding tools you find in RISE, including meditation and the mantram (he used "Rama"), one-pointed attention, training his mind, and serving others.[13] In doing so, he became a kind of "super" Type A, a person who uses his Type A characteristics to a positive advantage. We call this the Type A+ personality, a promising alternative to the self-destructive patterns usually associated with these characteristics.

In fact, recent research has shown that Type As can even put their aggressiveness to work for their health. Contrary to expectations, Type As who suffer a coronary attack have been found to be less likely to suffer a second heart attack than more passive Type Bs who have also had a coronary.[14] This has puzzled Type A researchers, but it may simply mean that Type As can use their drive and discipline to heal themselves ("I'm going to beat this if it kills me!"). As Gandhi showed, much depends on how well trained our minds are and on the vision we have of what a human being is and what he or she can become.

In Gandhi's case, his anger was transformed into a beneficial force on a large scale. His success can stand as a model for anyone tormented by aggression and anger. It can be argued that Gandhi used his to free the people of his impoverished country from the grip of the greatest empire the world has seen — without firing a shot.

Questions and Answers

- *Sometimes I feel as though I am repressing my anger when I use the mantram.*

The point of using your mantram when you get angry is to calm yourself in order to respond to the source of your anger. This could take some time. It does not mean you ignore the source of your anger, or even refuse to express it if the circumstances warrant that. But you are trying to avoid chronic explosions of anger as well as the slow, burning resentments that are detrimental to your health — not to speak of your relationships.

II. Wellness: Building a Hardy Lifestyle

Making Healthy Choices

"One of the things that RISE has taught me is how much of what you do is nothing but a habit. And you can focus on that, you can change that habit. It is not mandatory that you get this habit and you have to live with it for the rest of your life. You can change it." (Carol C.)

What lifestyle habits most affect our health? You probably know them as well as we do: diet, exercise, how we manage stress, the prevalence of high-risk behaviors like substance abuse and unsafe sexual practices. Nothing new here, no information the average adult hasn't been hearing about for at least the last decade. The real mystery is why more people don't lead healthier lives.

One long-term study at the School of Public Health at the University of California at Los Angeles followed the records of almost seven thousand people to find out what made the difference between good and poor health. The study established seven health "behaviors" that correlated positively with good health. We've listed them in the accompanying box. People in the study who observed these seven practices were demonstrably healthier than those who did not. Major illnesses were reduced. Life span increased. The study's results revealed that a forty-five-year-old male who followed all seven practices could

SEVEN BEHAVIORS FOR GOOD HEALTH

1. Get seven to eight hours sleep per night.

2. Eat breakfast regularly.

3. Do not eat between meals.

4. Keep within a few pounds of your ideal weight.

5. Engage regularly in active sports or exercise.

6. Drink moderately or not at all.

7. Don't smoke.

expect to live on the average eleven more years than the person who followed three practices or less.[1]

Lifestyle and Health

Lifestyle has been playing an increasingly significant role in maintaining health since the spectacular decline of infectious diseases during this century. Now that diseases like smallpox and cholera have virtually vanished from developed societies, the leading causes of premature death and disability are chronic diseases like heart disease, cancer, and strokes. These in turn have become increasingly linked to behavioral risk factors like smoking, overconsumption of alcohol, high-fat diets, lack of exercise, poor stress management, and, in the case of HIV illness, unsafe sexual practices.

A healthy lifestyle is an essential component to maintaining health. Habits, especially diet, exercise, and stress management, have become the cornerstone of lifestyle. In his book *The American Way of Life Need Not Be Hazardous to Your Health*, Dr. John Farquhar, director of the Stanford Center for Disease Prevention, writes, "By the way you live, you greatly determine not only the length of your life, but also the quality of your life."[2]

Like it or not, our health depends greatly on how sound, or unsound, our habits are.

The Failure of Lifestyle

Given the success of vaccines over most infectious diseases and the simplicity of the health prescriptions listed above, one would expect to find a relatively healthy population in the country today. Complying with the three "don'ts" and four "dos" from the UCLA study requires no special equipment, no large amounts of money or unreasonable amounts of time. Yet the health of the country entering the 1990s is surprisingly at risk. Sixty million adult Americans, for instance, are still at high risk for coronary disease because of high blood cholesterol levels due largely to diets high in fat. More than 150,000 annual fatalities are attributed directly to smoking, and another one million individuals suffer from significant degrees of pulmonary crippling because of cigarettes. Still, more than fifty million people continue to smoke. Some 700,000 Americans suffer non-fatal heart attacks and strokes each year, while almost 250,000 Americans under age seventy-five die "prematurely" from heart attacks and another 50,000 from strokes, 90 percent of which are preventable.[3]

In the cases of immune-related disease, impressive evidence has accumulated to show that cancer of the breast, colon, and rectum are related to longstanding dietary practices. Even in the case of HIV-related illness, where its causes are linked so clearly to unsafe sexual practices, understanding is not mirrored in practice. Researchers at the Center for AIDS Prevention Studies at the Medical School of the University of California at San Francisco have uncovered what they termed the "relapse" factor — about 20 percent of San Francisco gay men "fall off the safe-sex wagon" each year.[4]

Clearly, despite the massive evidence regarding high-risk behaviors, our unhealthy habits die hard.

Health and Habits

We talked at some length in Chapter One about why it is so difficult to make permanent changes in high-risk behavior. More than a third of the country's 51 million smokers tried to stop during one recent year, for example, but couldn't. Even "minor" urges like a craving for junk food or caffeine can bring a fierce and unexpected resistance when you try to alter them.

Most compulsive physical behavior, we said, is driven as much by emotional components as by physical ones. Emotional moods or states of mind like anxiety or depression can lend a "charge" to physical habits that makes them resistant to change. How you feel has much to do with how you act. Most habits carry an emotional force that drives them from below. Even strictly physical habits like smoking or overeating may represent only the tips of emotional icebergs. Driven by inner tensions we suddenly borrow a cigarette and light up though we haven't smoked in six weeks. The resistance to changing even a minor compulsive habit can be surprisingly strong. Sometimes, as with smoking, it seems far out of scale to the habit itself.

The Habit Knot

It may help to understand better these dynamics if we think of a physical habit as a kind of knot, a slip knot, to be precise. The knot is loose and slips easily in the beginning stages of a habit. We may not even notice it is there. What's one more gin and tonic? we think. An after-dinner smoke? But each time we indulge the craving, the habit knot cinches a little inside.

Then our doctor suggests some changes. "Stop smoking," she tells us. "Cut back on your drinking. Get some exercise."

All right, we reason, what's the big deal? We cut out the two martinis at lunch. Head down to the gym after work. For a week it's smooth sailing. Two weeks. Then we hear the rumblings from somewhere within: How long's this going to go on? Get a life! So we try just one martini at lunch or skip the workout today. And before we know how it happened, we begin to sense that a habit knot of some considerable size has formed somewhere inside.

Size alone is not what makes habit knots so difficult to loosen. There is also the depth to which they penetrate. Their strands trail far into the mind, through every level of the personality. It may help to understand our relapses better if we realize that we are fighting our habits on several levels of our personality at the same time, physical, mental, and emotional. This makes the fight a difficult one. Even an urge for sweets may run deep within us, echoing needs that have followed us since childhood. The craving itself triggers a more formidable array of forces that may sink far into the mind itself.

The power of a physical craving results from the physical, emotional, and mental forces it confronts us with all at once. It's hardly a fair fight! But it makes it more understandable, for instance, how the men in the UCSF study relapsed into unsafe sexual practices, despite the potentially fatal consequences. Sexual drives reach into the deepest level of the human psyche, urging us on against our better judgment, even into practices we may know are life-threatening.

Fighting Compulsive Behavior

At the heart of the problem of harmful lifestyles is compulsive behavior — our actions, emotional states, moods, and attitudes that lock us into behaviors that are harmful to our health. In RISE, we do not focus on particular habits. We leave it to you to decide which habits you may want to alter. Instead the RISE Response aims at compulsion itself, to loosen its grip on you. Training your attention strikes at the heart of compulsive behavior. Each time you return your attention to the meditation passage, for instance, you've strengthened your will at a deeper level of the mind, where compulsions begin.

You should view the need for lifestyle changes as a practical issue, not a moral one. It means striking a balance between encouraging yourself toward healthier behavior, while not maligning yourself for lapses. Breaking free from addictions and physical habits is seldom quick and rarely easy. You may be fighting years of conditioning from the media, advertising, and social pressures, as well as your own repetitive behavior. These will not stop just because you have decided to make some changes. Discretion, compassion, and common sense can go a long way to preserving a healthy balance.

Getting Started

The three areas of lifestyle that bear most significantly upon health are diet, fitness, and stress management. In the next two chapters we will treat each of these areas in detail, suggesting changes you may choose to make. But first we'll describe some guidelines that have helped hundreds of course participants begin to make meaningful lifestyle changes.

An engineer we know once pointed out that engineering is mainly a matter of solving a number of small problems. He designed bridges, and a bridge, he said, is mainly a succession of technical problems that, having been solved, get you across a river.

Changing lifestyle involves a similar process. Small changes, made in their proper time, form the stuff of human transformation. So start gradually. Avoid vows or sweeping resolutions. Gradualism has been shown to be the most effective and enduring method for making self-directed changes.[5]

Look for Trouble Spots

In small group discussions, course participants have talked about a number of trouble areas in which they found themselves vulnerable to compulsive behavior. Understanding and anticipating these helped many participants guard against relapses:

- *Speed.* Habits thrive on the times the mind is moving so fast you're not fully aware of what you're doing.

- *Transitional moments.* Watch out for the times when you have finished a task but have not yet begun another. Your focus is likely to be blurred during transitions, leaving your mind more susceptible to compulsive behavior.

- *When you're distracted or agitated.* Moments of agitation are open invitations to compulsions. A distracted mind is an easy prey to old habits.

- *Highs and lows.* Compulsive behavior often coincides with emotional highs and lows. Bad news comes and the mind wastes no time in taking advantage of your vulnerability: "You deserve a break," it whispers inside. "Something sweet!" Or you receive news of a promotion and along with your elation comes a similar message from the mind: "Indulge yourself. Go ahead, you've earned it."

Vitality

Another way to understand the power of compulsive behavior is through its connection with vitality. Vitality is energy, the elusive, hard-to-measure bridge between body, mind and spirit. Perhaps vitality can best be characterized as the total "energy" within the healing system. It represents the physical, sensory, emotional, and even "spiritual" energies at work on both the conscious and unconscious levels. Vitality is a central concept to our understanding the healing system. But it is difficult to document scientifically. Life would be impossible without vitality, but medical science still lacks a working definition for it.

Still, we know when we have an abundance of vitality. We can feel it. And we usually know when it's low. Even if we lack a scientific model to explain it, vitality is a physiologic reality. Conserving it is important, especially if you are coping with serious illness or disability.

Vitality is closely linked to our behavior. The food we eat, what kind, how much of it, the amount of exercise we get, how well we manage stress are related to our vitality. As such, vitality can be used as one indicator of the appropriateness of a lifestyle choice without invoking moral sanctions. Generally speaking, if a behavior or attitude or feeling tends to drain us, we should consider modifying it.

Vitality and the Mind

Vitality is connected with the entire healing system of body, mind, and emotions. So it is also affected by what we think and how we feel. Our sense of control, well-being, and self-esteem influence the level of our vitality, as do the quality of our relationships and our sense of purpose. Watch a friend in a depression, for instance. His listlessness and general torpor testify to the drain a depression places on the healing system. In fact, as we described in Chapter Nine, several studies have linked depression and helplessness to impaired immunity.

VITALITY EVALUATION CHART

Vitality and Lifestyle: Look at your eating habits, your work, entertainment, relationships, feelings and attitudes. Try to assess how they affect your sense of vitality. Do they enrich it and make you feel energized? Take a piece of paper and list them in the left-hand column below as shown below. Do they leave you feeling somewhat drained, tired, or listless? List them in the right-hand column. Vitality is a useful way to assess the appropriateness of lifestyle choices without invoking moral sanctions.

Activities and Experiences that Conserve and Enrich	*Activities and Experiences that Drain and Deplete*
[List]	[List]

Whether a particular activity drains or enriches our vitality seems to depend at least as much upon our mental attitude, as the nature of the activity itself. To help course participants more fully appreciate this connection, we ask them to evaluate their activities according to whether they are enriching or depleting.

In filling out the vitality chart we've reproduced here, participants list activities, feelings, and attitudes that seem either to enrich or deplete vitality, placing them to the right or left of the dividing line in the middle of the page. In most RISE classes, participants discover that a number of experiences and activities fall on both sides of the line. It's because they appear both to drain and enrich vitality. These fall most often in the areas of emotions, work, relationships, and sensory experiences. One class, for instance, decided that grief was an appropriate and healing reaction to loss. But if allowed to become chronic, they decided, grief could become devitalizing. This led to the general observation that moods and attitudes can be both vitalizing or devitalizing depending upon how intentional or compulsive they are. And the same with behavior.

Many alumni report that conscious, intentional behavior is more likely to enrich their vitality than automatic behavior. When they act mechanically, with little intention or out of habit, their experiences have depleted them. Participants have told us that being too rigid or too lax in their behavior, acting or thinking in extremes, generally devitalized them.

The most common terms that emerge from our classes to describe what best fosters vitality are "freedom," "choice," and "intention." To many RISE alumni, these have become useful guidelines to behavior, free from moral judgment. By increasing their capacity to act with freedom, they may well influence the level of their vitality. This may partly account for the results in our Denver study, which showed that course participants significantly increased their sense of well-being.

Conserving Vitality

Here are some general suggestions for conserving vitality.

1. *Meditation:* It may be that the most powerful tool we can develop to enhance vitality is a trained mind. With trained attention, we can reduce the amount of wasted energy from negative thinking and temper the exhausting mood swings that emotional stress brings.

2. *Slowing down:* Compulsive speed is one of the largest drains of vitality. Slowing down and becoming more intentional can reduce that drain.

3. *One-pointed attention:* Scattered, "polyphasic" thinking is another large drain. Staying "one-pointed" as much as you can will conserve vitality. One-pointedness is best cultivated by practicing the art of doing only one thing at a time.

4. *Physical habits:* Reducing addictive behavior, improving your diet, and getting adequate physical exercise can have a positive influence on your vitality. In the next chapter, we explain in detail how to begin to modify physical habits that may impair vitality and to cultivate habits that enhance it.

5. *Emotional habits:* Negative emotional states can deplete vitality. So can the ways we respond emotionally to stress. We cannot avoid stress, but we can alter our emotional reactions to

it so as to minimize their draining our vitality. Chapters Ten and Fifteen describe ways to use the tools to manage stress better.

6. *Purpose:* Having a purpose, coupled with a powerful will to live, can play a significant role in conserving vitality. Having a purpose and a strong will to live characterized a group of "long-term AIDS survivors" that were studied at the Medical Center of the University of California at San Francisco.[6]

7. *Likes and dislikes:* A surprising amount of vitality is consumed in the vacillations of the mind as it swings toward what it likes and away from what it doesn't like. In either case, vitality is consumed in quantity. Breaking loose of compulsive behaviors includes trying to pry ourselves loose a little from our more rigid tastes and opinions. Such a loosening can release surprising amounts of "captured" vitality.

Habits That Heal:
Diet, Nutrition, Fitness

Nutrition and Health

We all eat, for we all need to move around to one degree or another. How we eat and how much we exercise can have a significant bearing upon our health status. In light of this, you should begin to look closely at your own patterns of eating and exercise, evaluate them according to your specific health needs, and begin to bring them within the accepted scientific guidelines for optimal health. What are these?

The major chronic illnesses of industrialized societies are all related to diets characterized by a high intake of meat, with a preponderance of processed and refined foods that are high in fat, sugar, and salt and low in fiber.[1] These illnesses include the major "killer" diseases such as some cancers, diverticular disease, hypertension, and cardiovascular diseases like heart attacks and strokes. Together these account for more than 50 percent of adult deaths in the U.S.

Based upon studies carried out during the past two decades, a number of relationships have been established between diet and chronic illness that bear repeating. They include:

1. Increased dietary cholesterol and saturated fat (meat, eggs, and milk products form major sources) are closely related to cardiovascular diseases such as heart attack and strokes.

2. A high-fat diet has been identified as a risk factor in cancer, particularly of the breast and colon.[2]

3. Low fiber is a major risk factor for diverticular disease of the colon.

4. Obesity is a risk factor in cardiovascular disease, cancer, hypertension, and adult diabetes.[3] Large amounts of sugar

in the diet contribute to the development of heart disease as well.[4]

5. There is probably a relationship between development of adult onset diabetes in susceptible individuals and high sugar intake.

6. High sodium (salt) intake is probably related to the development of hypertension.[5]

The "Optimal" Diet

There is no single perfect diet. In fact, a variety of dietary styles can maintain adequate health. Nonetheless, the nutritional sciences can now speak with confidence, in broad terms anyway, of what can be considered the cornerstones of an optimum diet. People with AIDS require a much more specific nutritional management plan, which we outline in Chapter Fourteen. People who are HIV positive, but have shown no signs of "wasting" or other symptoms of illness, can safely follow the guidelines below. They should still consult with their primary care physician regarding their diet. Based upon the accumulated evidence, a recent surgeon general's report made the following recommendations for a diet for healthy individuals:

- Decrease dietary fat (especially saturated fats) to less than 30 percent of total dietary calories.

- Maintain a desirable body weight.

- Increase dietary intake of complex carbohydrates and fiber.

- Decrease dietary sodium intake (salt).

- Decrease, or preferably eliminate, alcohol intake.

What to Eat

There is no longer any mystery about what a nutritious diet looks like. It is high in dietary fiber, low in fat, salt, and sugar. Such a diet would emphasize the following foods, in descending order of importance:

- *Whole grain cereals:* including "dinner" grains like brown rice or polenta, and breads made from whole grain flour.

- *Fresh vegetables:* especially dark green leafy and yellow ones and "cruciferous" vegetables — the broccoli and cabbage family that protect against cancer.

- *Dried legumes:* lentils, split peas, azuki, and kidney beans. There is a great variety of them, and every ethnic cuisine has something to teach us about their preparation. Don't forget soybeans and their derivatives, tofu and tempeh.

- *Fresh and dried fruits:* the best possible way to satisfy a sweet tooth, while providing good sources of vitamins C and A, fiber, and some minerals.

- *Low-fat dairy products:* especially the cultured ones like yogurt and kefir.

For more specific dietary guidelines, consult one of the nutrition guidebooks we list at the end of the chapter. But if you do nothing more than begin today to add some of these foods to your diet, you'll be taking a step forward. All of them can be purchased in a supermarket, but you should also explore the offerings at a good natural foods store. You'll find ready-to-eat cereals made from whole grains, unsweetened or lightly seasoned with fruit concentrates. For the more adventurous, you'll find tofu and tempeh burgers, ready to broil or sauté, whole grain pastas, organically grown vegetables and fruits, and much more.

General Guidelines

As a general rule, we recommend the following simple formula, which can provide a safe, easy-to-understand plan for adequate nutrition. It includes three key ideas: eat a *variety* of *whole foods* in *moderation*.[6] Let's look at each of the key items in detail.

Variety simply means eating foods from all the major categories — leafy vegetables, roots, grains, fruits, and so on. If your diet includes enough variety, you need not worry about nutrients. This means choosing foods from as many different families as possible, and varying choices even within the families themselves. Eating spinach is fine, but an unvarying diet of spinach may lack nutrients found in other leafy greens like kale or chard. And a steady diet of spinach can become monotonous.

Adequate variety in your food choices can ensure that your nutritional needs will be met and that there won't be unknown gaps. We can safely say that if a substantial amount of your calories are drawn from a reasonable variety of unrefined grains and vegetables, you can hardly get too much fat or too little protein, vitamins, or minerals.

Whole foods are unrefined and unprocessed, coming to us in virtually their natural state. As such, they retain their full complement of nutrients. Foods that have been processed usually have lost some or most of their nutrients. White flour and other processed, separated foods have become the norm of the American diet. As a result, average Americans have a deficient intake of vitamins B_6, C, E, calcium, magnesium, iron, and zinc though their caloric needs may be met or even exceeded.[7] Even with enrichment, many Americans do not get enough vitamin B_6, for instance, because of their reliance upon refined white flour.

Refined foods create "empty" calories. Sugar or alcohol, for instance, meet caloric needs without providing the necessary nutrients that would have accompanied those calories in whole foods. The "empty" calories in a pastry tend to fill you up, but supply only a part of your nutritional requirements. Separated and processed foods usually contain chemicals to add color or shelf life. Too little is known today about the full effects of these chemicals to justify using them in abundance. Whenever possible purchase organically grown foods, which are becoming widely available and less costly.

We particularly recommend whole grains and cereals as staples for a healthy diet. Their nutritional contribution is both balanced and reliable. And they contain starch and protein in proportion to our energy and protein needs, while providing essential vitamins and minerals. Of course grains are high in both carbohydrates and fiber content.

Another consideration to bear in mind is freshness. Vegetables in particular lose nutrients from the time they are picked. The fresher the vegetable, the higher its vitamin content.

Moderation. Changes in eating habits can represent a major turnaround for many people. But you should not feel you have to achieve all these goals at once. After all, your current diet was formed over many years. Don't be impatient. Make small, incremental changes, one or two at a time. And avoid extremes.

There is no need to be rigid or excessive. Don't overwhelm or discourage yourself. Congratulate yourself at regular intervals!

Getting Started

Eating is a largely unintentional business, particularly today when the conventional meal patterns that used to give some coherence to what one ate are gone. Grazing through most of our waking hours has replaced sit-down meals and the obligatory soup-salad-and-veggie configurations of the past. It may by that the single greatest deterrent to good nutrition is speed itself. The easy availability of convenience foods, coupled with the pervasive sense that there simply isn't enough time to eat properly, are at the center of the country's poor eating habits.

Consequently, to decide you're actually going to plan what you eat, and plan according to current nutritional wisdom, is a big step. It requires time, but time that is well spent. Intentionality — slowing down enough to remember your choices and making appropriate ones — is the key here, just as it is in other areas of this program.

And be positive. Instead of dwelling on what you're giving up, concentrate on making new food discoveries. Get some good cookbooks and set aside time for trying out new recipes. (See our recommendations at the end of the chapter.) Get acquainted with unusual vegetables and fruits — explore tofu and tempeh, and find out what quinoa is.

You need to consider doing more of your own cooking. True, the extra time may seem like an imposition. But wait, look again. Cooking can be immensely pleasurable, especially if you give yourself time. The raw materials of a natural foods diet are beautiful, and the chopping, slicing, stirring, and steaming that go into a meal can leave you feeling calm, centered, and pleased with yourself. Once you get a couple of menus under control, you can start cooking for friends, and that kind of satisfaction is a subtle form of nourishment in itself.

Questions and Answers

- *Where do we begin to make changes?*

It's at this point in our courses that participants can become discouraged. Their habits cut a wide swath through all kinds of unhealthy behavior, and many of them tell us they can't possibly change everything at once. Indeed, if you try to change too much, too soon, you could get overwhelmed with a sense of overload. For this reason, we recommend an especially graduated approach. Select one physical habit you want to work on and begin there. Cut back on smoking or alcohol consumption or make a dietary change, or start getting more exercise. But don't try more than one at the same time.

A good start on making dietary changes, for example, would be to try one new vegetable a week, a dark, leafy green, this week, something a little exotic like kohlrabi next. It can be fun as well as pleasant. Or get one of the cookbooks listed in the "Helpful Reading" section at the end of this chapter (page 162) and read it through. You might find it inspiring. No need to revolutionize your life in one week!

If you can reestablish control in one area of your life — for example with food or exercise — you can extend this control gradually to other areas. Research indicates that increasing physical exercise often leads to the adoption of other lifestyle habits like eating less, quitting smoking, and coping more effectively with stress.[8] The leverage you gain over your mind by cutting back on sweets, can be used to tackle smoking or substance abuse. Each gain increases your confidence. Momentum builds.

Experiment

- *Diet:* Try a dietary change this week that can make your diet higher in dietary fiber or lower in fat, salt, or sugar. (Choose one.) Or try a new vegetable or a new recipe. Look at "Helpful Reading" at the end of the chapter for cookbook suggestions.

- *Sleep and rest:* In your journal assess: Do you plan for sleep or take it as it comes? When do you go to bed? When do you arise? Do you plan a time for rest and relaxation, or just "crash" when you have to? How much time do you spend on the couch watching TV? (A recent major study found that watching a lot of TV leaves you tense rather than relaxed.) Do you think you get too much sleep or too little?

Physical Fitness

Physical fitness is neither a luxury nor a panacea, and its appropriate place in contemporary life is often misunderstood. People seem to ignore fitness altogether (only one-third of Americans exercise regularly) or pursue it as an end in itself, sometimes with an obsessive preoccupation. A healthier perspective toward exercise views fitness as one essential component of a healthy lifestyle. Within this perspective such physical qualities as endurance, strength, flexibility, and agility are seen as necessary elements of optimum health.

We now know that appropriate physical exercise produces health benefits throughout the healing system. A recent study of more than five thousand Harvard alumni, ranging in age from twenty-one to eighty, demonstrated that "moderate exercise" — as little as twenty minutes three times a week — "produces lifelong benefits to health, including a reduction in cancer risk."[9] The study also concluded that such exercise would also serve as "a stress reliever and an antidote for stress-related illness and decreased performance." Vigorous exercise has also been shown to help lower plasma cholesterol and blood pressure levels, strengthen bones and help decrease the severity of diabetes.[10]

Other studies have found lower levels of depression and anxiety, fewer days sick, and increased work satisfaction reported for participants in aerobic fitness programs.[11] In their study of executives working under high stress, Kobasa and Maddi found that "vigorous exercise is a good anti-stress tool."[12] "Executives who work out," Kobasa writes, "stay healthier than those who don't."[13]

If your current health permits and your doctor approves, you should consider starting a fitness program. It does not have to include joining a club, or investing in expensive equipment. But you should find out what kinds of exercise are best for you and how much of it you need to achieve cardiovascular conditioning. We have listed several useful books at the end of the chapter that give detailed information on the benefits of a range of physical exercise.

Aerobic Fitness

Aerobic exercise is the most important kind of exercise for cardiovascular fitness. It includes any type of exercise that rhythmically uses the large muscle groups of the body and maintains the heart at 60–80 percent of its desirable maximum rate. Weight lifting and stretching do not improve cardiovascular fitness but they are good adjuncts to aerobic exercise.

Activities like swimming, fast walking, bicycling, rhythmic dancing, jogging, running, and tennis can improve aerobic conditioning if done regularly and for long enough periods. There is some controversy as to how much aerobic exercise is necessary to maintain cardiovascular fitness. The Stanford Center for Disease Prevention recommends at least twenty minutes three or four times a week.[14] Recent studies show, however, that the same health benefits can be gained by exercising in smaller increments throughout the day for a total of thirty minutes at least five days a week.[15] Coming from the U.S. Public Health Service, this recommendation is good news if you haven't been able to work in a regular fitness routine. Instead, you can work at getting a cumulative total of thirty minutes a day of exercise through normal activities in your day — walking up stairs, walking to work, raking leaves, dancing, long walks, to mention a few examples.

How Aerobics Exercise Works

We still believe that if you can build a routine of aerobic exercises into your week, you can ensure you cardiovascular fitness. So we have gone to some lengths below to help you do that. The word "aerobic" refers to the ability of the body to bring in and deliver oxygen to its muscles, blood vessels, heart, and lungs. The more fit you are the more oxygen you will be able to deliver to your body's working muscles and the more work your body will be able to do.

Aerobics exercise works because physical activity makes a demand on your system for extra energy. As you exercise, your energy system automatically starts working harder to meet the demand for oxygen. You can feel the system at work. Your lungs start breathing more, your heart pumps harder and faster, and oxygen-laden blood runs through your blood vessels to feed the energy fires.

HOW MUCH EXERCISE DO WE NEED?

Old Recommendation: That you engage in at least twenty minutes of continuous aerobic activity, which stimulates the heart and lungs, three to five days a week. Examples include jogging, tennis, aerobics, bicycling, swimming, fast walking, bicycling.

New Recommendation: That you engage in thirty minutes of moderate exercise intermittently during the course of the day, at least five days a week, without any special machinery or paraphernalia. Examples include going for a brisk five-minute walk, climbing stairs instead of taking elevators, dancing, and raking leaves.

Immediate effects come from the extra energy that builds as a result of the increased oxygen in your system. Long-term effects include better muscle tone, effective weight control, relief from stress, and increased resistance to illness. More specific benefits include the following:

Lungs. An aerobic exercise program increases your vital capacity because fit lungs can expand more fully and hold more air. You do not have to breathe as often. Smoking and aging decrease the capacity of the lungs, while exercise increases it.

Heart. A conditioned heart can expand more and hold and pump more blood and therefore does not have to beat as often to distribute the same amount of blood.

Cholesterol. The total amount of cholesterol in your blood as well as the ratio between good cholesterol (high-density) and bad (low-density) are the important factors in cardiovascular disease. Aerobic conditioning lowers the amount of total cholesterol in the blood and improves the ratio of high-density to low-density cholesterol.

Fat. Aerobic exercise works on fat in a number of ways. It burns up extra calories as you exercise, while it raises your metabolism for up to seven hours after an exercise session. A regular exercise program can change your metabolism and make it more active. While you are exercising at your training heart rate (see below, page 161, "How to Begin") your primary source of energy is fat.

Bones. Bones begin to demineralize when you do not exercise, so you need to maintain activity, especially weight-bearing activity, to keep your bones strong. Tendons and ligaments also remain strong when you are aerobically fit and are less prone to injury.

Brain. The brain likes sugar as a fuel. Therefore, aerobic exercise that uses fat (and not sugar) for energy spares sugar for the brain. It's going too far to say that aerobically fit people are smarter, but they do report better powers of concentration and more energy.

Nervous System. Aerobic exercise reduces the amount of the stress hormones like epinephrine in your system. Both subjectively and physiologically, aerobic exercise helps control stress.

Immune System. There's not enough data yet to draw conclusions about exercise and immune function, but it's reasonable to conclude that anything that reduces stress will have a positive effect on the immune system. Moreover, there are unconfirmed reports that regular exercise increases T-cell counts.

Aerobic Conditioning

To become aerobically fit, you should exercise according to the following "FIT" formula: Frequency, Intensity, Time.

Frequency. You need to exercise four or five times a week for ninety days. Once you reach the level of fitness appropriate for you, three thirty-minute sessions a week will maintain your fitness (and even two days will do in those weeks when you're cramped for time).

Intensity. Your training heart rate determines the intensity of your exercise. See below ("How to Begin") for calculating yours through the Karvonen formula, which takes your age into account. The key to safe, effective aerobic conditioning is not to exercise at your maximum capacity but to get up to about 60 to 80 percent of it.

Time. We suggest you begin with ten- to fifteen-minute exercise sessions. Aim to increase these to thirty-minute sessions, which include five minutes of warm-up and five minutes of cool down after you've finished.

How to Begin

1. Get a physical examination and an OK from your doctor to start an aerobic exercise program. Determine the percentage of your maximum heart rate at which you should train.

2. Determine your training heart rate. You need to know your resting heart rate: take your pulse for ten seconds; multiply by six. Then:

   • Subtract your age from 220. This is your maximum heart rate. (DO NOT EXERCISE AT THIS RATE!)

   • Subtract your resting heart rate from your maximum heart rate.

   • Multiply this by 65 percent (or less if your doctor recommends it).

   • Add your resting heart rate. The total equals your training heart rate. *Example:* forty-year-old with a resting heart rate of 70.

     a. 220 − 40 = 180 (maximum heart rate)

     b. 180 − 70 = 110

     c. 110 x .65 = 71.5 (72)

     d. 72 + 70 = 142 (training heart rate)

   • When you exercise, check your pulse to see what your heart rate is: count for ten seconds and multiply by six. Once you get a good feel for how hard you are breathing at your target heart rate, you will not need to keep checking. "Aerobic feel" has been described as medium hard.

3. Select your exercise. See "Helpful Reading" (page 164) for books that describe appropriate aerobic exercises.

Remember

Improved fitness comes with exercising longer, not harder. Do not try to get into shape too fast.

Be concerned with how long you exercise and what your pulse rate is. Don't overdo it, especially at first. Build up gradually but regularly, making sure you don't go over your targeted pulse rate.

Your exercise sessions:

- Should be steady and non-stop.

- Should last a minimum of twelve minutes.

- Should be maintained at the recommended training heart rate.

- If you are over forty years of age and unused to regular exercise, you may want to change your type of exercise day by day (example: jog M/W/F, swim T/Th). This saves on muscle wear-and-tear.

Experiment

- *Fitness:* Use this week to evaluate your fitness program (or lack of one). Your objective should be to move toward an aerobic program (your health status allowing it), that will bring you to a state of cardiovascular fitness.

Helpful Reading

Diet and Nutrition

We've listed below the titles of some books that have proven useful in guiding course participants through the dietary changes we suggested above. All are available through libraries or bookstores.

Whole Foods Cooking

The New Laurel's Kitchen, by Laurel Robertson, Carol Flinders, and Brian Ruppenthal (Berkeley, Calif.: Ten Speed Press, 1986). This provides the most complete and accessible nutrition guide to a whole foods diet that we know of. It discusses nutrition in lay people's language and offers hundreds of recipes for cooking with whole grains, preparing dark leafy greens, baking your own bread. Though a "vegetarian" cookbook, you by no means need to be vegetarian to benefit from this classic of whole foods cooking.

Another comprehensive source of whole foods recipes is *American Whole Foods Cuisine*, by Nikki and David Goldbeck (New York: New American Library, 1983.)

The first edition of *Diet For a Small Planet*, by Francis Moore Lappé (New York: Ballantine, 1986), started the vegetarian revolution and explained how eating more vegetarian dishes can better our health and the health of the planet too.

For more vegetarian recipes, see also *Recipes for a Small Planet*, by Ellen B. Ewald (New York: Ballantine, 1986). *The Enchanted Broccoli Forest*, by Mollie Katzen (Berkeley, Calif.: Ten Speed Press, 1983), adapts the cooking of other cultures to the U.S. dietary guidelines, established by the U.S. Department of Health and Human Services.

Diet Plans

The American Way of Life Need Not Be Hazardous to Your Health: Coping with Life's Seven Major Risk Factors, by John Farquhar, M.D. (Menlo Park, Calif.: Addison-Wesley Publishing Company, 1987) offers an excellent phased program for changing to a diet aimed at preventing the primary "killer" diseases discussed in Chapter Twelve. Dr. Farquhar writes from ten years of experience as the founder and director of the Stanford Center for Disease Prevention.

Transition to Vegetarianism: An Evolutionary Step, by Rudolph Ballantine, M.D. (Honesdale, Pa.: Himalayan Institute, 1987), is a useful guide to making the transition to a meatless diet.

Other books whose recipes are in line with the U.S. Dietary guidelines include *American Heart Association Cookbook* (New York: Ballantine, 1986); *Eat to Your Heart's Content: The Low Cholesterol Gourmet Cookbook*, by Gordon and Kay Heiss (New

York: New American Library, 1979); *The New American Diet: The Lifetime Family Eating Plan for Good Health,* by Sonja and William Connor (New York: Simon & Schuster, 1986); and *Jane Brody's Good Nutrition Book* (New York: Bantam, 1987).

Fitness

There are many excellent guides to fitness available in most bookstores. We recommend any of the following:

Aerobics

The New Aerobics (New York: Bantam, 1981), *The Aerobics Way* (New York: Bantam, 1981), and *The New Aerobics for Women* (New York: Bantam, 1988), by Kenneth Cooper M.D., M.P.H., are written by one of the landmark authors of the aerobics revolution. His extensive charts and aerobic point system give useful guides to equivalent amounts of exercise obtainable through various types of physical activity. Also see Dr. Cooper's *Total Well Being: The Complete Aerobics Program for Radiant Health through Exercise and Diet* (New York: M. Evans, 1982).

Running

Run to Health, by Peter D. Wood (New York: Grosset and Dunlap, 1980), gives solid information on the medical issues around running. *Runner's World* (Rodale Press) is a useful monthly periodical that carries articles on every conceivable topic of interest to runners.

Walking

The Complete Book of Exercise Walking, by Gary Yanker (Chicago: Contemporary Books, 1983), offers a thorough guide to safe walking. Also see *Walking My Way,* by John Merrill (Topsfield, Mass., c/o Merrimack Publishers' Circle; Chatto & Windus, Hogarth Press, 1984), and *The Complete Walker.* For the passionately committed, there is even a periodical dedicated solely to walking: *The Walking Magazine* (Rabin Publishing, 711 Boylston St., Boston, MA 02116).

Stretching

For a comprehensive and easily usable guide, see *Stretching,* by Bob Anderson (Bolinas, Calif.: Shelter Publications, 1980).

Wellness and HIV/AIDS:
Diet, Nutrition, and Fitness Guidelines

If you are HIV impacted, it is important to maintain as healthy a lifestyle as you can. We know that 3 percent of people infected by HIV develop AIDS three years after seroconversion, while a far higher percentage remain well for many more years. We do not know why some people live longer than others after becoming infected by HIV. But "long-term survivors" of HIV do share some characteristics that are worth mentioning here: they are realistic about the fatal nature of the illness, but are coping realistically to maintain optimal health; they are actively involved in their treatment; their relationship with their physician is a "positive partnership" rather than dependency; and they "take charge" of their treatment, seeking a range of treatments and interventions, rather than remaining passive.

And there are things you can do, and stop doing, to optimize your well-being. No one has been able to show that wellness factors — diet, exercise, and stress management — directly correlate to longevity for people living with HIV, but we do know that they improve quality of life. And there *is* evidence that smoking increases the risk of opportunistic infections like pneumocystis pneumonia, and, along with alcohol and drug use, speeds up the rate of progression to AIDS. Moderating or stopping these behaviors altogether can make a difference.

Nutrition is exceptionally important because weight loss is a common symptom of HIV illness, and maintaining an optimal nutritional status in the early course of the infection might delay weight loss. And there is evidence that malnourishment impairs the functioning of the immune system.

Nutrition and Immune Function

Good nutrition is necessary for proper functioning of the immune system. Inadequate intakes of protein and calories as well as imbalances in vitamins and minerals can all disturb the equilibrium of the immune system. Deficiencies of vitamins A, B, C, E, copper, iron, and zinc can all impair immune system functioning, as can megadoses of vitamin E, iron, and zinc.[1] Deficiencies of vitamin B_6, which is lost in refining flours, has been found to impair cellular immunity.[2] AIDS patients have been reported to have depressed levels of zinc,[3] and decreased vitamin B_{12} levels have been reported with HIV infection.[4]

Living with HIV

If you are HIV positive but have not progressed to AIDS, your daily regimen should be like those we give in Chapter Fourteen for active, healthy people. In general, for people impacted with HIV but who have not progressed to AIDS, we recommend the following wellness guidelines:

1. Eat a well-balanced diet with a variety of whole foods.

2. Maintain the ideal body weight for your height.

3. Take a daily vitamin/mineral supplement. The required amounts of vitamins and minerals will be adequately supplied in a varied whole foods diet, but because of infections, fevers, or medications, you may need a vitamin/mineral supplement that provides 100–200 percent of the Recommended Daily Allowance (RDA). Check with your physician or dietitian to avoid any possible interaction between the supplement and your medication.

4. Don't smoke. Smoking is now considered a cofactor in HIV illness and has been shown to increase the incidence of pneumocystis pneumonia.

5. Avoid alcohol and recreational drugs. They speed up the progression to AIDS, can interfere with food intake and adequate nutrient metabolism, and have been shown to depress the immune system.

6. Get adequate rest and exercise.

7. Avoid fads or "miracle" diets. Simply because a product is expensive does not mean that it is useful.

Nutrition and PWAs

People living with AIDS need to continually assess their nutritional requirements because they are often challenged throughout the progression of the illness by symptoms such as malabsorption, diarrhea, oral lesions, fever, nausea, vomiting, fatigue, and weight loss, each of which dictates altered nutritional plans. If you are affected by severe weight loss, for instance, the U.S. dietary guidelines against high-fat diets we explain in Chapter Twelve should give way to the overriding need for calories. In this case, caloric intake should take precedence over all other dietary considerations. Once a reasonable body weight is regained, a more moderate fat intake diet would again be appropriate. If you are experiencing chronic diarrhea, consider changing to white breads and refined cereals, which are easier to digest than high-fiber foods such as whole grains.

Many of the other common symptoms of AIDS — thrush, or mouth soreness, for instance — call for special dietary practices as well. *Nutrition and HIV Infection,* a report prepared for the Center for Food Safety and Applied Nutrition of the Food and Drug Administration (November 1990), examined all of the relevant studies carried out during the previous decade. It concluded that the body of knowledge derived from experimental studies on the role of nutrition in HIV infection and AIDS is limited and relies heavily on clinical observations and inductive reasoning rather than studies. Most of its summary conclusions simply document the obvious, but they may be worth reporting here briefly:

1. Nutrient deficiencies are a common occurrence in HIV infection, especially in the advanced stages of the disease.

2. The nutritional problems facing any patient with HIV infection should be given high priority as part of an aggressive clinical management strategy. Studies of aggressive nutrition interventions report a decrease in hospitalization stay and an increase in patients' quality of life with the use of an enteral formula in advanced AIDS patients.

3. Nutrition may impact on the course of HIV infection by (1) influencing specific systems involved in the progression of the disease, (2) influencing the susceptibility to opportunistic infections, and (3) contributing to the adequacy of response to HIV-related diseases.

4. Deficiencies and excesses of specific nutrients in addition to general malnutrition affect the function of various components of the immune system and influence resistance to infection. (This includes a chart on the effects of specific nutrients on immune function.)

5. Anecdotal information suggests that nutrition support in AIDS is not considered a priority in many hospital settings.

6. Unproven therapies like the use of large supplemental doses of specific nutrients may interfere with effective treatment. Numerous studies have evaluated some of the more common unproven nutritional therapies and unconventional diets used by patients with HIV infection. These include:

   Megadoses of vitamins A, E, C, B_{12}, selenium, zinc: Large doses of these nutrients have been recommended to restore cell-mediated immunity by increasing T-cell number and activity, but efficacy and outcomes of these interventions have not been established in controlled clinical trials. Toxicity can occur with chronic intakes of vitamin A, zinc, and selenium.

   Lecithin: The purported ability of this lipid to destroy HIV by "membrane fluidization" has not been demonstrated.

   Laetrile: Its lack of efficacy in a strict vegan diet has been demonstrated. The diet is low in energy and may supply inadequate amounts of some vitamins and minerals and excessive levels of others.

   Herbal remedies: So far, there have been relatively few studies to investigate the assertion that herbs can regenerate the immune system.

The report recommends a balanced diet incorporating individualized food preferences that include a variety of foods and that contain an adequate intake of protein and calories to pre-serve lean body mass. A multivitamin supplement that supplies 100 percent of the RDA for each nutrient is recommended, but the report cautions that there is no evidence that megadoses of any vitamin or mineral will alter the course of AIDS or fur-ther improve the nutritional status of the patient. If antifolate drugs are used in treating opportunistic infections, folic acid supplements may be necessary during treatment.[5]

Special Nutritional Needs of PWAs

As AIDS progresses, different conditions and symptoms may require special dietary adjustments. Below we make recommen-dations for some of the more common AIDS conditions.

Weight Loss/Anorexia

If you are experiencing significant weight loss, your caloric needs should take precedence over other dietary considerations. Eat foods as rich in fat as you can tolerate. And follow these suggestions:

- Eat small, frequent meals throughout the day. Having a small meal or snack every one or two hours can achieve the same nutritional goals as three large meals.

- Keep nutritious, high-calorie foods and beverages handy. Avoid filling up on low or non-calorie foods or beverages.

- Drink small amounts of liquids with your meals so you don't fill up before you've eaten enough.

- Take advantage of those times when your appetite is best to "catch up."

- Take a brisk walk if you can before eating.

- When possible, eat with friends or family, and eat in a pleasant, relaxing atmosphere.

- Choose foods you enjoy most.

- Select foods with faint odors and serve them at cool temper-atures since this tends to lessen their odor.

To boost calories and protein:

- Use whole milk, half-and-half, or cream.
- Add generous amounts of butter, cream cheese, sour cream, cheese, and mayonnaise to bread, pasta, rice, potatoes, vegetables, and other foods.
- Add whipped cream or frosting to desserts.
- Add sauce or gravy to foods.
- Use honey on toast and cereal and in coffee and tea.
- Add non-fat dry milk to foods for added calories and protein (mashed potatoes, cream soups, gravies, etc.).
- Add raisins, dates, dried fruit, chopped nuts, granola, and brown sugar to hot or cold cereals and to ice cream or other desserts.

Nausea and Vomiting

If eating causes nausea or vomiting, try these suggestions:

- Experiment with different foods until you find ones that you can eat without difficulty.
- When you are feeling good, eat complete meals to help tide you over during periods when you do not feel like eating.
- Eat smaller portions of food more frequently throughout the day.
- Drink clear, cool beverages and try clear soups (broth) between (instead of with) meals. Drink fluids through a straw.
- Avoid greasy, high-fat, and spicy foods.
- Eat saltier foods and avoid very sweet foods.
- Eat drier foods, such as toast or crackers.
- Eat bland or soft foods that are easier to tolerate such as rice, soft-cooked or poached eggs, apple juice, nectars, custards.
- Do not lie down right after eating.

Bowel Disease/Diarrhea

Diarrhea may be caused by infectious organisms, medications, or changes in the intestinal lining. It can cause dehydration and electrolyte imbalances (loss of fluids and minerals), and it can cause malabsorption (inability to absorb nutrients). It is important to eat and especially to drink when you are experiencing frequent bouts of diarrhea. If it becomes severe, contact your physician. To manage a serious problem with diarrhea

- Drink plenty of liquids, including water, diluted fruit juices and flavored drink mixes. Try fruit-flavored popsicles.

- Eat small, frequent meals served at room temperature. Try to have your maximum intake earlier in the day.

- Eat and drink caffeine-free foods and beverages. Avoid coffee, chocolate, and caffeinated colas. Caffeine tends to irritate the bowel muscles.

- Use low-lactose foods such as cultured yogurt or aged cheese, since lactose (milk sugar) is not easy to digest during intestinal upsets and draws water into the bowel.

- Eat high-potassium foods like bananas, mangos, diluted orange and nectar juices, or potatoes to replace minerals you may have lost.

- Eat white rice, white bread, and cooked fruits and vegetables without the skin, rather than high-fiber foods like whole wheat or raw fruits.

- If fats seem to cause diarrhea, use the leaner types of foods such as low-fat cottage cheese and low-fat milk.

- If cramping is a problem, avoid foods that may cause gas or cramps, like beans, cabbage, broccoli, cauliflower, highly spiced foods, or too many sweet or carbonated drinks.

Mouth Soreness/Difficulty Chewing and Swallowing

Mouth pain or sores can make it hard for you to eat because of pain or difficulty in swallowing. Small amounts of fluids with meals can improve the ability to chew and swallow. Foods served at cold temperatures are generally more soothing. Good oral and dental hygiene also helps maximize your food intake. Some helpful hints to avoid mouth pain:

- Eat foods served at moderate temperatures.

- If acidic foods (oranges, lemons, cranberries, grapefruit) cause a burning feeling in your mouth, choose mild foods and drinks, such as apple, apricot, or pear juices.

- Limit spices and salted foods when you have open mouth sores.

- Dunk your toast, cookies, and crackers in liquids to make them softer.

- Eat non-abrasive foods like puddings, eggs, canned fruits, soft cheeses, noodle dishes, ice cream.

- Popsicles can be a tasty way to numb the pain.

Difficulty Swallowing

When you have trouble swallowing, your main concern should be to eat foods that will not irritate your throat. Here's what you can do:

- Choose single-texture foods (mashed potatoes, oatmeal) rather than combination foods (stews) since similar textures will be easier to swallow.

- Avoid sticky, dry foods (peanut butter) that can be hard to swallow, as well as slippery foods (macaroni, Jello).

- Use a straw to help when you are drinking.

- Try tilting your head back or moving it forward to make swallowing easier.

Thrush

Oral thrush, or candidiasis, causes lesions in the mouth and esophagus, making it difficult to eat and painful to swallow. It can also cause foods to taste different. If thrush is a problem:

- Try soft, non-irritating foods: eggs, cream soups, ice cream, puddings, ground meats, baked fish, soft cheeses, etc.

- Avoid spicy and acidic foods (citric fruits and juices, tomatoes, pickles, vinegar, etc.). Salty foods can cause discomfort too.

- Try cold and room-temperature foods and avoid very hot foods.

Eating Defensively: Rules of Food Safety

People with HIV infection are at much higher risk than others for food-borne infections from microorganisms in food and must therefore be especially careful in the preparation of their foods. A person with HIV, for instance, is much more likely to contract salmonella. Food-borne disease can cause harmful and even life-threatening illnesses to people with HIV. Most such diseases come from your own kitchen. (The video *Eating Defensively: Food Safety Advice for People with AIDS*, gives excellent advice on safety precautions for preparing food. It is available free from the National AIDS Information Clearinghouse at (800) 458-5231. Or call Sharar Kuperman, FDA Office of Public Affairs, (301) 443-3220.)

To protect yourself from food-borne infections follow these guidelines: All animal-derived foods (meat, fish, poultry, cheese) should be considered infected and used only after taking the following precautions:

- *Cook all meats* (including fish and poultry) until well done. Use a meat thermometer and make sure that the item is up to desired temperature throughout. When using a microwave oven, observe the standing time to be sure that the item is cooked through.

- *Keep hot foods hot.* Cook at 165–212 degrees F. Hold at 140–165 degrees F.

- *Keep cold foods cold.* Refrigerators should be kept below 40–45 degrees F. Cover foods well.

- *Do not eat raw meats* or foods with raw-meat-derived ingredients (sushi, hollandaise sauce, homemade ice cream). Make sure that eggs are well cooked (scrambled eggs or omelets should not be "runny").

- *Wash all fruits and vegetables thoroughly* with water. Keep refrigerated. Store in small covered containers.

- *Use pasteurized milk.* Raw, unpasteurized milk products can carry both TB and salmonella. Avoid soft-ripened cheeses like Brie and Camembert, and use cheeses made only from pasteurized milk.

- *If a food looks or smells "funny," throw it out.* Your nose is a highly sensitive instrument for detecting spoiled food.

- *Wash your hands thoroughly after touching raw meat,* especially if you have open cuts on your hands.

- *Use plastic cutting boards* and wash them thoroughly after each use.

Questions and Answers

- *What about nutritional supplements?*

Vitamin and mineral supplements may be necessary at various stages of AIDS because of poor intake or malabsorption in the intestinal tract. A good dietitian or physician can evaluate the need for supplementation based on nutritional assessments and laboratory blood values. In general, though, we recommend a well-balanced diet and a multivitamin with minerals at a level equal to the RDA.

Megadoses of vitamins and minerals have not been shown to be effective in AIDS treatment. Many studies show the importance of certain nutrients in increasing immune function, but these are at quantities that can be easily acquired in a well-regulated diet of whole foods. Taking too much of one vitamin, mineral, or amino acid can upset the balance of nutrients and even cause deficiencies of other nutrients that compete with those supplemented.

If you are unable to consume adequate foods, a commercial supplement that includes calories as well as vitamins and minerals may be helpful. But it should used as an adjunct to an overall dietary plan that includes as many foods as you are able to eat. Products are available in either powdered or ready-to-use forms that can be consumed as is, mixed into milk or water, or added to recipes. You should consult with a dietitian about which product would best fit your needs.

- *What about specialized diets?*

Be wary of any overly restrictive diet. At certain levels the macrobiotic diet, the Immune Power diet, or the Yeast-Controlled diet may result in inadequate intakes of calories, protein, vitamins, or minerals.

The following guidelines may be helpful in evaluating special diets. They:

- should not contain substances in amounts that may be physically harmful;

- should allow adequate consumption of calories and protein;
- should allow a variety of foods from all the major food families to meet the minimum requirements for a diet balanced in all of the nutrients.

Fitness and HIV/AIDS

Aerobic Exercise and HIV

With regard to HIV illness and exercise, it is far too early to draw conclusions on the appropriateness of various forms of exercise for people with HIV. For asymptomatic HIV-positive individuals, we recommend aerobic exercise done in consultation with their primary care physician. Although no significant or extensive research exists at this time, one study reported that newly diagnosed HIV-positive men who participated in a ten-week course that included aerobics had moderate increases in levels of T-4 cells.[6] It should be noted that the group also participated in relaxation techniques and altered diet patterns, so exercise may not be the whole story. Still, aerobic exercise is both safe and recommended for healthy HIV-positive individuals.

Fitness for PWAs

If you have AIDS, your exercise program should correspond to your overall health status and energy level. Consider that exercise is basically a matter of getting more movement than you normally get, whether this means walking more, or faster, or developing light workouts under the guidance of your physician. If you are bedridden or cannot leave the house, you should aim at some regimen of stretching or gentle range of motion exercises to maintain flexibility and to conserve energy. *Be sure to consult with your physician about the types and levels of exercise appropriate for your physical condition.*

III. Meeting the Challenges of the Workplace

Chapter Fifteen

RISE in the Workplace: Beyond Stress Reduction

It is axiomatic but still bears repeating: the workplace is a far more stressful environment now for the average worker and manager than it used to be. A series of developments during the past decade have contributed to an escalation of pressures: corporate downsizing and cost-cutting, a dizzying array of new technologies that speed up the pace of work, increase expectations, and create information overload; the new competitive pressures of a global economy; increasing violence in the workplace environment; and the emergence of a workplace culture that almost requires that you become a Type A personality in order to succeed. "What's frightening," Dr. Meyer Friedman says, "is how much the environment is nourishing Type A behavior now."[1]

The toll this is taking on our health is striking. Work-related anxiety has become endemic to the workplace and increasingly severe in its effects. Stress-related workers' compensation claims, for instance, were almost non-existent ten years ago. According to the California Worker's Compensation Institute, mental stress claims in the state skyrocketed 700 percent during the 1980s at time when disabling injuries on the whole fell 9 percent.

The Acceleration Syndrome

One major contributor to work-related stress and anxiety is hurry sickness. Because of increased expectations and pressures, most people in the workplace live with the chronic sense of time urgency — feeling they always have more to do than time allows — which Drs. Rosenman and Friedman described two decades ago as a component of Type A behavior. One newspaper editor described an extreme but not uncommon, example of it in a recent article on the acceleration syndrome: "You don't really live in the present anymore. You're never fully engaged...because what you really want to do is finish it, in order to get on to something else."[2]

To help our course participants identify the extent to which they are driven by this syndrome, we ask them a few rhetorical questions. We'll repeat some of them here for you:

- Do you have trouble falling asleep at night because you can't "turn off" your mind?

- Do you ever eat standing up?

- Do you carry aspirin or ibuprofen with you? (One New York designer/socialite confesses happily that she lives, "on Advil and Big Macs.")

- Do you carry on conversations while opening your mail or watching TV?

- Do you feel increasingly irritable?

If you've answered yes to any of these questions you should probably take a look at the suggestions we gave in Chapter Four on how to slow down.

Meeting the Challenge of the Workplace: The Hardy Personality

It doesn't look as though the workplace environment is likely to change for the better in the near future, since downsizing and increased competitive pressures from global markets are only going to get more intense. Consequently it is up to us to build strategies that can withstand these pressures and buffer us from its stresses. Fortunately, there is evidence to suggest that this can be done: certain stress-resistant traits can be learned that will keep us healthy even while facing the constant pressures of a changing workplace.

During the mid-1980s researchers Suzanne Kobasa and Salvatore Maddi studied two hundred executive managers in a major corporation undergoing stressful change. Of the executives studied, a hundred reported numerous symptoms of illness, while the others had few signs. Kobasa identified three traits in particular that distinguished members of the healthy group from those of the unhealthy one. They were:

1. *Control:* The healthier executives had a sense that they could control their lives — at least the impact of stress problems before them, if not the problems themselves.

2. *Challenge:* They saw change, good or bad, as inevitable and an opportunity for growth rather than a threat to their security.

3. *Commitment:* They were deeply involved in their work and families, a commitment that gave them a sense of meaning, direction, and excitement.[3]

Kobasa's study suggested that the executives with all three of these "hardiness" traits had a less than a one in ten chance of suffering a severe illness in the near future. On the other hand, for the managers who had none of the hardiness traits, who felt little or no support, and did not exercise, the probability for severe illness was more than nine chances in ten.

Perhaps more important, Kobasa and Maddi's research also suggests that "hardy" personality types may actually *increase* their interactions with stressful events, rather than avoid them, "exploring, controlling, and learning from them." Kobasa calls this "transformational coping" and suggests that such "stress-resistant" types can turn negative, stress-inducing events into positive experiences for growth and understanding.[4]

The RISE Approach: A Response for All Seasons

Stress-reduction programs abound in the corporate and workplace environments, but they tend to break down behavior into discreet activities and treat each one separately, rather than as parts of an integrated whole. The programs they offer in exercise, diet and nutrition, smoking cessation, and "stress management" have value as far as they go, but they treat the individual in the workplace as distinct from the same individual at home — as though personal problems will not invade the workplace, or problems at work can easily be left at the office.

RISE addresses the individual as a whole person who, in order to remain healthy, needs to function with equal ease and adaptability in the workplace, at home, anywhere. The RISE Response is global; its effects can be felt along most levels of human experience. For our course participants who were coping with challenges in both their private and professional lives — and this included most of them — the tools became a bridge between these two primary arenas of stress, affecting both the interior environment of the mind and emotions and external arenas of work and activity.

The worker or manager who can maintain equilibrium in the face of unrelenting pressures, who recovers quickly from emotional turmoil, whose mental clarity allows for setting realistic priorities stays healthier. When you become proficient in the use of the RISE tools, you can enter the work environment with an armory of stress-resistant skills we sometimes call (with apologies to Kobasa) the five Cs. They are:

- *Calmness:* A calm mind can maintain its focus even in the midst of the tensions and pressures of the modern office

- *Concentration:* This is the heart of high-performance and creativity as we discussed in Chapter Five on one-pointed attention.

- *Clarity:* A calm, focused mind will be able to see more easily the choices in any given situation.

- *Compassion:* As our vision clears, we begin to gain access to deeper resources, like compassion, that can enrich our relationships and help us understand and sympathize more easily both with others and with our own shortcomings.

- *Control:* Mastery of the RISE Response puts us in the driver's seat of our own lives. We experience a robust sense of control over our own reactions to the challenges in our work and lives.

Much is being made in management circles today about the need for a new paradigm, the need for workers to feel empowered enough to participate in the decisions that affect their work environments. In order for this to happen, both management and workers have to learn to move from automatic pilot to take conscious control of their attention and their choices. In this case, the RISE Response may be critical to such a paradigm, for it empowers us from within to meet on more favorable terms the challenges that work or life may bring us.

I work for a big hotel and sometimes I'll be setting up for a banquet with the guests arriving in fifteen minutes, and I still have twenty-five minutes worth of work to do! I start the mantram and I'm able to be completely focused on what I have to do, instead of losing my cool about it. I've developed great organizational skills and I know it's because of my meditation. The job is still stressful, of course, but it doesn't wipe me out." (Edward S.)

To manage stress effectively both in the workplace and outside it, you need a rapid-response, short-term strategy for managing emotional crises, and long-term life-management skills to build a hardy, stress-resistant personality. Below we've outlined RISE responses to both kinds of challenges, "RISE Crisis Management" for the short term and "The Seven Rs" for the long term.

RISE Crisis Management

In RISE, we define a stressful crisis as one in which an emotional challenge has caused you to lose control over your attention and triggered the automatic, health-damaging stress reactions we described in Chapter Nine. RISE crisis management aims at recalling your attention before you react automatically, before you "lose it," or "freak out," or simply revert to chronic feelings of helplessness or anxiety. The RISE Response helps you avoid going on automatic pilot and clears your thinking long enough to look at what is happening to you so that you can make conscious choices.

It's easy to write about, but quite another matter to keep calm in the grip of a powerful emotion like anger or high anxiety. Slowing down, one-pointed focus, and passage meditation all help to build your capacity to keep calm. Repeating your mantram during high stress is a strategic rapid-focusing tool. It can help clear your thinking and quickly restore your composure. You may remember that repeating the mantram elicits a "relaxation response" that acts as a balancing counterpart to stress. Your heart rate and blood pressure drop as your breathing rate and oxygen consumption decline. Brain waves shift to a more relaxed alpha-rhythm, and blood is sent to the brain and skin producing a feeling of "rested mental alertness."[5]

Emotional crises will occur during the normal working day. You can't avoid them, but you can learn to protect yourself against the stress they produce. Here are four strategies you can use to buffer you during intense emotional crises:

1. Buy Yourself Time

Try not to react automatically. Recapture your attention with the mantram so that you can assess the source of your distress. Many RISE participants have reported that the mantram helped them regain their attention and abort an automatic reaction.

Become physical if you can to help discharge the tension. If possible, take a fast mantram walk or do some vigorous exercise. Or close your office door and march in place to discharge tension. This can help to restore your natural breathing rhythm and bring you more calmness and clarity.

2. Assess Your Choices

There are probably more choices in a given crisis than you think at the time. Remind yourself that you do not have to react automatically. Ask yourself how you will benefit from your conditioned reactions. And look at all your options:

- Is the stressor actual or are you perceiving it as stressful?

- Can the circumstance wait for a reaction until you regain your equilibrium?

- Does it require an immediate reaction? Does it really require *any* response? (Or do you simply think it does?)

- What are some things you can do to change the circumstances, defuse the tension?

If you can't change the circumstances, then your best response may be simply to keep your emotional composure. The mantram can help to maintain your equilibrium. Once you decide what your response will be, keep that as your point of focus.

3. Conserve Your Vitality

The most appropriate choices (that is, the most healthy) are those that best conserve your vitality and do not needlessly drain it. Be sure you get adequate physical exercise and that your diet falls within the guidelines we've detailed in Chapter Thirteen.

4. Keep One-Pointed

Be aware that the strong emotions you feel in a crisis will pull your attention away from your point of focus. Keep your attention from returning unconsciously to the stressor. When it does, go back to step one, repeat your mantram, or engage in an absorbing task to buy more time. Don't allow the stressor to recapture your attention.

Focused attention helps restore a balance to your nervous system and reduce the conflicting signals your body may be receiving (Fight? Flee? Go limp?). When your attention is under your control, so also, to some extent, are the automatic stress responses that cause damage. One mechanism that keeps the stress response activated is your wandering mental focus. As it moves toward past or future "threats," it tells the nervous system to respond to circumstances that may or may not exist. It's a waste of energy, since only responses in the present are under your control.

Stay focused on the present moment. You maintain a more balanced rhythm in this state of rested alertness. You can more appropriately assess the meaning of the stress and try to deal with it.

The Seven Basic Rs:
A Plan for Long-Term Stress Management[6]

Any attempt to buffer yourself from the long-term effects of stress has to include a comprehensive management program that addresses the full range of human behavior. We've outlined a program below that can, in time, help you create a truly stress-resistant personality that can withstand the stresses of the workplace, and enable you to thrive in the midst of stress.

1. Responsibility

The first level of intervention in managing the effects of stress is to accept responsibility for how you cope. Remember: you may or may not be able to influence what happens to you, but you can influence what happens inside where stress does its damage. Taking responsibility leads to personal empowerment.

2. RISE

Practicing the four RISE tools — meditation, mantram, slowing down, one-pointed focus — can build and maintain your conscious attention so that you can cope more effectively with everyday emotional crises as well as maintain a stress-resistant lifestyle. The RISE tools are designed for personal engineering.

3. Reflection

Honest self-reflection is the next step in stress management. By becoming more aware of inner dialogues and more sensitive to your emotional reactions, you can become aware of what are your most common sources of stress. This increased awareness often leads to the realization that you have more choices than you thought in deciding how to respond in a stressful situation. As you see your choices broaden beyond just the automatic, your sense of inner control increases and displaces feelings of being overwhelmed and helpless. This in turn decreases the unhealthy stress reactions that accompany such feelings.

This means, of course, that you have to give up blaming others for your stress, which is to your advantage, since the less you feel that the sources of stress are outside you, the more empowered you will feel to modify them. Ask yourself:

- *How do I contribute to the stress in my life?* (Taking on more than you can handle, saying yes when you should say no, contributing to conflict in relationships, etc.?)

- *Am I doing all I can to minimize the effects of stress on my mind, body, and emotions?*

- *Do I secretly enjoy the benefits of being "stressed out"?* (People in high-intensity occupations such as ICU staffs should be careful not to become "adrenalin junkies," needing the rush of excitement to feel productive and useful.)

4. Relationships

For many of us, the most difficult stresses relate to significant people in our lives: supervisors, colleagues, clients, and employees at work; spouses, lovers, friends, family members at home. At work, speed and time urgency make healthy relationships difficult. As a television executive characterized the environment at a major network, "It was moving at such a velocity that the centrifugal force really just tore asunder people and relationships.... The fact is that people find it's not economical to spend time on personal transactions."[7] Notice that even personal relationships have been monetized to "transactions."

We should examine our relationships and acknowledge our part in perpetuating whatever strains that may exist. The stresses may relate to poor communication (because of hurry), a failure to be assertive, or assumptions and expectations that have not been clarified.

In relationships we should try to express ourselves clearly (see Chapter Sixteen), to be understanding and compassionate toward others, and to find constructive ways of relating, while avoiding relationships that are negative or destructive.

5. Recreation

Re-creation is important in mending the wear and tear of life's stresses. Try to make healthy recreation a standard part of your week's schedule, and try to share it with others — loved ones, friends, relatives, co-workers. It helps to enhance the quality of life, and if it is regularly shared with others it can enhance your relationships too. It can include passive forms of recreation such as listening to good music, or attending the theater, or more active forms like taking long walks or playing tennis. Exercise itself can be included as recreation too.

6. Refueling

Changing your diet according to the guidelines we suggest in Chapter Thirteen can become a strong ally in your ability to reduce the harmful effects of stress. Medical research is finding increasing links between diet and stress-related illnesses such as heart disease, hypertension, ulcers, asthma, colitis, and PMS.

7. Relaxation

Proper relaxation allows mind and body to repair themselves from the wear and tear of stress. Relaxation is the physiological release of tension particularly from muscles, joints, and internal organs. Relaxing while alert can be more reparative than sleep. Sleeping the right amount, neither too little nor too much, is important. It is better to relax willfully for one-half hour and sleep a half-hour less. (For an excellent guide to relaxation techniques, see Dr. John Farquhar's book listed in "Helpful Reading" below.)

Helpful Reading

Stress Management

Farquhar, John, M.D. *The American Way of Life Need Not Be Hazardous to Your Health: Coping with Life's Seven Major Risk Factors.* Menlo Park, Calif.: Addison-Wesley Publishing Company, 1987. This includes an excellent chapter on stress management, which is a good supplement to the guidelines we give in Chapter Fifteen.

Nuernberger, Phil, Ph.D. *Freedom from Stress: A Holistic Approach.* Honesdale, Pa.: Himalayan International Institute Press, 1981. This is a well-written and comprehensive discussion of stress, habits, and attention.

Understanding Stress

Baldwin, Bruce A., Ph.D. *It's All in Your Head.* Wilmington, N.C.: Direction Dynamics, 1985.

Borysenko, Joan, Ph.D. *Minding the Body, Mending the Mind.* Menlo Park, Calif.: Addison-Wesley, 1987.

Justice, Blair, Ph.D. *Who Gets Sick?* Houston: Peak Press, 1987.

Ornstein, Robert, Ph.D., and Paul Ehrlich. *New World, New Mind.* New York: Doubleday, 1989.

Ornstein, Robert, Ph.D., and David Sobel, M.D. *The Healing Brain.* New York: Simon and Schuster, 1987.

Pelletier, Kenneth, Ph.D. *Holistic Medicine.* New York: Dell, 1979.

─────. *Mind as Healer, Mind as Slayer.* New York: Dell, 1977.

Selye, Hans. *Stress without Distress.* New York: J. B. Lippincott, 1974.

Chapter Sixteen

Skilled Communication

Madeline Gershwin, R.N., M.A.

"No one would talk much in society, if he only knew how often he misunderstood others."

—Goethe

Although it is common to complain about lack of communication, it is, in fact, impossible not to communicate. We exchange messages whether we speak or keep silent. And like it or not, the vehicle for human interaction is language, both verbal and non-verbal. When we complain about lack of communication, we often mean that we do not feel heard, understood, appreciated, or respected.[1]

Impact and Intent

The objective of communication is to get your message across the way you mean it. The impact of what you say should equal its intended impact. In any interaction you are both sending and receiving messages. If two people are cooperating to insure that their intent equals their impact, they do not have to guess at what's being said, they do not make assumptions, and they pay attention to clarifying exchanges.

Effective communication occurs when people pay attention to the process of exchanging messages. If you have been using the RISE tools for some time, you might have noticed that you are paying more attention to what you say and how you say it. Each person brings to any interaction all of his or her conditioning, which includes attitudes, values, beliefs, and experiences. These are the filters through which messages have to pass on both the outgoing and incoming sides. Such filters obviously affect the way a message is sent as well as the way in which it is heard and perceived. We rarely think about the art of communication, nor do we usually reflect on its mechanics; but when we feel misunderstood, unappreciated, or unheard, we are being affected by this art (or lack of it) in ways that capture our attention.

Miscommunication

There are some common miscommunication styles that generate negative feelings. By becoming aware of your own miscommunication habits you can start to modify them and become a more effective communicator. Just as the RISE Response can help you make more beneficial choices in other areas of your life, they can also help you communicate differently than you do now, more constructively. Here are the most common miscommunication styles:

Sidetracking

Conversation begins with one issue but quickly moves to other, only vaguely related issues without closure or resolution on any issue. At its worst, totally unrelated issues are dragged in from "left field" completely muddling the interaction.

History Reporting

A defensive review of past events to justify current behavior ("and there was that time five years ago that you.... ").

Cross-Complaining

One complaint begets another until the interaction consists solely of a list of complaints. This invariably escalates unless one or both parties decide to apply the RISE approach — focus on one issue at a time.

Mind Reading

This involves:

- proceeding on assumptions about another's thoughts, feelings, reactions, needs, and wants. ("I know what you're thinking.")

- expecting that someone else should know your wants, needs, feelings, thoughts, and reactions without having to be told. ("If you really cared, you would know what I want.")

Character Assassination or Personality Labeling

This is the attribution of some insulting or negative characteristic(s) to another person's character. ("If you weren't so lazy....")

Yes, buts...

Every effort to state an opinion or point of view or offer a suggestion is met with the response, "Yes, but...", implying rejection and minimizing or discounting what the person has said.

Generalizations and Global Statements

"You always," "You never," "He doesn't care," "She has no respect for me." All of these miscommunication habits, when chronic, generate frustration, anger, resentment, and generally stressful conflict in relationships.

Guidelines for Effective Communication

The most important key to good communication is active listening. That means paying attention to what is being said and how it is being said and asking questions that are designed to increase your full appreciation for the intent of the speaker. It means giving constructive feedback about how you are perceiving the message. Good listening includes:

- *paraphrasing and summarizing* what you hear so that the speaker knows what kind of message you're receiving and can make the necessary clarification.

- *validation of feelings:* This is easy to do when you are in agreement but not so easy when you disagree. Suppose a friend is telling you that he was upset with you for canceling a dinner plan at the last minute. The tendency would be to become defensive — trying to explain and justify your reasons. A more constructive approach would be to express some understanding for how it felt for your friend to have a last minute change. That is validation.

- *asking clarifying questions.*

Sending Skills

Since we are always both listener and sender in our communications with other people, it is important to develop effective sending skills. These include:

- *using short, clear messages:* too much wordiness often loses the point.

- *eliminating* insulting, hostile, sarcastic, destructive, or accusing statements.

- *taking responsibility* for making clear, direct, open, honest statements of your feelings, opinions, and concerns.

It has been demonstrated that the power of any message comes more from non-verbal behavior than from the spoken content. When there is a discrepancy between the verbal and non-verbal, we are always more influenced by the non-verbal. Therefore, in order for communication to be truly effective, our non-verbal behavior must be congruent with our spoken message. Non-verbal behavior includes the following:

- *body movements and eye contact:* these are culturally influenced, but in Western cultures we generally value direct eye contact as a sign of sincerity, honesty, and openness. In some cultures however, direct eye contact is a sign of defiant disrespect.

- *facial expressions*

- *gestures*

- *posture and breathing*

- *spatial relationships:* how close you stand to people when you talk to them.

Not quite non-verbal, but not exactly verbal either are qualities of voice that affect the communication process. These qualities include volume, inflection, timbre, and tone.

Helpful Reading

Many books on communications skills are available on the market, while workshops, seminars, and college courses are devoted to understanding and improving communication. Understanding and skill development are important to forming effective communication skills, but even more critical is the capacity to pay attention and to become aware of habits that are not constructive. This requires the use of the RISE Response in order to make healthier choices in all spheres of our lives, including the way we communicate.

Two particularly useful books on communications skills are:

Gottman, John, et al. *A Couple's Guide to Communication.* Champaign, Ill.: Research Press, 1976.

McKay, M., M. Davis, and P. Fanning. *Messages: The Communication Book.* New York: New Harbinger, 1984.

IV. Spirituality and Self-Empowerment

Quiet Mind, Ample Heart

Rick Flinders, M.D.

...it was youth's ample heart that was now up for betrayal.

—*Arthur Miller*

"What the program has done has kind of opened doors that were closed for me in the past, made me turn inward and see what I'm really about, and what my potential is as a person. I've turned back to the religion that I was brought up in, and I feel very connected in that sense. It's a very big thing for me." (Lynne M.)

Rick and I used to spend summers along a dark-watered river that looped without much notice through the foothills of middle California and into pools that grew warm and mysterious in the sunlight. One of the pools lay at the foot of a rock that rose from the streambed forty feet or so above the water and seemed to glare at us. The pool was deep and the rock pitted, so that you could climb to the top if you wanted to, and (if you wanted to) jump.

We aimed for the still patches in the current. Locking our arms to our sides, we could sink straight through to the sand at the bottom and root ourselves there, stump-like, just above the bedrock. We'd stay down as long we could — gape into the river *above* us, and watch the air bubbles slide up shafts of sunlight to the top. *This was it*, we told ourselves each time. We'd stay right there as long as we could, hidden at the clear core of the river.

Even now, I can't remember a moment of such unmixed delight. Part of it came from the thrill of the long drop through the sky, part from the dazzling mystery at the bottom. But this went deeper than pleasure, for without knowing it we had flung ourselves into the heart of a metaphor that was closer to us than we knew. We had touched more than the hidden rock of the river; we had glimpsed, perhaps, our own clear, glowing core.

I won't press this too far — after all, we didn't stay down there, much as we'd have liked to. We ran out of breath, and finally out of interest. As hormones sprouted and ambitions flowered, the river ceased to be a concern. But we *were* up to more than we knew about at the time: we climbed to reach heights, ours as well as the rock's; and we jumped to test the depths, the river's, our own. We were unconsciously answering the call within all young persons, *to get to the bottom of things*, to pry out of the world, and themselves, *what is there*.

And the metaphor lingered. Though we left the river one summer and never went back, the stirrings we felt in its glittering pools left their traces — the longing for self-mastery and meaning, the need for deep and abiding delight. We all start life as pilgrims of a sort, seekers driven toward mastery and meaning. Then that urge dims and finally slips away altogether under the crush of pursuits for career, achievement, and security. Not that we should spend the rest of our lives looking for meanings inscribed at the bottom of dark pools. But that we should stop looking altogether is a regrettable loss.

And if the mind-body research we described in earlier chapters is accurate about the healing benefits of altruism, caring, and purpose, it may prove to be a health-threatening loss as well. You might recall, for instance, that the "hardy" executives in Kobasa's studies during the 1980s shared a level of commitment that gave them a sense of meaning and direction. So strong a cofactor was this commitment in predicting the healthier executives that it became one of Kobasa's three criteria for describing the hardy, stress-resistant personality.[1] Several other studies suggest that "being religious" improves health, according to Dr. Redford Williams, Director of Behavioral Research at Duke University Medical Center. In his latest book, *Anger Kills,* Dr. Williams describes the "survival skills" he recommends for protecting ourselves from the hostility and cynicism that threaten our health — such injunctions as, "Be Tolerant," "Forgive," "Listen," "Increase Your Empathy," "Become More Religious."[2] Almost twenty years ago, Hans Selye, the pioneer of stress research, called purposelessness "the worst of all modern social stresses."

Having a purpose in life may help protect us from the ravages of modern stress. But there is a better reason to keep the search for it an active force in our lives. The "call" for meaning comes from deep within and is silenced only with the loss of a very real part of our deepest selves. Answering the call in some way in our lives, here, now, may take us a long way toward the fulfillment we seek. "This is the true joy in life, George Bernard Shaw wrote at the turn of the century: "the being used for a purpose recognized by yourself as a mighty one."

In *Minding the Body, Mending the Mind* cell biologist Joan Borysenko writes about a young physician with AIDS named Sam, who recounted to her how the disease had started him thinking in new ways: "All my life I've searched for meaning in the things I could accomplish," he told her from his hospital bed. "I became a physician — a good one. . . . I spent my life getting secure, acquiring the things we all think of as important. A house, a car, enough money to do the things I want . . . but somehow all those things don't seem to be enough. Part of me is empty, longing for something. I don't seem to have any peace. . . . " And then he asks her: "Is there really some way to experience peace of mind?"[3]

The story of Sam's last year of life, which Dr. Borysenko describes, is a moving and, finally, successful search for the peace and meaning he sought. We've heard similar stories from RISE participants, telling us how their illnesses, as unwelcome as they were, had brought them unexpected meaning and, in some cases, peace. Their stories can serve as cautionary tales for those of us who have allowed our own youthful idealism and need for purpose to be eclipsed by career, ambition, or simple carelessness.

What *are* we capable of? How much wisdom, clarity, compassion, peace, *wellness* can we attain? We scarcely know since we've rarely been encouraged to find out. It's odd, when you think about it. With a little help we can calculate the composition of starlight a trillion light-years away, figure it down to the last infinitesimal glimmer. But to our own glimmerings we are like the blind. Our hearts have been formed wide and deep, with ample resources to live our lives in fullness and serenity. But we lose sight of the fact as easily as yesterday's news. "There is radiance and glory in the darkness could we but see," a medieval Italian friar implores in a passage you'll find in Chapter Eighteen, "and to see we have only to look."

Many RISE course participants have been content to use the RISE tools strictly as aids to help them cope with illness, disability, or stress — and to leave it at that. We welcome and support them, and we know they receive measurable benefits. But for those who feel the need for more meaning in their lives and greater access to their deeper selves, RISE can become a kind of ultimate recovery program that can help them look for and begin to release some of their deepest inner resources — calm and equilibrium, tolerance, compassion, greater clarity, forgiveness — back into their lives.

The key to this recovery is meditation on self-selected inspirational passages from traditional spiritual sources. Sri Easwaran first developed this technique for the audiences he spoke to as a Fulbright scholar at the University of California in Berkeley during the early 1960s, thinking, rightly, that they would respond to a language-based, rationally supportable form of meditation. As a result, this powerful blending of traditional wisdom and rational choice allows you to enter fully into the heart of any spiritual tradition, East or West, while remaining consistent with your own predilections for or against religions in general. You can select passages that speak directly to your own highest image of yourself (Fearless? Compassionate?) and stamp it upon your unconscious in meditation. Echoes begin to chime from within, memories stir. These qualities begin to penetrate your thinking and then your behavior: you *do* act fearless one day, you begin to feel in greater control of your life. And you start to suspect, like many RISE participants, that you have a far greater capacity for health and wellness than you thought.

We have seen hundreds of RISE participants — traditional, new age, orthodox, agnostic, atheists — use passage meditation with equal ease to touch spiritual depths within themselves that they were delighted to find. Many orthodox Christians have found it surprisingly congenial to their beliefs and practices. They've told us that meditating on a passage from a medieval mystic or using a verse from the Beatitudes helped them rediscover the spiritual riches of their tradition. In his recent book, *Life of the Beloved*, Father Henry Nouwen, a widely read Catholic writer, eloquently describes how passage meditation enhanced his own spiritual practices:

> The Hindu spiritual writer Eknath Easwaran showed me the great value of learning a sacred text by heart and repeating it slowly in the mind, word by word, sentence by sentence. In this way, listening to the voice of love becomes not just a passive waiting, but an active attentiveness to the voice that speaks to us through the words of the Scriptures.[4]

A surprising number of *former* practicing Christians have told us how passage meditation helped them recover an understanding of their former faith. And there are the many skeptics (our number is legion) who — with some reluctance — "tried" a passage with traditional language for a few weeks and found a surprising taste develop for it.

This does not necessarily mean the RISE tools will bring you these kinds of results — or that you would even want them to. But the unique flexibility of passage meditation allows for a wonderful range of possibilities. In this sense, we see RISE as a tentative first step toward a fuller spirituality — but only a first step. If you want to follow a spiritual path more thoroughly, you should find the guidance of an experienced teacher. RISE is, first of all, a program for coping with the stresses of illness and life. But its tools can help you begin to address a fuller range of human needs — physical, emotional, and spiritual — and in ways that can accommodate the widely varying needs of believers and skeptics alike.

As I touched upon in the introduction, it is no coincidence that the word "holy" is cognate with the old English word "wholle." They seem intrinsically linked. For as we develop our deeper resources and become more wholly ourselves, we are moving closer to our deepest self — reaching, inescapably, and at the same time, toward a greater self-empowerment and a fuller spirituality. "More than anything," Sri Easwaran quotes the Buddha:

> "I want your physical, emotional, and spiritual health to improve, your life to be always fresh, your relationships always rich, your contribution always valued. And I want you to have the good opinion of the person whose approval is most difficult to win: yourself." Then we can say, as the Buddha did toward the end of his life, "I am the happiest of mortals. No one is happier than I.' "[5]

Chapter Eighteen ————————————————

Inspirational Passages
for Meditation

DISCOURSE ON GOOD WILL ————————————————

1.

May all beings be filled with joy and peace.
May all beings everywhere,
The strong and the weak,
The great and the small,
The mean and the powerful,
The short and the long,
The subtle and the gross:

May all beings everywhere,
Seen and unseen,
Dwelling far off or nearby,
Being or waiting to become,
May all be filled with lasting joy.

2.

Let no one deceive another,
Let no one anywhere despise another,
Let no one out of anger or resentment
Wish suffering on anyone at all.

Just as a mother with her own life
Protects her child, her only child, from harm,
So within yourself let grow
A boundless love for all creatures.

For a wide selection of passages chosen especially for meditation, see E. Easwaran, *God Makes the Rivers to Flow* (Petaluma, Calif.: Nilgiri Press, 1991).

3.

Let your love flow outward through the universe,
To its height, its depth, its broad extent,
A limitless love, without hatred or enmity.

Then as you stand or walk,
Sit or lie down,
As long as you are awake,
Strive for this with a one-pointed mind;
Your life will bring heaven to earth.

> — *From the Buddhist canon*

THE HIGHEST GOOD ————————————————

The highest good is like water.
Water gives life to the 10,000 things and does not strive.
It flows in places men reject and so is like the Tao.
In dwelling, be close to the land.
In meditation, go deep in the heart.
In dealing with others, be gentle and kind.
In speech, be true.
In ruling, be just.
In business, be competent.
In action, watch the timing.
No fight...no blame.

> — *From the Buddhist canon*

TAO TE CHING ————————————————————

The universe had a beginning
Called the Mother of All Things.
Once you have found the Mother
You can know her children.
Having known the children,
Hold tightly to the mother.
Your whole life will be preserved from peril.

Open up the openings,
Multiply your affairs,
Your whole life will become a burden.

He who sees the small is called clear-headed,
He who holds to gentleness is called strong.

Use the light.
Come home to your true nature.
Don't cause yourself injury:
This is known as seizing truth.

— *Lao Tze*

THE 10,000 THINGS _____

1.
Empty yourself of everything.
Let the mind rest at peace.
The 10,000 things rise and fall
While the self watches their return.

2.
They grow and flourish and then return to the source.
Returning to the source is stillness, which is the way of nature.
The way of nature is unchanging.

3.
Knowing constancy is insight.
Not knowing constancy leads to disaster.
Knowing constancy, the mind is open.

4.
With an open mind, you will be open-hearted.
Being open-hearted, you will act royally.
Being royal, you will attain the divine.
Being divine, you will be at one with the Tao.
Being at one with the Tao is eternal.
And though the body dies, the Tao will never pass away.

5.
Break into the peace within.
Hold fast to stillness.
And in daily life,
You will ably manage the 10,000 things.

— *From the Buddhist canon*

THE TWIN VERSES _____

1.

All that we are is a result of what we have thought:
we are formed and molded by our thoughts.
The man whose mind is shaped by selfish thoughts
causes misery when he speaks or acts.
Sorrow rolls over him as the wheels of a cart
roll over the tracks of the bullock that draws it.

All that we are is the result of what we have thought:
we are formed and molded by our thoughts.
The man whose mind is shaped by selfless thoughts
gives joy whenever he thinks or acts.
Joy follows him like a shadow that never leaves him.

2.

"He insulted me, he struck me, he cheated me, he robbed me":
those caught in resentful thoughts never find peace.

"He insulted me, he struck me, he cheated me, he robbed me":
those who give up resentful thoughts find peace.

3.

The selfish man suffers here, and he suffers there;
he suffers wherever he goes.
He suffers and frets over the damage he has done.

The selfless man rejoices here, and he rejoices there; he rejoices
wherever he goes.
He rejoices and delights in the good he as done.

For hatred does not cease by hatred at any time: hatred ceases
by love.
This is an unalterable law.

— *From the Dhammapada*

In my house there is a cave.
And in the cave,
Nothing at All.
Pure, wondrous, empty,
Resplendent with a light like the sun.
Simple greens will nourish this body,

Humble clothes will protect it.
Let a thousand saints appear before me.
I have the Buddha of truth!

    — *Han Shan*

    1.

Your real nature is, in highest truth,
Empty of self, silent, pure.
It is glorious, mysterious, peaceful joy —
That is all.
Enter into it by awakening to it in yourself.
All that is before you is your real nature,
Whole, full, complete.
Other than this, there is nothing at all.

    2.

The place of precious things is the Mind,
Original essence, treasure of our real nature.
The piles of glittering jewels there cannot be measured.
It is a place to which no one can direct you.
All we can say is, it is close by.
It cannot be described.
But look within yourself —
It is there.

    — *Huang Po*

Lord, where shall I find thee?
High and hidden is your place.
And where shall I not find you?
The world is full of your glory.
I have sought your nearness,
With all my heart I called you,
And going out to meet you,
I found you coming toward me.

    — *Halevi*

PRAYER OF ST. FRANCIS ————————————————————————

Lord, make me an instrument of your peace.
Where there is hatred, let me sow love;
Where there is injury, pardon;
Where there is doubt, faith;
Where there is despair, hope;
Where there is darkness, light;
Where there is sadness, joy.

Oh Lord, grant that I may seek not so much,
To be consoled, as to console,
To be understood as to understand,
To be loved, as to love.

For it is in giving that we receive;
It is in pardoning that we are pardoned;
It is forgetting ourselves that we come to life.

ON PATIENCE ————————————————————————————

Let nothing trouble you.
Let nothing frighten you.
Everything is changing,
God alone is changeless.
Patience attains all.
Who knows God needs nothing.
God alone suffices.

> — *Teresa of Avila*

THE GIFT ———————————————————————————————

1.
There is nothing I can give you
which you do not have,
but there is much that while I cannot give it,
you can take.
No heaven can come to us
unless our hearts find rest in it today.
Take heaven.
No peace lies in the future

which is not hidden in this present instant.
Take peace.

  2.

The gloom of the world
is but a shadow behind it,
yet within reach is joy.
There is radiance and glory in the darkness
could we but see,
and to see we have only to look.
I beseech you to look.

  — *Fra Giovanni*

PRAYER FOR PEACE _____

O loving presence,
You who are within and without,
Above and below and all around,
You who are interpenetrating
Every cell of my being;
You who are the eye of my eyes,
The ear of my ears,
The heart of my heart,
The mind of my mind,
The life of my life,
The soul of my soul,
Bless us, dear God, to be aware of your presence
Now and here.

OH, GREAT SPIRIT _____

  1.

Oh, Great Spirit, whose voice I hear in the winds,
And whose breath gives life to all the world—
Hear me.

I come before you, one of your many children.
I am small and weak,
I need your strength and wisdom.

2.

Let me walk in beauty, and make my eyes ever behold,
The red and purple sunset.
Make my hands respect the things you have made,
My ears sharp to hear your voice.
Make me wise so that I may know the things,
You have taught my people,
The lesson you have hidden in every leaf and rock.

3.

I seek strength
Not to be superior to my brother,
But to be able to master myself.

Make me ever ready to come to you
With clean hands and straight eyes,
So when life fades as a fading sunset,
My spirit may come to you without shame.

— *Yellow Lark, Sioux Indian Chief*

PRAYER OF OFFERING _____

1.

Grandfather, Great Spirit,
You have been always,
And before you no one has been.
There is no other one to pray to but you.
You yourself, everything has been made by you ...

2.

Grandfather, Great Spirit,
Lean close to the earth
That you may hear the voice I send.
You towards where the sun goes down, behold me ...
And you, Mother Earth, the only Mother,
You who have shown mercy to your children!

3.

Hear me, four quarters of the world — A relative I am!
Give me the strength to understand,
That I may be like you.
With your power only can I face the winds.

4.

Great Spirit, Great Spirit, my Grandfather,
All over the earth the faces of living things are all alike.
With tenderness have these come up out of the ground.
Look upon these faces of children without number
And with children in their arms,
That they may face the winds
And walk the good road to the day of quiet.
This is my prayer. Hear me!

— *Black Elk*

PRAYER OF BLACK ELK _____

Grandfather, Great Spirit,
Once more behold me on earth
And learn to hear my feeble voice.

You lived first, and you are older than all need,
Older than all prayer.
All things belong to you —
The two-leggeds, the four-leggeds,
The wings of the air
And all green things that live.

You have set the powers of the four quarters
To cross each other.
The good road and the road of difficulties
You have made to cross;
And where they cross, the place is holy.
Day in and day out, Forever,
You are the life of things.

A PRAYER OF AWARENESS
(Native American) _____

Now Talking God
With your feet I walk
I walk with your limbs
I carry forth your body
For me your mind thinks
Your voice speaks for me

Beauty is before me
And beauty behind me
Above and below me hovers the beautiful
I am surrounded by it
I am immersed in it
In my youth I am aware of it
And in old age I shall walk quietly
The beautiful trail.

POEMS OF KABIR _____

1.

The Lord is in me, the Lord is in you,
As life is in every seed.
O servant, put false pride away,
And seek for him within you.

2.

A million suns are ablaze with light,
The sea of blue spreads in the sky;
The fever of life is stilled,
And all stains are washed away,
When I sit in the midst of that world.

3.

How blessed is Kabir, that midst this great joy,
He sings within his own vessel.
It is the music of the meeting of soul with soul;
It is the music of the forgetting of sorrows;
It is the music that transcends all coming in,
And all going forth.

FROM THE VEDAS _____

God makes the rivers to flow.
They tire not, nor do they cease from flowing.
May the river of my life
flow into the sea of love that is the Lord.

May the thread of my song be not cut
before my life merges in the sea of love.

FROM THE PSALMS _____

Let the heaven rejoice, let the earth be glad.
Let the sea and all it contains roar in praise....
Let the sea roar, and all its creatures;
The world and its inhabitants.
Let the rivers burst into applause,
Let the mountains join in acclaim with joy.
The Lord is coming to sustain the earth.
He will sustain the earth with kindness,
Its people with graciousness...
Your works, O Lord, make me glad;
I sing with the joy of Your creation.
How vast Your works, O Lord.
Your designs are beyond our grasp...

    — *Psalms 96, 98, 92*

The Lord is my shepherd; I shall not want.
He makes me to lie down in green pastures:
He leads me beside the still waters.
He restores my soul:
He leads me in the paths of righteousness for his name's sake.
Yea, though I walk through the valley of the shadow of death,
I will fear no evil: for you are with me;
Your rod and your staff comfort me.
You prepare a table before me in the presence of my enemies:
You anoint my head with oil; my cup runs over.
Surely goodness and mercy will follow me
all the days of my life:
And I will dwell in the house of the Lord for ever.

    — *Psalm 23*

WITH ALL MY STRENGTH _____

With all my strength and spirit,
I adore you, Truth,
aloud and in my secret core.
I hoard your name. And who can rob this spoil?
He is my love. What other could I crave?

He is my light. How could my lamp need oil?
How can I falter, leaning on such a stave?...
Source of my life, your praise shall sound as long
As I can breathe my fervor into song.

    — *Halevi*

FROM THE UPANISHADS _____

1.

Hear O children of immortal bliss!
You were born to be united with the Self.
Follow the paths of the enlightened sages,
And you will be united with the Self.

2.

The Self is hidden in the hearts of all.
Draw it out of the body in meditation,
As you would draw the seed from a stalk of grass.
Know your Self to be pure and immortal!
Know your Self to be pure and immortal!

3.

Hidden in the heart of every creature
Exists the Self, subtler than the subtlest,
Greater than the greatest. They go beyond
Sorrow who behold the glory of the Self.

4.

The ruler supreme, inner Self of all,
Multiplies its oneness into many.
Eternal joy is theirs who see the Self
In their own hearts.
To none else does it come!

Changeless among the things that pass away,
Pure consciousness in all who are conscious,
The Self answers the prayers of many.
Eternal peace is theirs who see the Self
In their own hearts.
To none else does it come!

5.

The effulgent Self, who is beyond thought,
Shines in the greatest, shines in the smallest,
Shines in the farthest, shines in the nearest,
Shines in the secret chamber of the heart.

Beyond the reach of the senses is the Self,
But not beyond the reach of a mind stilled
Through the practice of deep meditation.

Research Abstracts

**Abstract presented at the
Sixth International AIDS Conference,
June 21, 1990, San Francisco**

PSYCHOSOCIAL ADJUSTMENT TO HIV INFECTION:
EFFICACY OF DIFFERENT GROUP INTERVENTIONS
IN GAY AND BISEXUAL MEN

W. Earl, R. Flinders, M. Flahive, B. Bartholow, J. Kobayashi,
D. Cohn

Denver Health and Hospitals, Denver, Colo., RISE Program
Management

Objective

To establish the level of distress experienced by HIV-infected
gay and bisexual men and to assess the efficacy of psychosocial
interventions in preventing maladaptive adjustment to living
with HIV infection and AIDS.

Methods

Psychosocial inventories were administered to four groups
(n=179) of HIV-infected men. (1) participants in the Longitudinal Cohort Study (LCS) who received no treatment but were
followed for a six-month period of time (n=50); (2) traditional
psychotherapy groups (n=29); (3) traditional stress management groups (n=50); (4) RISE participants who underwent
self-stewardship training using meditation as a central discipline (n=50). All groups were of ten weeks duration. Patients
were measured by the Brief Symptom Inventory (BSI, Dero-
gatis, 1979) at the start and conclusion of treatment. The LCS
received their second evaluation after six months.

Results

On subscales evaluating levels of depression and the adaptive scales of hostility, anxiety, phobic anxiety, and paranoia, the RISE intervention was more efficacious as it presents movement within a cluster of adaptive skills, while the other interventions showed improved function on isolated subscales. General well-being was improved in the RISE participants at a significant level ($p < 0.01$) and the level of distress (number of items reported and level of distress indicated) was significant to $p < .0001$.

Conclusion

Men who completed the RISE program reported less distress and showed improvement in a cluster of coping skills (reduced anxiety, hostility, and social isolation) that suggested the more beneficial adjustment was made by the men in the RISE program, though all interventions improved some aspect of the client's perception of coping ability. This study report is limited to within-group movement and BSI profiles that emerge from a given intervention. Sufficient numbers have not been accumulated in the comparison groups to make a cross-correlation meaningful.

1. *Denver Longitudinal Cohort:* evidenced a decrease in psychotic distress and depression.

2. *Traditional therapy:* produced a reduction in paranoia and depression.

3. *Traditional stress management:* reduced obsessive compulsive distress.

4. *RISE:* lowered distress across subscales describing social sensitivity, depression, anxiety, hostility, phobic anxiety, paranoia, and psychotic distress.

Abstract Presented at the
Seventh International AIDS Conference
June 17, 1991, Florence, Italy

REDUCTION OF RISKY SEXUAL BEHAVIOR
IN GAY AND BISEXUAL MEN

R. Flinders, M.D., D. Cohn, B. Ruppenthal, C. J. Martindale, E. M. Freeman, V. J. Cole, M. Flahive

The RISE Institute, Davies Medical Center, San Francisco; California, Denver Disease Control Service, Denver, Colorado

Objective

To investigate high-risk sexual practices and substance abuse behaviors before and after participation in group, individual support, and educational programs.

Methods

From a longitudinal cohort of gay men, three group programs were explored; RISE, a ten-week program for "self-stewardship" using attention-training techniques; a support group emphasizing community service' and two ongoing support groups using stress management training. Cohort members in individual psychotherapy and without group membership were also analyzed. Behavioral outcomes were measured by questionnaire every six months and were compared before and after participation. Change scores were analyzed by one-way ANOVA.

					p-values/post-hoc comparisons		
Results	#	N	Mean Score*		Dunett	REGWF	Williams
RISE	1	10	18.76		.010		
Community Service	2	12	50.11	1<2	.050	.0079	.005
Stress Management	3	12	44.45	1<3	.010	.0212	.005
Psychotherapy	4	12	45.56	1<4	.010	.0612	.005
No Group	5	19	51.49	1<5	.010	.0055	.005

$F = 4.066$, $p = 0.005$. *Scores indicate levels of post-program sexual behavior. Only RISE was significant in pair-wise comparisons ($p < .05$). There were no differences between groups for changes in substance abuse.

Conclusion

Of the programs compared in this study, RISE appears to be promising for reducing risky sexual behavior in gay men.

Appendix B

The Voices of RISE

We interviewed a number of RISE alumni and asked them to speak about their experiences with the tools. Their words have been placed throughout the book as samples of how some participants feel that the RISE tools met their needs. We have altered their names to protect anonymity.

Carl F.: Carl is in his late thirties and is an information systems specialist for a major medical center. He came to RISE after deciding that he wanted to manage his life better and deal more positively with his HIV status.

Carol C.: Carol is in her forties. Testing positive for HIV shifted her priorities and changed her focus. She feels that the RISE training has transformed her life.

Cecily E.: Cecily developed an obscure disease of the spinal cord and has undergone multiple major surgeries. She has had chronic pain, a drug problem related to pain management, and impaired physical functioning. As a result of her illness she is totally disabled and unable to work. She was referred to RISE to help her deal with anger and fear.

Chris O.: Chris is in his early thirties and a recovering alcoholic. He is a triathlete and active in gay athletic organizations. Chris works with people with developmental disabilities.

Doug C.: Doug is in his late fifties and tested positive for HIV. He has a business as manufacturer's representative for lighting fixtures, and he and his wife, Carol C., have been prominent members of their community.

Edward S.: Twenty-three years old, born in Texas, Edward has been HIV positive for seven years and was recently diagnosed for Kaposi's sarcoma. He works in a hotel and felt recharged by his diagnosis to deal with his condition in "a new way," which is what brought him to RISE.

Helen P.: A middle-aged Iranian woman with teen-aged children, Helen took RISE to deal with emotional stress.

James R.: James is fifty-eight, a grandfather, and a person living with AIDS. He is a prominent labor negotiator and developer of a popular southern California program for helping people manage HIV illness.

Kyle B.: Kyle was one of the first RISE graduates. Diagnosed with AIDS in 1986, he transformed his attitude toward his illness and was an inspiration to all of us who knew him. Kyle died of an infection in 1989.

Lynne M.: Lynne is an administrative nurse with extensive experience in managing intensive care and trauma units in a major metropolitan hospital. She took RISE to help manage the high levels of stress in her workplace and found that the tools helped reawaken a dormant spiritual life.

Mark V.: Mark is in his late forties, a grade school teacher who took RISE to support his wife. He suffered a heart attack during his RISE training and used the RISE tools to manage the anxiety that accompanied his illness.

Mort B.: Mort is in his mid-fifties and was an early participant in RISE as a support to his HIV-positive lover. He decided to take RISE for himself and became a stanch alumnus.

Penny V.: Penny is a grade school teacher who developed a panic disorder. The RISE tools played a significant role in helping her cope with her disorder.

Rick E.: Rick was one of the founders of the Los Angeles AIDS network in the early 1980s and a long-term AIDS survivor. He survived numerous opportunistic infections over a period of several years, while leading an active life as a landscape architect and school board member in northern California. Rick died of an infection in July 1991.

Roger S.: A decorator in his mid-thirties, Roger lost two family members to AIDS.

Sandra H.: Married with four children, Sandra has systemic lupus and comes from a highly dysfunctional background, including long-term sexual abuse.

Terry A.: Terry is in his late twenties, an aerobic exercise instructor and personal fitness trainer. He took RISE initially to slow down and help him deal with anger.

Walt S.: Walt is a computer technician who took the RISE course at the insistence of his wife, a RISE alumna. They have several children and feel that the RISE program has had a significant effect on their entire family.

Notes

Introduction

1. W. Earl, Rick Flinders, M.D., B. Bartholow, J. Kobayashi, D. Cohn, M. Flahive, "Abstract," presented at the Sixth International AIDS Conference, June 21, 1990, San Francisco (see page 211). The study was conducted within the Longitudinal Cohort Study (LCS) funded by the Centers for Disease Control (CDC) through the AIDS Prevention Program of the Denver Public Health Department. The LCS has been following twelve hundred persons at risk for HIV in the Denver area. Participants in the LCS were randomly assigned to several interventions including RISE. The study found that RISE participants significantly (p-0.01) improved their general sense of well-being and significantly (p-.0001) reduced their levels of distress. The results suggest that RISE is more effective in providing coping skills to persons affected by HIV than comparable ten-week group psychotherapy and stress-management programs.

2. R. Flinders, M.D., D. Cohn, B. Ruppenthal, C. J. Martindale, E. M. Freeman, et al., "Abstract," presented at the Seventh International Conference on AIDS, June 17, 1991, Florence, Italy (see page 213). The purpose of this study was to quantify and compare high-risk sexual behavior before and after participation in group, individual support, and educational programs. Three group programs in the LCS were compared: RISE, a support group emphasizing community service, and two ongoing support groups using stress management training. Data from cohort members in individual psychotherapy and without group membership were also analyzed. Serial measurement of sexual behaviors by questionnaire at six-month intervals, analyzed by one-way ANOVA of contrasts and by logistic regression of binary outcomes, indicated that the RISE program was associated with significant pre/post lowering of behavioral risks while the other programs were not. Treatment groups were homogeneous on HIV status, initial behavior, ethnicity, income, and psychological measures.

3. See, for instance, R. Ader, L. J. Grota, et al., "Conditioning Phenomena and Immune Function," *Annals of the New York Academy of Sciences* (1987): 496–532; H. O. Besedovsky, A. del Rey, et al., "Immunoregulatory Feedback between Interleukin-1 and Glucocorticoid Hormones, *Science* 233 (1986): 652–54; D. L. Felten, et al., "Noradrenergic Sympathetic Neural Interactions with the Immune System: Structure and Function," *Immunology Review* 100 (1987): 225–60; C. B. Pert, et al., "Neuropeptides and Their Receptors: A Psychosomatic Network," *Journal of Immunology* 135 (1985): 820–26; M. Stein, et al., "Stress and Immunomodulation: The Role of Depression and

Neuroendocrine Function," *Journal of Immunology* 135 (1985): 827–33. For a review of the more significant PNI research see Norman Cousins, *Journal of the American Medical Association* 260, no. 11 (September 16, 1988): 1610.

4. M. Irwin, M. Daniels, et al., "Plasma Cortisol and Natural Killer Cell Activity during Bereavement," *Biological Psychiatry* 24 (1988): 173–78; Jo A. Wegmann, "Hospice Home Death, Hospital Death, and Coping Abilities of Widows," dissertation, Claremont Graduate School, 1985, abstracted in *Dissertation Abstracts International* 46 (8-A), 1986: 2457; S. J. Schleifer, et al., "Suppression of Lymphocyte Stimulation during Bereavement," *Journal of the American Medical Association* 250, no. 3 (1983): 374; R. Glaser, J. K. Kiecolt-Glaser, et al., "Psychosocial Modifiers of Immunocompetence in Medical Students," *Psychosomatic Medicine* 46, no. 7 (1984).

5. M. Stein, S. E. Deller, and S. J. Schleifer, "Stress and Immunomodulation: The Role of Depression and Neuroendocrine Function," *Journal of Immunology* 135 (1985): 827–33; M. Irwin and T. Patterson, "Reduction of Immune Function in Life Stress and Depression," *Biological Psychiatry* 27 (1990): 22–30.

6. Stein, et al., "Stress and Immunomodulation," *Journal of Immunology* 135 (1985): 827–33.

7. M. L. Laudenslager, S. M. Ryan, et al., "Coping and Immunosuppression: Inescapable but Not Escapable Shock Suppresses Lymphocyte Proliferation," *Science* 221 (1983): 568–70; M. Borysenko and J. Borysenko, "Stress, Behavior, and Immunity: Animal Models and Mediating Mechanisms," *General Hospital Psychiatry* 4 (1982): 59–67, quoted in Blair Justice, Ph.D., *Who Gets Sick?* (Houston: Peak Press, 1987), 64.

8. C. Peterson and A. J. Stunkard, "Personal Control and Health Promotion," *Society of Scientific Medicine* (Great Britain) 28, no. 8 (1989): 819–28; Michael H. Antoni, paper presented at the annual meeting of the American Association for the Advancement of Science, San Francisco, January 15, 1989, quoted in *New York Times*, January 16, 1989.

9. Laudenslager, Ryan, et al., "Coping and Immunosuppression."

10. C. Peterson, M. E. P. Seligman, and G. E. Vaillant, *Journal of Personality and Social Psychology* 55, no. 1 (1988): 23–27.

11. Jon Kabat-Zinn, *Full Catastrophe Living: Using the Wisdom of Your Body and Mind to Face Stress, Pain, and Illness* (New York: Delta, 1990), 201.

12. *Healthy People: The Surgeon General's Report on Health Promotion and Disease Prevention* (DHEW Publication no. 7 9-55071). Washington: Government Printing Office, 1988.

13. R. Ader, "Clinical Implications of Psychoneuroimmunology," *Developmental Behavior Pediatrics* 8 (1987): 357–58; M. H. Antoni, N. Schneiderman, M. A. Fletcher, et al., "Psychoneuroimmunology and HIV-1," *Journal of Clinical Psychology* 58 (1990): 38–49; G. F. Solomon, L. Temoshok, et al., "An Intensive Psychoimmunologic Study of Long-Surviving Persons with AIDS," *Annals of the New York Academy of Sciences* (1987): 647–55; G. F. Solomon, "Psychoimmunology and Human Immunodeficiency Virus Infection," *Psychiatric Medicine* 7 (1989): 47–57.

14. J. K. Kiecolt-Glaser and R. Glaser, "Behavioral Influences on Immune Function: Evidence for the Interplay between Stress and Health," in T. Field, L. McCabe, and N. Schneiderman, eds., _Stress and Coping_, vol. 2 (Hillsdale, N.J.: Lawrence Erlbaum Associates, 1985).

15. B. Gruber, N. Hall, S. Hersh, et al., "Immune System and Psychologic Changes in Metastatic Cancer Patients Using Ritualized Relaxation and Guided Imagery," _Scandinavian Journal of Behavioral Therapy_ 17 (1988): 25–45.

16. A. Laperrier, P. O'Hearn, et al., "Exercise and Immune Function in Healthy HIV-1 Antibody Negative and Positive Gay Males," presented at the Ninth Annual Scientific Meeting of the Society of Behavioral Medicine, Boston, April 1988.

17. David Spiegel, quoted in "Health Front," _Prevention_ 42 (February 1990): 14–16.

18. S. C. Kobasa, "Stressful Life Events, Personality and Health: An Inquiry into Hardiness," _Journal of Personality and Social Psychology_ 37, no. 1 (1984): 1–11.

19. S. C. Kobasa, "Test for Hardiness: How Much Stress Can You Survive?" _American Health_, September 1984, 64.

Chapter One: The Problem of the Mind

1. John Farquhar, M.D., _The American Way of Life Need Not Be Hazardous to Your Health: Coping with Life's Seven Major Risk Factors_ (Menlo Park, Calif.: Addison-Wesley, 1987), 24.

2. Ibid., 3.

3. Randy Shilts, "Falling Off the Safe-Sex Wagon," _San Francisco Chronicle_, May 22, 1989, A8. Studies at the University of California at San Francisco have found that about 20 percent of local gay men fall off the safe-sex wagon per year.

4. Farquhar, _The American Way of Life_, 24.

5. E. F. Schumacher, _Guide for the Perplexed_ (New York: E. P. Dutton, 1978), p. 72.

6. Ibid.

Chapter Two: Passage Meditation

1. See Eknath Easwaran, _Meditation_ (Petaluma, Calif.: Nilgiri Press, 1978). This book gives a fuller description of meditation on an inspirational passage and of Sri Easwaran's eight-point spiritual program.

2. E. Easwaran, _The Bhagavad Gita for Daily Living_ (Petaluma, Calif.: Nilgiri Press, 1975), 16.

3. Easwaran, _Meditation_, 33.

4. Ibid., 37–38.

5. E. F. Schumacher, _Guide for the Perplexed_ (New York: Dutton, 1978), 66–67.

6. E. Easwaran, _Meditation_, 33.

Chapter Three: Using a Mantram

1. For a more thorough treatment of mantrams, see E. Easwaran, *The Unstruck Bell* (Petaluma, Calif.: Nilgiri Press, 1993).
2. P. Carrington, *Clinically Standardized Meditation* (Kendall Park, N.J.: Pace Systems, 1978), in D. H. Shapiro, Jr., and R. N. Walsh, eds., *Meditation: Classic and Contemporary Perspectives* (New York: Aldine, 1984), 550; D. H. Shapiro and D. Giber, "Meditation and Psychotherapeutic Effects: Self-Regulation Strategy and Altered States of Consciousness," *Archives of General Psychiatry* 35 (1978): 294–302.
3. Shapiro and Giber, "Meditation and Psychotherapeutic Effects."
4. R. L. Woofolk, "Psychological Correlates of Meditation," *Archives of General Psychiatry* 32 (1975): 1326–33.
5. Shapiro and Walsh, *Meditation*, 550.
6. H. Benson, with M. A. Klipper, *The Relaxation Response* (New York: William Morrow, 1975).
7. J. Borysenko, with L. Rothstein, *Minding the Body, Mending the Mind* (Reading, Mass.: Addison-Wesley, 1987), 13.
8. Ibid.

Chapter Four: Slowing Down/Seeing Clearly

1. Redford Williams, M.D., *The Trusting Heart: Great News about Type A Behavior* (New York: Times Books, 1989). See Dr. Williams's introduction for an excellent history of the development of the Type A theory, and its subsequent rise, fall, and recent resurrection among the scientific community. Dr. Williams argues that hostility is the only aspect of the Type A personality cluster that is toxic in isolation.
2. See M. Friedman and D. Ulmer, *Treating Type A Behavior and Your Heart* (New York: Knopf, 1984).
3. Jane Brody, *The New York Times Guide to Personal Health* (New York: Times Books, 1982), 143.
4. Ibid., 144.

Chapter Five: One-Pointed Focus

1. See M. Friedman and D. Ulmer, *Treating Type A Behavior and Your Heart* (New York: Knopf, 1984), 40–41.
2. D. Wood, et al., "The Prevalence of Attention Deficit Disorder, Residual Type, or Minimal Brain Dysfunction, in a Population of Male Alcoholic Patients," *American Journal of Psychiatry* 140, no. 1 (1983): 95–98.
3. Jo A. Wegmann, "Hospice Home Death, Hospital Death, and Coping Abilities of Widows," dissertation, Claremont Graduate School, 1985, abstracted in *Dissertation Abstracts International* 46 (8-A), 1986: 2457; R. W. Bartrop, et al., "Depressed Lymphocyte Function after Bereavement," *Lancet* 1, no. 8016 (1977): 834–36; S. J. Schleifer, et al. "Suppression of Lymphocyte

Stimulation during Bereavement," *Journal of the American Medical Association* 250 (1983): 374–77.

4. E. Langer and A. Benevento, "Self-Induced Dependence," *Journal of Personality and Social Psychology* 36, no. 8 (1978): 886–93; J. Avorn and E. Langer, "Induced Disability in Nursing Home Patients: A Controlled Trial," *Journal of the American Geriatrics Society* 30, no. 6 (1982): 397–400.

5. William James, *Principles of Psychology* (Cambridge, Mass.: Harvard University Press, 1981), 275.

6. E. Langer, et al. "Environmental Determinants of Memory Improvement in Late Adulthood," *Journal of Personality and Social Psychology* 37, no. 11 (1979): 2003–13. See also E. Langer, et al., "An Exploration of Relationships among Mindfulness, Longevity, and Senility," *Academic Psychology Bulletin* 6 no. 2 (1984): 211–26.

7. Daniel Goleman, "Concentration," *Vogue*, September 1985, 345.

8. C. P. Snow, *Variety of Men* (New York: Charles Scribner's Sons, 1966), 97.

9. Carl Howard, "Leonard Bernstein: The Man and the Artist," *San Francisco Chronicle*, August 14, 1981, 9C.

10. *Writers at Work: The Paris Review Interviews*, 2d series, intro. by Van Wyck Brooks (New York: Viking Press, 1963), 221.

11. Joseph Renzulli, *The Enrichment Triad Model* (Wethersfield, Conn.: Creative Learning Press, 1977), 34–35.

Chapter Six: Healthy Ties

1. J. Borysenko, with L. Rothstein, *Minding the Body, Mending the Mind* (Reading, Mass.: Addison-Wesley, 1987), 25.

2. Ibid.; Blair Justice, Ph.D., *Who Gets Sick?* (Houston: Peak Press, 1987), 43–44, 204.

3. Ibid., 44, 204.

4. Ibid., 131.

5. Borysenko, *Minding the Body, Mending the Mind*, 25–26.

6. J. H. Medalie and U. Goldbourt, "Angina Pectoris among 10,000 Men, II: Psychosocial and Other Risk Factors," *American Journal of Medicine* 60 (1976): 910–21.

7. M. M. Burg, J. A. Blumenthal, et al., "Social Support as a Buffer against the Development of Coronary Artery Disease," paper presented at the annual meeting of the Society of Behavioral Medicine, San Francisco, 1986, in Justice, *Who Gets Sick?* 6.

8. E. R. Growald and A. Luks, "A Reason to Be Nice: It's Healthy," *San Francisco Chronicle*, March 4, 1988.

9. M. G. Marmot, "Stress, Social Support and Cultural Variations in Heart Disease," *Journal of Psychosomatic Research* 27, no. 5 (1983): 377–84.

10. D. C. McClelland, et al., "The Effect of an Academic Examination on Salivary Norepinephrine and Immunoglobulin Levels," *Journal of Human Stress* 11, no. 2 (1985): 52–59, in Justice, *Who Gets Sick?* 249.

11. Borysenko, *Minding the Body, Mending the Mind*, 25–25.

12. Ibid., 24.

13. T. H. Holmes, "Multidiscipline Studies of Tuberculosis," in Sparer, ed., *Personality, Stress and Tuberculosis* (New York: International Universities Press, 1956), 65–151.

14. Borysenko, *Minding the Body, Mending the Mind,* 25.

15. Graham Scherwitz, et al., "Self-Involvement and Coronary Heart Disease Incidence in the Multiple Risk Factor Intervention Trial," *Psychosomatic Medicine* 48, nos. 3/4 (March/April 1986).

16. J. Fischman, "Type A on Trial," *Psychology Today,* February 1987, 48.

17. Ibid.

18. Justice, *Who Gets Sick?* 258.

19. Growald and Luks, "A Reason to Be Nice: It's Healthy."

20. Ibid.

21. Ibid.

22. Ibid.

23. M. Minkler (speaker), "Social Networks and Health: People Need People," series on the Healing Brain, cassette recording no. T57 (Los Altos, Calif.: Institute for Study of Human Knowledge, 1987); N. Angier, "Four-legged Therapists," *Discover* (1983): 86–89, in Justice, *Who Gets Sick?* 258.

24. E. J. Langer and J. Rodin, "The Effects of Choice and Enhanced Personal Responsibility for the Aged: A Field Experiment in an Institutional Setting," *Journal of Personality and Social Psychology* 34, no. 2 (1976): 191–98, in Justice, *Who Gets Sick?* 142.

25. J. Rodin and E. Langer, "Long-term Effects of a Control-relevant Intervention with the Institutionalized Aged," *Journal of Personality and Social Psychology* 35, no. 3 (1977): 897–902.

26. Growald and Luks, "A Reason to Be Nice: It's Healthy."

27. S. Gore, "The Effect of Social Support in Moderating the Health Consequences of Unemployment," *Journal of Health and Social Behavior* 19 (1978): 157–65.

28. J. Kiecolt-Glaser, R. Glaser, et al., "Clinical Psycho-neuroimmunology: Basic Principles and Experimental Advances," presentation at the meeting of the Society of Behavioral Medicine, New Orleans, 1986, in Justice, *Who Gets Sick?* 134.

29. Ibid.

30. Ibid., 135.

31. D. Thomas, et al., "Effect of Social Support on Stress-Related Changes in Cholesterol Level, Uric Acid Level, and Immune Function in an Elderly Sample," *American Journal of Psychiatry* 142, no. 6 (1985): 735–37.

32. Borysenko, *Minding the Body, Mending the Mind,* 25–25.

Chapter Eight: HIV/AIDS, RISE, and the Mind-Body Connection

1. See, for instance, R. Ader, L. J. Grota, et al., "Conditioning Phenomena and Immune Function," *Annals of the New York Academy of Sciences* (1987): 496–532; H. O. Besedovsky, A. del Rey, et al., "Immunoregulatory Feedback between Interleukin-1 and Glucocorticoid Hormones," *Science* 233 (1986): 652–54; D. L. Felten, et al., "Noradrenergic Sympathetic Neural Interactions with the Immune System: Structure and Function," *Immunology Review* 100 (1987): 225–60; C. B. Pert, et al., "Neuropeptides and Their Receptors: A Psychosomatic Network," *Journal of Immunology* 135 (1985): 820–26; M. Stein, et al., "Stress and Immunomodulation: The Role of Depression and Neuroendocrine Function," *Journal of Immunology* 135 (1985): 827–33.

2. For an interesting review of the more significant PNI research see Norman Cousins, *Journal of the American Medical Association* 260, no. 11 (September 16, 1988): 1610.

3. R. Glaser, J. K. Kiecolt-Glaser, et al., "Psychosocial Modifiers of Immunocompetence in Medical Students," *Psychosomatic Medicine* 46, no. 7 (1984).

4. Ibid., 7.

5. M. Irwin, M. Daniels, et al., "Plasma Cortisol and Natural Killer Cell Activity during Bereavement," *Biological Psychiatry* 24 (1988): 173–78.

6. M. Irwin and T. Patterson, "Reduction of Immune Function in Life Stress and Depression," *Biological Psychiatry* 27 (1990): 22–30.

7. M. Stein, et al., "Stress and Immunomodulation: The Role of Depression and Neuroendocrine Function," *Journal of Immunology* 135 (1985): 827–33.

8. M. Kemeny, "Psychological and Immunological Predictions of Recurrence in Herpes Simplex II," paper presented at the annual meeting of the American Psychological Association, Toronto, August 1984, in Blair Justice, Ph.D., *Who Gets Sick?* (Houston: Peak Press, 1987), 157.

9. Malcolm W. Browne, *New York Times*, January 16, 1989. Papers suggesting a link between psychological factors and AIDS were presented by Dr. Karl Goodkin of the University of Texas; Dr. Ronald Glaser and Dr. Janice K. Kiecolt-Glaser of Ohio State University College of Medicine; Dr. George F. Solomon of the University of California, Los Angeles; Dr. Lydia Temoshok of the University of California at San Francisco; and Dr. Michael H. Antoni of the University of Miami.

10. C. Peterson and A. J. Stunkard, "Personal Control and Health Promotion," *Society of Scientific Medicine* (Great Britain) 28, no. 8 (1989): 819–28.

11. Michael H. Antoni, paper presented at the annual meeting of the American Association for the Advancement of Science, San Francisco, January 15, 1989, quoted in *New York Times*, January 16, 1989.

12. M. Borysenko and J. Borysenko, "Stress, Behavior, and Immunity: Animal Models and Mediating Mechanisms," *General Hospital Psychiatry* 4 (1982): 59–67, quoted in Justice, Blair, Ph.D., *Who Gets Sick?* (Houston: Peak Press, 1987), 64.

13. M. L. Laudenslager, S. M. Ryan, et al., "Coping and Immunosuppression: Inescapable but Not Escapable Shock Suppresses Lymphocyte Proliferation," *Science* 221 (1983): 568–70.

14. C. Peterson, M. E. P. Seligman, and G. E. Vaillant, *Journal of Personality and Social Psychology* 55, no. 1 (1988): 23–27.

15. R. Ader, "Clinical Implications of Psychoneuroimmunology," *Developmental Behavior Pediatrics* 8 (1987): 357–58; M. H. Antoni, N. Schneiderman, M. A. Fletcher, et al., "Psychoneuroimmunology and HIV-1," *Journal of Consulting Clinical Psychology* 58 (1990): 38–49; G. F. Solomon, L. Temoshok, et al., "An Intensive Psychoimmunologic Study of Long-Surviving Persons with AIDS," *Annals of the New York Academy of Sciences* (1987): 647–55; G. F. Solomon, "Psychoimmunology and Human Immunodeficiency Virus Infection," *Psychiatric Medicine* 7 (1989): 47–57.

16. J. K. Kiecolt-Glaser and R. Glaser, "Behavioral Influences on Immune Function: Evidence for the Interplay between Stress and Health," in T. Field, L. McCabe, and N. Schneiderman, eds., *Stress and Coping,* vol. 2 (Hillsdale, N.J.: Lawrence Erlbaum Associates, 1985).

17. B. Gruber, N. Hall, S. Hersh, et al., "Immune System and Psychologic Changes in Metastatic Cancer Patients Using Ritualized Relaxation and Guided Imagery," *Scandinavian Journal of Behavioral Therapy* 17 (1988): 25–45.

18. M. D. Fawzy, N. Cousins, et al., *Archives of General Psychiatry,* August 1990.

19. A. Laperrier, P. O'Hearn, et al., "Exercise and Immune Function in Healthy HIV-1 Antibody Negative and Positive Gay Males," presented at the Ninth Annual Scientific Meeting of the Society of Behavioral Medicine, Boston, April 1988.

20. David Spiegel, quoted in "Health Front," *Prevention* 42 (February 1990): 14–16.

21. R. Glaser, unpublished report, in Bruce Bower, *Science News* 139 (April 6, 1991): 217.

22. Spiegel, quoted in "Health Front," 14–16.

23. N. Cousins, "Intangibles in Medicine: An Attempt at a Balancing Perspective," *Journal of the American Medical Association* 260, no. 11 (September 16, 1988), 1612.

24. W. Earl, et al., "Abstract," 1990. See Introduction, note 1, for a description of this paper.

25. R. Flinders, et al., "Abstract," 1991. See Introduction, note 2, for a description of this paper.

Chapter Nine: Understanding Stress

1. William James, from *The Varieties of Religious Experience,* quoted in W. G. Allen, *William James: A Biography* (New York: Viking Press, 1967), 166. Actually, James's published version of the episode disguises it as that of a Frenchman rather than his own. Many years later William James's son Henry revealed that a traumatic experience presented in *Varieties of Religious Expe-*

rience as that of a Frenchman was actually James's experience, by his own admission to his son (165).

2. Allen, *William James: A Biography*, 165.

3. Ibid., 168. James defined the process at the time of his depression as "the sustaining of a thought because I chose to when I might have other thoughts." It was only later that he began to call this selective attention.

4. V. A. Price, *Type A Behavior Pattern: A Model for Research and Practice* (New York: Academic Press, 1982); D. Ornish, *Stress, Diet and Your Heart* (New York: Signet, 1982); R. B. Williams, Jr., et al., "Type A Behavior and Elevated Physiological and Neuroendocrine Responses to Cognitive Tasks," *Science*, 218, no. 4571 (1982): 483–85, in Justice, *Who Gets Sick?* 84.

5. H. Selye, *Stress in Health and Disease* (Boston: Butterworths, 1968), in Justice, *Who Gets Sick?* 68.

6. Price, *Type A Behavior Pattern*; Ornish, *Stress, Diet and Your Heart*; and Williams, et al., "Type A Behavior and Elevated Physiological and Neuroendocrine Responses to Cognitive Tasks." RISE participants with diagnoses of AIDS and ARC have frequently reported major life stresses shortly prior to getting sick.

7. Justice, *Who Gets Sick?* 84.

8. Joan Borysenko, "Behavioral-Physiological Factors in the Development and Management of Cancer," *General Hospital Psychiatry* 4, 69–74. Also see Phil Nuernberger, Ph.D., *Freedom from Stress: A Holistic Approach* (Honesdale, Pa.: Himalayan International Institute Press, 1981).

9. See Nuernberger, *Freedom from Stress*.

10. S. C. Kobasa, "Test for Hardiness: How Much Stress Can You Survive?" *American Health*, September 1984, 64.

11. D. C. McClelland, et al., "Stressed Power Motivation, Sympathetic Activation, Immune Function, and Illness," *Journal of Human Stress* 6, no. 2 (1980): 11–19; D. C. McClelland, et al., "The Effect of an Academic Examination on Salivary Norepinephrine and Immunoglobulin Levels," *Journal of Human Stress* 11, no. 2 (1985): 52–59, in Justice, *Who Gets Sick?*; J. B. Jemmott III, J. Z. Borysenko, et al., "Academic Stress, Power Motivation, and Decrease in Secretion Rate of Salivary Secretory Immunoglobulin A," *Lancet* 1, no. 8339 (1983): 1400–1402, in Justice, *Who Gets Sick?* 249.

12. Kobasa, "Test for Hardiness," 64.

13. S. R. Maddi and S. C. Kobasa, *The Hardy Executive: Health under Stress* (Homewood, Ill.: Dow Jones-Irwin, 1984).

14. Justice, *Who Gets Sick?* 1987, 42.

Chapter Ten: Managing Emotional Stress

1. See M. Friedman and D. Ulmer, *Treating Type A Behavior and Your Heart* (New York: Knopf, 1984), 223. Dr. Friedman, who helped pioneer the work on the Type A personality, hypothesizes that anger can be addictive because of the strong and seductive flow of adrenaline it releases. Hostile Type As under his treatment have frequently reported difficulty overcoming

their hostility because they equate this adrenaline surge with a perceived success.

2. R. W. Bartrop, L. Lazarus, et al., "Depressed Lymphocyte Function after Bereavement," *Lancet* 1, no. 8016 (1977): 834–36; S. J. Schleifer, et al., "Suppression of Lymphocyte Stimulation during Bereavement," *Journal of the American Medical Association* 250, no. 3 (1983): 374–77; B. S. Linn, et al., "Degree of Depression and Immune Responsiveness" (abstract), *Psychosomatic Medicine* 44, no. 1 (1982): 128–29, in Justice, *Who Gets Sick?* 188–89.

3. S. E. Locke, et al., "Life Change Stress and Killer Cell Activity," (research report), Department of Biological Sciences and Psychosomatic Medicine, Division of Psychiatry, Boston University School of Medicine, in Justice, *Who Gets Sick?* (Houston: Peak Press, 1987), 239.

4. J. K. Kiecolt-Glaser, et al., "Modulation of Cellular Immunity in Medical Students, *Journal of Behavioral Medicine* 9, no. 1 (1986): 5–21.

5. See A. T. Beck, M.D., et al., *Cognitive Therapy of Depression* (New York: Guilford Press, 1979); and G. Emery, Ph.D., and J. Campbell, M.D., *Rapid Relief from Emotional Distress* (New York: Rawson Associates, 1986).

6. Ibid.

7. J. Borysenko, with L. Rothstein, *Minding the Body, Mending the Mind* (Reading, Mass.: Addison-Wesley, 1987), 13.

8. Justice, *Who Gets Sick?* 221.

9. Ibid.

10. S. M. Levy, "Emotional Expression and Survival in Breast Cancer Patients: Immunological Correlates," paper presented at the meeting of the American Psychological Association, Anaheim, Calif., 1983, in Justice, *Who Gets Sick?* 190.

11. J. Achterberg, O. C. Simonton, "Psychology of the Exceptional Cancer Patient: A Description of Patients Who Outlive Life Expectancies," *Psychotherapy: Theory, Research and Practice* 41 (1985): 416–22.

12. Norman Cousins, *Anatomy of an Illness* (New York: W. W. Norton, 1979).

13. M. A. Chesney and R. H. Rosenman, "Specificity in Stress Models: Examples Drawn from Type A Behavior," in C. L. Cooper, ed., *Stress Research* (New York: Wiley, 1983), 21–34, in Justice, *Who Gets Sick?* 221.

14. S. Maier, M. Laudenslager, and S. Ryan, "Stressor Control-Ability, Immune Function, and Endogenous Opiates," in J. Overmeier and S. Brush, eds., *Affect, Conditioning and Cognition: Essays on the Determinants of Behavior* (Hillsdale, N.J.: Lawrence Erlbaum Associates), 183–201, in Justice, *Who Gets Sick?* 190.

15. T. Holmes and R. Rahe, *The Holmes-Rahe Scale of Stresses*, in S. C. Kobasa, "Test for Hardiness: How Much Stress Can You Survive?" *American Health*, September 1984, 67. (On a scale of 0–100, marriage is assigned a point value of 50, marital separation a value of 65.)

16. Holmes and Rahe, *The Holmes-Rahe Scale of Stresses*, 67. Marital reconciliation rates 45 points; being fired at work, 47.

17. Borysenko, *Minding the Body, Mending the Mind*, 177.

Chapter Eleven: The Problem of Anger

1. See M. Friedman and D. Ulmer, *Treating Type A Behavior and Your Heart* (New York: Knopf, 1984), 36.
2. Ibid., 222.
3. J. C. Barefoot, W. G. Dahlstrom, R. B. Williams, "Hostility, Coronary Heart Disease Incidence, and Total Mortality: A 25-year Follow-up Study of 255 Physicians," *Psychosomatic Medicine* 45, no. 1 (1983): 59–63. These researchers interpret the hostility score on the Cook and Medley as a more accurate measure of cynicism, singling out people who were resentful, jealous, bitter and suspicious (in J. Fischman, "Type A on Trial," *Psychology Today*, February 1987, 48).
4. Redford Williams, M.D., *The Trusting Heart: Great News about Type A Behavior* (New York: Times Books, 1989), 49ff.
5. Ibid., 62–63.
6. Ibid., 70.
7. Friedman and Ulmer, *Treating Type A Behavior and Your Heart*, 152–53.
8. Ibid., 222–23.
9. Ibid., 223.
10. Ibid., 230–43.
11. J. Borysenko, with L. Rothstein, *Minding the Body, Mending the Mind* (Reading, Mass.: Addison-Wesley, 1987), 13.
12. Eknath Easwaran, *Gandhi the Man* (Petaluma, Calif.: Nilgiri Press, 1978), 74.
13. See ibid. This is an inspiring biography that traces Gandhi's transformation.
14. R. Brand, *New England Journal of Medicine*, 318, no. 2 (January 14, 1988): 65.

Chapter Twelve: Making Healthy Choices

1. *San Francisco Chronicle*, August 18, 1980, 2.
2. John Farquhar, M.D., *The American Way of Life Need Not Be Hazardous to Your Health: Coping with Life's Seven Major Risk Factors* (Menlo Park, Calif.: Addison-Wesley, 1987), 3.
3. Ibid., 3.
4. *San Francisco Chronicle*, May 22, 1989, A8.
5. Farquhar, *The American Way of Life*, 80.
6. G. F. Solomon, L. Temoshok, et al., "An Intensive Psychoimmunologic Study of Long-Surviving Persons with AIDS," *Annals of the New York Academy of Sciences* (1987): 647–55.

Chapter Thirteen: Habits That Heal

1. Epidemiological studies show that these diseases are much less prominent in underdeveloped countries where the average diet typically includes high amounts of fiber and complex carbohydrates and much less fat. Total

calorie intake is much lower, reducing the incidence of obesity (a major risk factor for chronic illness). When populations migrate from undeveloped to industrialized societies, they tend to adopt the typical mainstream diet and, as they do, begin to acquire the diet-associated diseases as well.

2. John Farquhar, M.D., *The American Way of Life Need Not Be Hazardous to Your Health: Coping with Life's Seven Major Risk Factors* (Menlo Park, Calif.: Addison-Wesley, 1987), 101–5. The National Research Council reviewed the evidence for a direct effect of diet on the development of cardiovascular disease and issued a major document, *Diet, Nutrition and Cancer,* concluding that dietary changes can indeed help prevent many forms of cardiovascular illness. The American Heart Association advises that no more than 8 percent of total calories consumed should be derived from saturated fat. High blood cholesterol levels are associated with increased heart attack rates, and studies indicate that both cholesterol levels and heart attack rates increase proportionately as the percentage of calories in the diet from saturated fat increases. For example, the average blood cholesterol level of the Japanese (3 percent fat of total calories consumed) was about one-half that of the Finns (20 percent fat of total calories). And the Japanese heart attack rate was one-tenth of the Finns.

3. Farquhar, *The American Way of Life,* 3.

4. Large amounts of refined sugar in the diet can impair the body's healthy functioning in several ways. Refined sugar tends to increase triglyceride levels in the blood and with them the low-density lipoproteins that are associated with atherosclerosis. Also sugar-rich foods promote obesity, and when more than 10 or 15 percent of total calories consumed are derived from sugar (the U.S. national average is 24 percent) nutritionally valuable foods may be displaced. Refined sugar results in empty calories: it has no nutritive value. Foods rich in complex carbohydrates (vegetables, grains) that sugar tends to replace, are rich in essential nutrients including balanced proteins and chromium, and are lower in caloric density than fatty or sugary foods. Sugar also tends to displace fiber-rich foods like whole grains, fruits, vegetables, and legumes. Processing removes the fiber. And high fiber, low-fat diets are associated with a low incidence of cardiovascular disease as well as with lowered rates of cancer of the colon, rectum, and breast. Researchers at the National Cancer Institute have estimated that at least 25,000 out of 100,000 deaths per year from certain cancers could be prevented by substitutions of high-fiber vegetable foods for high-saturated fat foods.

5. Farquhar, *The American Way of Life,* 104. Studies have repeatedly shown that even a modest salt limitation (reducing intake from 11 to 5 grams a day) was accompanied by a decrease in blood pressure. Moreover, the most effective drugs for treating moderate degrees of high blood pressure are diuretics, which increase the kidneys' excretion of sodium.

6. Readers of *The New Laurel's Kitchen* (Berkeley, Calif.: Ten Speed Press, 1986) will recognize our indebtedness to this landmark work on diet and nutrition. Our thanks to the publishers and the authors.

7. N. Sims, "Contributions of the US Department of Agriculture," *American Journal of Clinical Nutrition* 47, no. 329 (1988).

8. Farquhar, *The American Way of Life*, 80.

9. Ibid., 80.

10. C. M. Agress, M.D., "Exercise and Cardiovascular Disease," *Primary Cardiology*, October 1983, 17.

11. *New York Times*, April 20, 1989.

12. S. C. Kobasa, "Test for Hardiness: How Much Stress Can You Survive?" *American Health*, September 1984, 73.

13. Ibid., 73.

14. Farquhar, *The American Way of Life*, 80.

15. Reported in the *San Francisco Chronicle*, July 30, 1993, A1, A19.

Chapter Fourteen: Wellness and HIV/AIDS

1. M. E. Shills, *Modern Nutrition in Health and Disease* (Philadelphia, 1988), 7.

2. *Journal of the American Medical Association* 259 (1988): 817, 839; 260 (1988): 1881. Depressed thymus hormone levels in these patients can be returned to normal by the addition of zinc.

3. Victor Herbert, M.D, J.D., "B_{12} Deficiency in AIDS" (letter), *Journal of the American Medical Association* 260 (1988): 2837. Dr. Herbert, of the Mount Sinai School of Medicine, reports: "Our data thus tend to support the concepts that negative vitamin B_{12} balance is present in about one-third of patients with AIDS and that it is due to defective absorption."

4. *Nutrition* 5, no. 1 (January/February 1989).

5. *Nutrition and HIV Infection*, prepared for the Center for Food Safety and Applied Nutrition, Food and Drug Administration, November 1990. This provides an excellent summary of the studies that have been reported as of 1990, and assesses non-scientific claims as well. The reports are technical, but some useful charts give helpful information regarding nutrient loss, and vitamin and mineral deficiencies. These include the nutritional interactions of common HIV-related medications (36, 37) and the effects of specific nutrients on immune function.

6. *New York Times*, April 20, 1989. The study was conducted by Mary Ann Fletcher of the University of Miami. She reported that the immune measures were comparable to those observed in some studies of AZT.

Chapter Fifteen: RISE in the Workplace

1. Tony Schwartz, "The Acceleration Syndrome," *Vanity Fair*, October 1988, 186.

2. Ibid.

3. S. R. Maddi and S. C. Kobasa, *The Hardy Executive: Health under Stress* (Homewood, Ill.: Dow Jones-Irwin, 1984).

4. In J. Borysenko, with L. Rothstein, *Minding the Body, Mending the Mind* (Reading, Mass.: Addison-Wesley, 1987), 13.

5. Justice, *Who Gets Sick?* (Houston: Peak Press, 1987), 42.

6. Adapted from "Stewardship of the Self: A Program for Self Mastery." Our thanks to Warren Gershwin, M.D., for his permission to use and adapt this material.

7. Schwartz, "The Acceleration Syndrome," 188.

Chapter Sixteen: Skilled Communication

1. See John Gottmann, et al. *A Couple's Guide to Communication* (Champaign, Ill.: Research Press, 1976).

Chapter Seventeen: Quiet Mind, Ample Heart

1. S. R. Maddi and S. C. Kobasa, *The Hardy Executive: Health under Stress* (Homewood, Ill.: Dow Jones-Irwin, 1984).

2. W. Redford, M.D., and V. Williams, Ph.D., *Anger Kills* (New York: Times Books, 1993).

3. J. Borysenko, with L. Rothstein, *Minding the Body, Mending the Mind* (Reading, Mass.: Addison-Wesley, 1987), 186.

4. Henri Nouwen, *Life of the Beloved* (New York: Crossroad, 1992), 64.

5. Eknath Easwaran, *Conquest of Mind* (Petaluma, Calif.: Nilgiri Press, 1988), 104.

The RISE Institute

Publications and Materials

The Rise Institute produces instructional materials to support people who are using the RISE tools, including audio instructional tapes. You can receive a brochure describing our material by writing to:

> The RISE Institute
> P.O. Box 2733
> Petaluma, CA 94973

Programs

The institute also sponsors courses, workshops, and seminars designed to introduce people and agencies to the RISE tools or to provide follow-up and ongoing support for people already using them. Separate workshops address the specific needs of people coping with illness, those wanting to make healthier lifestyle changes, and those facing the challenges of the workplace. If you would like information about the institute's programs or would like to facilitate a RISE study circle, of if you want to know if there is a course or study circle near you, write to:

> The RISE Institute
> Programs Division
> 4362 Bonita Road, Ste. 404
> Bonita, CA 92002

Eight-Point Program for Spiritual Living

If you would like more information about Sri Eknath Easwaran's Eight-Point Program for Spiritual Living, from which the RISE tools were adapted, write to the Blue Mountain Center of Meditation, P.O. Box 256, Tomales, CA 94971, or call (707) 878-2369.